Cultivating Leadership in Schools

Connecting People, Purpose, and Practice

GORDON A. DONALDSON, JR.

FOREWORD BY
MICHAEL G. FULLAN

Teachers College, Columbia University
New York and London

Published by Teachers College Press, 1234 Amsterdam Avenue, New York, NY 10027

Library of Congress Cataloging-in-Publication Data

Donaldson, Gordon A.
    Cultivating leadership in schools : connecting people, purpose, and practice. / Gordon A. Donaldson.
        p. cm.
    Includes bibliographical references and index.
    ISBN 0-8077-4003-9 (cloth)—ISBN 0-8077-4002-0 (pbk.)
        1. Educational leadership—United States. 2. School improvement programs—United States.
    3. Teacher participation in administration—United States.

    LB2822.82 .D65 2000
    371.2′00973—dc21

                                                                                        00-044336

ISBN 0-8077-4002-0 (paper)
ISBN 0-8077-4003-9 (cloth)

Printed on acid-free paper

Manufactured in the United States of America

08   07   06   05   04   03   8   7   6   5   4   3

Contents

Foreword

There are many books about educational leadership, but none captures the depth of issues in clear, practical, and comprehensive terms as does *Cultivating Leadership in Schools*. Donaldson's book is at once deeply theoretical and moral, as it is replete with practical examples and action advice for how to tackle complex matters of reform.

The book's main theme—mobilizing people for moral purpose—is a powerful lever for understanding and doing something about leadership. In presenting a fresh model for school leadership, Donaldson wipes clean the old slate, once crowded only with images of administrators, and opens up broad new possibilities for the shared leadership that is so necessary in high-performing schools. His ideas about teacher leadership and how it complements the leadership and management of principals are fresh and useful. Readers will find opportunities throughout this book for understanding their own important roles in the leadership of their schools.

The model, based on three streams, is both simple and generative. "Building relationships," "mutual moral purpose," and "shared belief in action" are the three streams that Donaldson pursues at many levels. At one level the book is inspiring because of the value and clarity of the message; at another, it unpacks the complexity of working with the three streams in day-to-day practice with numerous examples.

Having set the stage with an analysis of the model in practice, Donaldson then takes on the much more challenging question of "how to grow leadership," which he answers in three chapters that bring to life what it will take to develop, nurture, and sustain leadership in educational reform.

At a time when leadership for schools has never been so critical, there is also a growing shortage of people who are willing to take on the responsibility. *Cultivating Leadership in Schools* inspires and points the way by highlighting the importance, excitement, and worthwhile challenges of reform. It could not have come at a better time for all educators interested in the well being and effectiveness of schools in complex times.

Michael G. Fullan

Preface

Can a public school be led? It's such an obvious question, especially in an era when everybody assumes our schools *must* be led. It has taken an embarrassingly long time, though, for me to even ask it. I have always believed that schools could be led. As a teacher in Philadelphia, Boston, and Maine, I thought I'd experienced—and even participated in—school leadership. I became a principal and described myself as an administrator, all the while thinking of myself as the leader of the school. I moved from practice to the professorship to prepare school administrators. And, of course, I thought of my work no longer as preparing administrators but as cultivating leaders—principal leadership, instructional leaders, moral leaders, and, more recently, teacher leaders.

But my 30 years as a public educator have been rife with claims that schools, in general, have not been led well. Our schools have "put our nation at risk." Wave after wave of reform has broken upon our schoolhouses, each with its own map for change with its leadership responsibilities. And when these waves have receded, we've been told we're still at risk, that our schools' outcomes are still below standard. Although I haven't always agreed that our schools are failing, I have been very personally involved in helping aspiring leaders to prepare for their important work and in assisting schools to reculture their own leadership. With all the teeth-gnashing about school performance, it finally occurred to me to ask, "So, can schools be led?"

My journey to this book has forced me to ask a number of questions of myself that I expect have occurred to many others concerned about our public schools. What is it that we expect of school leaders? Exactly how is it that we want them to *lead*—as distinct from "manage" or "run"—our schools? Given the realities of public school, can true leadership thrive in an American public school? My answers to these questions took me to the foot of a new mountain where I realized that the uniqueness of public schools required a similarly unique model of leadership. This book is the result of my explorations into such a model.

Writing *Cultivating Leadership in Schools* has been a pivotal intellectual and professional journey for me. It has helped me to understand how our past (and continuing) models of leadership do not fit the conditions of many public schools. I have grown to appreciate how the classical leadership paradigm has not only contributed to the failure of school reform but has as well convinced capable educators—

principals and teachers both—that they do not belong among the ranks of our leaders. Leadership, I discovered, is about the blending of three streams of organizational life—relationships, purpose, and action-in-common—into a dynamic current that will carry a school toward improved teaching and learning. For schools to have leadership, I further discovered, they need leade*r*s—not a single leader. This book is about the integration of teacher and principal leadership into a coherent process that marks the success of leadership by the quality of learning in the school.

I hesitate to say that my discoveries are fresh or even earth-shaking. They are, rather, sense-making for me. They will, I hope, bring a fresh kind of sense about school leadership to principals and teachers, to the superintendents and school boards who shape the conditions for school leadership, and to professors and others who play powerful roles in leadership development. The three-stream model has a simplicity about it (at one level at least) that makes it applicable in the midst of meetings, classrooms, walks through school corridors, or while reading, writing, and reflecting. I trust that it will stimulate conversation and discussion among teachers, principals, central office staff, professors, and others, for it is from such dialogues that the relational leadership model will move from the pages of this book into the action of the school.

Untold numbers of people have contributed to this work. Colleagues, students, and parents shaped my own experiences as a teacher and leader in three special schools where I believe leadership lived: The Pennsylvania Advancement School, Philadelphia; the North Haven Community School, North Haven, Maine; and Boggy Brook Vocational School, Ellsworth, Maine. So too have colleagues in two stellar professional leadership programs been my inspiration and my teachers: The Maine Academy for School Leaders and the Maine Principals' Academy. Finally, it has been my good fortune to be a member of a small collaborative team at the University of Maine that has, in our proud corner of the country, pushed the envelope consistently on the concept of school leadership and on the development of school leaders.

I extend thanks to Becky van der Bogert, Roland Barth, Dave Brown, Anne Marie Read, Dick Barnes, Joe Richardson, and Gary Whiteley for their contributions to my learning. I am particularly grateful for the wise counsel, good humor, and insightful feedback of four special friends and colleagues: Richard Ackerman, Sally Mackenzie, George Marnik, and David Sanderson. And, as always, I could not have completed this work without Cynthia's love, partnership, and patience with the clutter it has spread through our house for the past two years.

Cultivating Leadership in Schools

Connecting People, Purpose, and Practice

CHAPTER 1

Public School Leadership Reconsidered

Nobody here really wants me to be a leader except the central office and the school board. The teachers want me to leave them alone. The students want me to leave them alone, too. And the parents want me to solve every one of their problems. When I try to put [the statewide learning standards] on the table, everybody looks the other way.

—A Maine principal

Schools need leaders. Or do they? We are so accustomed to the idea that every school needs a principal that it is practically heretical to suggest otherwise. Of course a school needs a principal! Who else would I call to dismiss my child early? Who would see to it that kids toed the line, that the school did not slip into juvenile or adolescent chaos? How would the school survive parents' night? basketball games? fundraising activities? the school fair? Who would call the substitute teachers? Who would make sure teachers did what they did and that buses ran on time?

But I said *leaders*. Sure, schools need people to structure and manage the daily life of the school. With teachers busy teaching, counselors busy counseling, custodians minding the building, and secretaries handling the ebb and flow, the school's machinery must run smoothly and safely. By default, however, we have come to define these principalship functions as "school leadership." To states, superintendents, and school boards, leadership has meant the enforcement of their policies and carrying the torch for district and state goals. To pragmatists, it has meant a principal who uses his executive authority to respond to the unexpected and make on-the-spot decisions. To school staffs, the leader-principal "handles the public", presents the school well to the outside world, and buffers those inside the school from those outside.

But is this the work of a leader? As important as these individual functions are, simply satisfying our century-old conventions does not a leader make. Keeping the master schedule, the bus routes, the attendance and disciplinary systems well greased and oiled does not by itself match most conceptions of leadership. Neither does carrying out directives "from above." Being a "man of action" and an on-the-spot decision-maker, although matching the classical leader mold, emphasizes too heavily the reactive, short-term aspects of leadership. So too does the public representative role seem insufficient: Prowling the community and handling politicians and

1

parents with aplomb serve practical and symbolic purposes, but they do not constitute all of what we hope for in a leader.

When principals fulfill the major requirements of their roles, they often fail to provide the leadership we need in schools (Barth, 1990; Darling-Hammond, 1997; Goodlad, 1984). Larry Cuban (1988) said it succinctly: "Within the school and district workplaces, the managerial imperative, not the impulse toward leadership, dominates behavior" (p. xx). This realization has led in the past two decades to numerous attempts to reconfigure the principal's role as "instructional," "transformational," "constructivist," and "moral" leader (Lambert, Walker, Zimmerman, Cooper, Lambert, Gardner, & Slack, 1995; Murphy, 1992; Sergiovanni, 1992). Significantly, it has led as well to pushing beyond the principalship to consider teachers as leaders (Little, 1988; Wasley, 1991) and even to reconceive of school leadership as a "community of leaders" function (Barth, 1988).

What these attempts share is an ambition to find a model of leadership that will enable schools to improve their service to children and community, not merely to maintain and react. As Joe Murphy (1992) put it,

> [The] challenges to schools of the past, of today, and of tomorrow [have led to] a belief that society needs better schools. The first corollary . . . is that if "we want better schools, we are going to have to manage and lead differently" (Sergiovanni, 1992, p. x). The second corollary is that different leadership will require a transformation of our conception of administration, that leaders and leadership in the postindustrial age must look radically different from what they have looked like in the past. (pp. 123–124).

This book's central purpose is to develop a model of leadership for American public schools that stays true to the ambitious notion that true leadership enables organizations to grow more effective. In seeking a more fitting model of leadership, I will take Murphy's advice and, from the beginning, set aside our past conceptions of who school leaders are: principals, assistant principals, department heads, athletic administrators, and others with formal titles. Instead of picturing what these people do as "school leadership," I will begin with a definition of leadership that I have found helpful: *the mobilization of people to adapt a school's practices and beliefs so that it more fully achieves its mission with all children.*

Past models of school leadership have come largely from corporate and political settings (Rost, 1993; Sergiovanni, 1996). Yet, as I argue in Chapters 2 and 3, the realities of public schools have never matched the characteristics of the private corporate organizations for which these classical leadership models were designed. In fact, public schools are fairly unusual among American organizations. They have many disparate, idealistic, and often vague purposes. Their "raw material"—that is, children—is endlessly varied and idiosyncratic. The methods and techniques of their work resist standardization and instead require great sensitivity, discretion, and artistry from the key frontline workers, teachers. Their products defy accurate measurement or standardization. Their cultures reflect diverse community customs and attitudes even as they bear the uniform, bureaucratic traces of our national system of schooling.

The need for a new model of leadership, then, stems from the fact that leadership as we have attempted it has not usually mobilized staff to adapt their practices and beliefs to emerging student and societal needs. When we have assumed that schools would respond to leadership the way a business, a platoon, a football team, or even a political party responds to classical leaders, we have doomed ourselves to failure. The tragedy is that, with each failure, more people have grown skeptical that schools can be led at all. The double tragedy is that those who tried to lead feel that the failure is theirs. Without a more fitting model for their important work, many have withdrawn and a serious leadership vacuum has continued to grow (Evans, 1995).

Regardless of how difficult it is to pin down how leadership operates in an American school, we need to cultivate greater leadership in everyone of them. The past 15 years of criticism have made it clear that many people want our schools to do better by all their students. From inside schools as well comes a steady call for improvement, for not settling for last year's curriculum or last year's outmoded staff development or practices that don't serve all children. Only those who urge abandonment of our universal education system could argue that we do not need inspired leadership merely to move our public schools from "partway there" to "closer to fulfillment."

SCHOOL LEADERSHIP: AN EVOLVING CONCEPT

Our past understanding of school leadership has failed to meet two functional tests in recent decades: that it successfully promote organizational improvement and that it be sustainable for the leaders themselves. For the purposes of this book, these two tests will be the guiding criteria for a new model of school leadership. The way we understand school leadership must permit and encourage new knowledge, new attitudes, and new practices so that, as children's and society's needs evolve, public schools can change to meet them. And the way we enact school leadership must be healthful and replenishing for those who lead.

Historically, as schools and districts grew in size and as curriculum and other services became formalized by states, "principal teachers" were appointed to serve these largely managerial functions. Early designers of the role borrowed from the emerging field of business management to create principals and superintendents in the image of public executives (Callahan, 1962; Cubberly, 1916). The classical leadership model was considered suitable for schools in four respects:

- Formal authority must be vested in specific roles to assure school-wide safety, orderliness, and productivity.
- The people in these roles must be able to organize a rational institutional process so that the school's core work with students is uniform and meets state standards.
- Leaders must be well informed, have access to governing and funding bodies, and be able to control personnel.
- Leaders must be able to shape the school to meet emerging needs in its environment and among its students.

During the first half of the 20th century, school-level leadership came to be accepted as primarily a middle-management function executed by male principals in schools of mostly female faculty and staff (Biklin,1995; Shakeshaft,1989). Important decisions were made "above" the school level; a good school leader ran a tight but humane ship and met the immediate requirements of the central office and community board. This system appears to have satisfied many needs until the 1960s (Tyack & Hansot, 1982).

Curiously, the word "leadership" did not come to be widely applied to schools until the 1970s and 1980s (Cunningham, 1990). That, in itself, is quite remarkable: We seem to have been satisfied with "administration" running our schools until we came face-to-face with the challenge of educating more successfully whole subpopulations of neglected Americans. The same thing was happening in other public service arenas, leading in the 1980s and 1990s to the emergence of the first programs of graduate study focusing on leadership and how it functions (Rost, 1993). Given the infancy of this field, it is not surprising that it is littered with unarticulated assumptions and definitions and, as Joseph Rost put it, that "leadership is a word that has come to mean all things to all people" (1993, p. 7). Clearly, exploring what it is about schools that requires leadership is central to the advancement of both practice and the theories that guide it.

In the rush to offer models of leadership to schools, we looked in the late 1970s and early 1980s to two sources: the business literature and the effective schools literature (Cunningham, 1990). In both cases, we were inclined to prescribe new models and checklists of leadership tasks and strategies. Hailing the need, for example, for principals to become "instructional leaders," we applied the results of scant research from the effective schools movement to our efforts to reconceive the principalship under the halo of leadership (Hallinger & Murphy; 1991; Persell & Cookson, 1982). Or we offered workshops and textbook revisions detailing the latest management science breakthroughs as if they would lead to the rebirth of principals as "quality leaders."

These efforts have so far failed to implicate themselves widely into the practice of American school leaders, in some cases because they were proffered so prescriptively but more often because conditions in schools proved hostile or resistant to them. Principals who tried the new models not only bucked the cultures and politics of their schools, they struggled to stretch their personal and professional competencies to meet these new challenges (Donaldson, 1991; Murphy, 1992). Schools did not operate the way businesses did when it came to change (Fullan & Miles, 1992). Principals could not single-handedly initiate a reform in their schools any more than they could single-handedly make themselves over in a new leadership image. The position, authority, and context of the office simply did not permit it.

The failure of these efforts to recast administration as leadership have raised deep concerns that our best educators are avoiding leadership roles because they are so stressful and difficult (Evans, 1995). It has also spawned in the 1990s a rich array of school-level experimentation, writing, and professional development. As we seek to understand how leadership can function to improve schools, we are exploring what teacher leadership means, both in its formally appointed form and in its informal, natural form. We are also learning how historically male and hierarchical models constrain our thinking and our practice and what the possibilities are to work free of these (Foster, 1989; Lambert et al., 1995; Shakeshaft, 1989). Universities have invested in new ways to educate administrators and teachers in leadership (Milstein et al., 1993; Murphy, 1993). Principals' centers and academies now have a proud 20-year history of supporting leadership development by listening to principals and helping them to reinvent themselves by understanding more deeply their colleagues, themselves, and their schools (Donaldson & Marnik, 1995; Wimpelberg, 1990). Indeed, the times are ripe for widening the lens in search of a model of school leadership that is both more productive for schools and more sustainable for those who aspire to lead.

THE CORE CONCEPT: A RELATIONSHIP THAT MOBILIZES

What *is* leadership? Leadership satisfies a basic function for the group or organization: It mobilizes members to *think, believe, and behave in a manner that satisfies emerging organizational needs, not simply their individual needs or wants.* When leadership is present, we can detect it in the synchronicity of members' thoughts, words, actions, and outcomes. We can say, after visiting a business or school or volunteer group where leadership is alive and well, "Those folks are on the same page and you can see it in what that place has accomplished." It is important to point out that the synchronicity among members does not mean that their beliefs, their knowledge, their values, and their behaviors are identical. It means that their many unique actions and interactions work together in a systematic manner so that what they do as individuals *creates a collective effect greater than the sum of all those individual efforts.*

This fundamental premise—that leadership mobilizes people for organizational adaptation—is supported by theoreticians and by common sense. Leadership, as Burns (1978) and others have argued, enables a group or organization to conduct its collective business with its environment in such a way that the environment continues to support it. Ronald Heifetz (1994) understands this interaction as fundamentally symbiotic: The organization performs a function within society that is useful enough for society to support its continued life; if it grows useless, society's support shrivels and it either adapts or dies. In this context, leadership plays a vital "adaptive" role as it makes the difference—through mobilizing people to act in common—in the organization's ability to change to meet environmental needs.

A team, a business, a church group, or a school can operate routinely in patterns it has developed over time, with each member carrying out roles in a manner that made the group successful at some past time. Applying the adaptive definition of leadership, such a group does not need leadership so much as it needs management. As the world changes around it to a point where those routine operations no longer satisfy the environment's need, the organization faces "adaptive challenges" usually characterized by growing stress, uncertainty, and evidence of failure. These are the times when leadership can and must perform its unique function. Schools have often been portrayed as 19th-century institutional forms hanging on for dear life in, now, a 21st-century world. Our failed learners are presented as evidence that educators and communities have not adapted to the "realities" of learning, child development, and preparation for a 21st-century future. From *A Nation at Risk* (1983) to the many reform programs that now dot our national landscape, citizens, politicians, businesspeople, and educators urge schools to restructure, to transform, to reculture. The gnashing of teeth, the casting of blame, the rising needs and plunging resource base, and the many state and local attempts at reform all signal the adaptive challenges we face—and the need for leadership within and around our public schools.

School leadership's function, then, is to mobilize people to change how they themselves work so that they collectively serve better the emerging needs of children and demands of society. This basic concept of leadership forms the backdrop of my search for a more appropriate model of how school leadership works. As I first examine the realities of teachers and other adults in our public schools, I ask, "Can leadership thrive here? Can people be mobilized in schools? Can they be mobilized so that their beliefs, values, and actions adapt the school to better meet the changing needs of students, their families, and society as a whole?"

We have grown frustrated with the prospects for leadership in schools in large part because the models of leadership that have governed leader activities are not properly sensitive to the unique realities of our schools or our democratic values. Our "imported" models of leadership fundamentally violate the professional culture and social fabric of most public schools (Sergiovanni, 1996). Where school activities are loosely connected by nature, leaders have tried to tightly force all parts into a seamless system. Where teaching requires immense discretion and flexibility, leaders have strived for uniform "best" practices. Where children and families seek individual care and attention, leaders have thrust them into programs, schedules, and now performance testing geared to the norm. Where teachers, parents, and students say, "We know what needs to be done," leaders have too often said, "But the policy says it needs to be done this way."

In exploring a leadership model more fitting for schools, I investigate how principals and teachers can build from existing professional, social, and practical realities a new way jointly to mobilize themselves to address the evolving mission of their schools. This exploration hinges on recognizing that leadership is a *relational, not an individual, phenomenon.* Leadership, that is, does not reside in the individual; it resides in the interpersonal networks among the members of the group, the faculty, the workforce, the nation. Many theoreticians (Bolman & Deal, 1991; Burns, 1978; Heifetz, 1994; Rost, 1993; Wheatley, 1992) as well as increasing numbers of practitioners and observers (Barth, 1990; Darling-Hammond, 1997; Lambert et al., 1995) now offer evidence supporting this notion.

Among other things, this relational quality permits a uniquely democratic value base to creep into our thinking about leadership: The mobilization of people emerges from their numerous, diverse contributions to the task of developing a better way to function together to meet their purposes. It broadens our understanding of who school leaders are; they are people who invest in the leadership relationship and can include teachers (whether designated as "leaders" or not), principals (despite their formal designations), and many others (Berry & Ginsburg, 1990). And it expands our view of what leaders do and how they grow through cultivating their own interpersonal and intrapersonal skills and learning (Donaldson & Marnik, 1995).

The model I develop posits that leadership activity occurs in three essential dimensions:

1. The Relational: fostering mutual openness, trust, and affirmation sufficient for the players to influence and be influenced willingly by one another.
2. The Purposive: marrying individual commitment and organizational purposes that are deemed morally beneficial by the membership.
3. The Action-In-Common: nurturing a shared belief, reinforced by shared experience and action, that together the group or organization can act to accomplish goals more successfully than individuals can alone.

The model not only invites all who are willing into the leadership relationship but also places special emphasis on three qualities of American public schools that can nurture and enliven this relational leadership: their egalitarian ethos, their moral purpose, and their bias for action. Here, I argue, we have the heart of a leadership model that, because it is fitting for our public schools, can unlock the potential of our schools to improve themselves.

THE READER'S ITINERARY

The book has two distinct parts. The next three chapters consider the challenges of school leadership and develop a leadership model compatible with the realities of American public schools. The rest of the book looks more practically into how principals, teacher leaders, and others can cultivate a strong leadership relationship in their schools and the skills and qualities in themselves to be part of that relationship.

Chapters 2 and 3 cull from research about teachers, teaching, and schools to *identify features of school life that appear to impinge most on leadership*. The view that emerges is not pretty and, to a hopeful leader or school reformer, may be even downright depressing. But these realities make the case that American public schools were not designed to be led in the ways that we now exhort leaders to attempt. These two chapters establish the groundwork for a new leadership model that is better adapted to contemporary conditions in American public schools.

Chapter 4 is the pivot point in the book's argument where *I present the model and its justification*. The model's three "streams" of leadership—the relational, the purposive, and the action—shape the school's capacity to mobilize for improvement. It describes each stream and explores briefly how their strengths and their complementarity constitute the quality of leadership. Chapter 4 permits a reexamination of school realities with an eye toward identifying new ways that principals, teachers, and others can participate in leadership.

Chapters 5, 6, and 7 turn our lens to the *activities that are central to leadership practice* in each of the three streams and then *to principals' and teacher leaders' prospects for engaging in them*. Principals, by dint of their formal position and legal obligations, find themselves both constrained and enabled with respect to forming leadership relationships with others, contributing to purposive commitment, and shaping a belief in action-in-common. Teacher leaders, often because they are not formally appointed, find themselves constrained and enabled in ways different from those of principals. All together, these three chapters help educators and those who hire, supervise, and rely on them to understand more clearly what special potentials—and what special pitfalls—come with being a principal or a teacher who seeks to lead.

Chapters 8, 9, and 10 focus more fully on *leaders and the core activities they engage in to "grow leadership" in their schools*: putting relationships at the center of their work, facing the challenges confronting the school and through that process renewing the commitment to school purposes, and blending learning with action in an upwardly spiraling process of improvement. Each chapter describes leaders' core activities and then *explores the skills, knowledge, and personal qualities that are important to success*. These chapters most specifically describe what leaders—whether principals, formally appointed teacher leaders, informal teacher leaders, or other staff or parents—do to foster school leadership in the image of the book's model.

The final chapter returns briefly to the question, "In what ways does a school need to be—and can be—led?" I summarize some practical features of schoolwork, among them the intractability of roles, the lack of time for planning and leading, and the press of central office, district, and community that can often hamper relational leadership. I conclude, however, that where educators and others resolve to lead together, their capacity to form strong relationships and to nourish a robust sense of purpose and commitment will lead to productive action. Leadership of this sort moves like a steady river through a school's life, promoting critical thought, creative action, and a focus on student learning.

CHAPTER 2

A Conspiracy of Busyness
The Structural Context for Leadership

Teachers and administrators are both bosses and subordinates. They direct others while obeying orders. They are solo practitioners. They prize autonomy. They manage conflict. They are also expected to lead.

Cuban (1988), p. xix

Schools have forever been vessels for their constituents' dreams. Parents, students, taxpayers, educational reformers, and politicians want their schools to be better, be different. Schools are populated with caring, committed educators, people who in most instances hold dearly their obligation to respond to the dreams and concerns of community members. Indeed, as vehicles for enlightenment and social and economic mobility, schools were invented to carry dreams for families, individuals, and society. Why then do schools struggle so to change?

This same question might be posed of leaders. Why do leaders struggle so to help their schools change? The dreams and problems of the school's constituencies are the domain of the leader—be he or she a principal, a teacher, or a parent volunteer. They materialize everywhere: faculty meetings; parent phone calls; a teacher's note; the school board's long-range planning document. Through each question, complaint, suggestion, and crisis shines the ray of one's hope and dream for his child, her students, their school.

Leaders in our schools attract these hopes and dreams much the way lightning rods attract lightning. We look for leaders to share their problems and suggestions, seeking a route for their dreams to play out in action. Leaders, reciprocally, look for people in the school community with whom they can share others' problems and suggestions, others' dreams. Leaders cannot solve every problem and fulfill every dream (though many have tried). They need others to respond along with them, to carry out if they will the action necessary to effect the change. This collecting of lightning bolts and transforming them into action through others is one of the essences of leadership work. It is also, ironically, a central, abiding frustration of school leadership. Everyone knows the principal's office phone number. Every teacher knows how to alert the team leader or building rep if he or she has a concern. Every superintendent and school board keeps the channels "down" the hierarchy busy.

Lightning can find the rod whenever the electron buildup reaches its trigger level. But how does the leader channel the energy and heat into productive action?

In my first year as a high school principal, I recall a moment in late September when I congratulated myself for getting the school year launched. Walking the halls, I proudly noted that every adult and child was in his or her place (as far as I could tell, at least). This, indeed, was often my goal as a principal: to keep everyone in classrooms, busily engaged in something! It took me several years to discover that reaching this goal created a huge paradox: *They* were all busy doing the work of educating but they were not available for me to lead. Where were the people with whom to share the pressing issues facing the school as a whole? Leaders who succeed at maximizing time on task for both students and staff find themselves impaled on their own pikes, their own attempts at leadership thwarted by a conspiracy of busyness.

I have since learned that most American public schools operate in ways that make people largely inaccessible to leaders. Thus the classic leader's assumption that he or she can assemble, organize, and shape the staff in order to mold their work to his or her vision often proves wrong for schools (Bolman & Heller, 1995). The principal, like me, who wants to convene committees, involve faculty and parents in decision-making, and impose institutional priorities on teachers' classroom practices works against a sturdy "architecture" of cultural patterns and work structures. In many ways, this architecture is unfriendly to classical, bureaucratic leadership of the kind I tried—and many others continue to try. The apparent failure of imposed restructuring and reform solutions stands as frustrating proof of this point.

This chapter and Chapter 3 explore the major attributes of schools that contribute to this leadership-resistant architecture. In this chapter, I discuss six structural characteristics of the work life of adults in school that significantly shape leaders' attempts to influence their schools in positive ways:

- There is no time to convene people to plan, organize, and follow through.
- Contact and the transaction of business are "on the fly."
- When staff gather formally, their interactions and effectiveness are curtailed.
- Informal collegial connections and conversations are rich.
- Important information is communicated informally and sometimes haphazardly.
- The larger the school, the more complex and impersonal the leadership environment.

Be forewarned that the image that emerges is a disappointing and even depressing one. Indeed, it explains why leadership as we have attempted to enact it using centralized, single-source models has not only failed to mobilize schools but has also burned out many talented principals and teacher leaders. But while the work-life patterns of schools make many of them inhospitable places for administrative leadership, they do not rule out leadership. Indeed, a more suitable model of leadership will need not only to embrace the busyness of our schools but offer ways to harness it as well.

NO TIME, NO WAY

The major reason both principal and teacher leaders have so few opportunities for direct leadership activity is that their most significant partners in action are busy all day with students. Teachers are simultaneously the leader's most powerful and least available partner. Questions, complaints, suggestions, or directives falling into the hands of the principal, team leader, or activities director nearly always require the cooperation or compliance of a teacher. Yet teachers are busy teaching, busy preparing, busy relaxing, busy conferring, busy eating lunch.

Consider first what teachers are doing during the instructional day; call it 6½ hours while students are "in class." The typical public elementary school teacher works directly with students—teaching and standing duties—for all but 30 minutes, or 8%, of the student day (Carnegie Foundation, 1990). High school teachers and many middle school teachers average more like 75 minutes, or 19% (Goodlad, 1984). Of their nonstudent time, roughly 25 minutes—nearly all of the elementary teacher's time—is for lunch.

Consider next the buffer periods just before and after instructional time—what we typically refer to as "before and after school." In the roughly 30 minutes before students arrive in the classroom, most teachers are preparing their rooms and lessons, talking with an early arrival or a colleague, focusing their energies on the long day that is just beginning. For many teachers, the after-school time is the optimal opportunity to work with individual students or talk with parents, extending it many days to a half hour or even an hour. In middle and high schools, after-school time is often unavailable for coaches and activities advisors. Thus, for most American teachers who have a minimum in-school workday of 8 hours, between 7 and 7 1/2 hours of that time is booked for instruction, student-related activities, duties, and lunch. Beyond this time commitment, 64% of American teachers reported in 1990 that they had less than 1 hour daily of scheduled preparation time (Carnegie Foundation, 1990). That is, most teachers have no time or insufficent time each day for any sort of collective organizational or leadership activity.

But even this total is misleading. Although a few minutes of planning time may exist for some teachers, these do not usually coincide with other teachers' minutes or the principals' minutes. Nor do they occur in a single block of time that makes it possible to think through a problem or a plan carefully. If the leader needs to assemble more than one teacher to confer or problem-solve, those teachers must not only have time to assemble but also their times must coincide! And if the leader is a teacher him or herself, the only time to engage in direct leadership work is when he or she is free.

In short, opportunities for leadership through direct collective activity are rare and often need to be forced into the school day. From the standpoint of engaging students all day in productive activities, these patterns make a great deal of sense to teachers, to parents, to accountability-conscious administrators and school boards, and to efficiency-minded taxpayers. Ironically, the inaccessibility of teachers created by their attention to duty is a major obstacle to leadership and to institutional change (Louis and Kruse, 1995).

ON THE FLY

The inevitable result of this reality is that the vast majority of direct leadership activity occurs either "on the fly" with individuals or at infrequent group meetings before or after the student day. Although principals generally have more control of their schedules than do teacher leaders, they must be experts at grabbing moments here and there, now and then, to be leaders with their colleagues during the school day. Teacher leaders, unless they work in teams with those they lead, are at the mercy of their own teaching schedules and often must catch leadership time either before or after school.

What does this "on the fly" time look like? Most often, leaders are interrupting teachers', counselors', and others' more immediate activities with students. When the principal catches a teacher heading to his or her lab to inquire about, say, a student referral, the teacher's mind is on the lab. When a teacher flags down the principal in the lunchroom to confer about this afternoon's curriculum alignment session, the principal is monitoring the lunchroom. When three teachers are huddled with their team leader before school, they have today's lessons or yesterday's incident foremost in their minds—not necessarily the long-range planning they have assembled to do.

In this regard, an essential quality of leadership time in schools is its fragmentation. It is splattered into dribs and drabs as principals and teacher leaders catch colleagues, students, and parents in the moments between first-priority activities. And even in these precious face-to-face conversations, the attention of participants is apt to be fractured by the press of multiple and often more immediate agendas: a student, a phone call, a missing book, a conversation with a colleague, a moment off duty. When the topic of the conversations involves other people, as it often does, it is difficult to resolve an issue or agree on action because other essential partners are missing. Needless to say, these conditions are hardly optimal for leadership in the classic sense.

Again, the busyness of school—unquestionably a positive attribute of a responsive, student-centered school—conspires against the model of leadership that requires regular, concentrated time from all constituents for communication, planning, coordination of efforts and policy, and uniformity of practice. In private corporations, employees are removed from production for retraining, problem-solving, and planning. Managers' workdays consist of meetings to analyze performance and procedures, to plan, and to strategize. In public schools, each employee is fully engaged most of the day with students. Individual planning occurs beyond this. No time is left for organizational communication and planning. And the resource base that causes this pattern is unlikely to change radically. Hence we need to rethink what it means to lead and to understand how "leading on the fly" in those short, fragmented interchanges play an important role in the development of the school. As we see in future chapters, the focus-on-action these interchanges provides can be a very potent opportunity for learning and planning.

THE LIMITED CONFINES OF FORMAL MEETINGS

Most school leaders schedule meetings in an effort to transact the business they are unable to accomplish through individual or informal contacts. These take two distinct forms: whole-faculty meetings and committee or team meetings. As with these other forms of direct leadership, precious little opportunity exists even for formal meetings. With teachers booked for 7 to 7 1/2 hours of a typical 8-hour in-school day, formal meetings typically extend the day and conflict with an after-school period crowded with students, co-curricular activities, other meetings, and planning. Viewed as an imposition by some teachers, these meetings have, in many districts, been limited in number and duration by the negotiated contract (where, significantly, they are viewed as "working conditions," not as an imperative professional responsibility). Hence most school leaders—teachers and administrators alike—seek to minimize the number and duration of meetings.

Adding to this tendency are two trends. First, the number of meetings in schools has mushroomed in the last decade or two, the result largely of reform activities and of special education procedures. State and federal school improvement protocols such as Goals 2000 grants, mandated results-based curriculum, or school site councils demand regular time, energy, and commitment from teachers and administrators. Similarly, teachers and principals are professionally and legally obligated to attend Pupil Evaluation Team meetings. Second, as the number of meetings is expanding, so are after-school student activities requiring faculty supervision. As schools have moved to fill latchkey children's empty afternoons with more sports, more music, more clubs, and even organized service and academic activities, teachers and principals are needed to staff and to supervise these activities. The result is that they are less available for school-wide planning and decision-making.

The result of these conditions is that whole-faculty meetings are usually suboptimal leadership events. They cannot happen frequently enough to maintain continuity from one to the next. Their length is curtailed by contract or fatigue. Participation is often piecemeal, with faculty coming and going. In many instances, the interpersonal dynamic among faculty and between faculty and administrators discourages open discourse and full involvement from all those present. Many principals, in response to these realities, schedule agendas tightly, hoping to use the precious time of the group as efficiently as possible. So, too, do department chairs, team leaders, and teacher association presidents. The result is a meeting that is directive and task-oriented in style. These accomplish some important organizational tasks: The faculty learns exactly how the new schedule will go next week; the sixth-grade team coordinates its parent phone calls; the faculty selects students for the annual achievement awards.

But they stymy other equally or more important professional deliberations: exploring the benefits of manipulatives for the teaching of arithmetic; examining student achievement data and planning from that information; taking stock of how the new discipline procedures are working. Formal meetings in many schools have come to be seen by all participants as unfriendly to long-range philosophical or evaluative discussions—the type that might invite dissenting views and speculative thinking. The task orientation, fatigue levels, and uncertain commitment of faculty combine to make whole-school gatherings inimical to true collaboration. It is typical of teachers to view faculty meetings as "the principal's time" and, given their uncertain benefit to the classroom or even to the school as a whole, commitment to attendance and participation in them can spiral downward.

Scheduled team and committee meetings are typically more fruitful than large or compulsory meetings. These small group sessions can more easily fit the parameters of effective collaborative groups than can large formal gatherings. Their purpose is usually more clearly defined (e.g., to review the science curriculum or frame a new policy about retention). Their members are more apt both to have expertise about the topic and to be committed to the task of the team or committee than is the case in large faculty meetings. The smaller size makes scheduling times and dividing up tasks easier, as well. Judith Warren Little's (1982) research demonstrates how teachers are professionally rewarded by team and committee work that integrates closely with their teaching. Here is an opportunity not only to engage teachers in continuous thinking, learning, and planning but to help them shape better ways of working with students, parents, and each other.

Leaders who seek to "get everyone on the same page" by calling them together are often frustrated by the competing forces on faculty time, energy, and commitments. Whether their intent is to direct staff toward uniform practices and compliance to rules (in the classical bureaucratic model) or to invite and reward their participation in decisions (in the collaborative management model), there is never enough "quality time." Principals and formally appointed teacher leaders find themselves driven to "lead by memo" and executive decision simply because they cannot reach everyone frequently enough any other way.

RICH COLLEGIAL CONVERSATION

Although formal meetings are questionable arenas for leadership, other less formal opportunities for faculty conversation offer greater potential for mobilizing staff. In some schools, staff development time and regularly scheduled planning time for instructional teams are more conducive to leadership than are more forced assemblages of staff. Similarly, when teachers themselves gather informally during the day, week, and month, important behavioral and attitudinal norms are set and affirmed and influential opinions are formed.

Staff development has undergone a long, arduous evolution from prescribed "training" sessions to staff-initiated agendas where information-sharing, skill-building, and professional growth can occur (Louis, Kruse, & Bryk, 1995). Unfortunately, these sorts of activities are rare, often relegated to one of five or six whole-day sessions during the contract year. Some schools, however, have woven half-day sessions throughout the year where student assessment and planning occur synergistically and where long-term improvement efforts can be sustained. Others have lengthened staff work calendars to include 2 weeks of planning and team work. The professional tone and student-centered focus of such teacher gatherings make them rich opportunities for both principals and teachers to engage in leadership (Darling-Hammond, 1997).

Staff who work in teams or belong to committees form working relationships with one another that can be extraordinary influences on the school. Meetings become opportunities for problem-solving or for wide-reaching discussion about mission or new practices. Here, staff can create together a philosophical commitment to an idea, an approach to working with students, or a preference for a new way to organize the school. The informal connections, spawned by conversations around and during meetings, are the cement in these small communities of interest (Frech, 1997). If conditions are ripe for it, a team that has coalesced can implement their philosophy directly with the students they serve. If conditions inhibit them, a team or committee can become a flashpoint for advocacy and action within the school or district. In either case, the conversation and connections among staff present a very potent opportunity for coalescing leadership.

Informal connections also abound in schools. Teachers, counselors, secretaries, social workers, and other staff stop by one another's rooms routinely to chat or share a cup of coffee. They congregate in the teachers' room, the office, and the lunchroom. They coach together, collaborate on holiday programs, and share rides to work. Groups of staff debrief together at a local bar or socialize on the weekend. Although these informal gatherings are not organized centrally for a purpose, they are the most continuous means of communication, opinion-setting, and relationship-building in most schools. They shape the culture that shapes a staff's beliefs and attitudes about their work and their actions with students, parents, and administrators (Sarason, 1982). Largely inaccessible and even resistant to leaders' formal attempts to guide and structure it, this informal culture is a very potent milieu for leadership (Blase & Anderson, 1995; Evans, 1996).

IMPORTANT COMMUNICATIONS ARE INFORMAL

Schools, as we have seen in this chapter, do not offer many opportunities for face-to-face whole-staff communication. In fact, most communications are in pairs and small groups. They are unplanned and the topics discussed are determined by the participants quite independently of the formal leadership's agenda. Except in our smallest schools, the effort of bringing everyone together on a weekly or even bi-weekly basis simply outweighs the projected benefits.

Principals—the school's "official leaders"—use formal communication channels to distribute information and direct people: the public address system; memoranda; weekly newsletters to staff, students, and parents; notes in mailboxes or on e-mail. These channels are distinctly one-way; they are designed for mass information (or they soon come to be understood that way). These systems often function well for management purposes. With the exception of e-mail, however, none approaches the form of a dialogue or conversation—the types of communication in which important leadership relationships and processes can occur.

School leaders, in most cases, find they must pursue more individual and informal means of communication. Studies of effective leadership find that principals spend the great majority of their time in face-to-face (or ear-to-ear) conversation with staff, parents, central office, and students (Persell & Cookson, 1982; Sergiovanni, 1996). "Management by Walking Around" has been adopted by many principals. Forced to transact their business "on the fly," teacher leaders as well squeeze important decisions and information-sharing into passing conversations in the hallway, lunchroom, or carpooling to work. The natural networks of friendships and alliances serve as the best grapevine not only for communication of information but for sharing judgments about how to respond to that information. Although these forms of communication are often personally meaningful, they are often too rushed and too infrequent to constitute a systematic way for a leader to mobilize staff.

As opportunities for leadership, these realities encourage "dumping" rather than dialogue. Their one-way character and their brevity offer both leaders and others the chance to have their say, make their complaint, raise their issue, present their suggestion. The implicit relationship is directive: "Let me tell you what I think you should do" or "This is broken; you fix it." School communications leave little opportunity for fact-finding, perspective-sharing, and joint problem-solving. They tend to disintegrate the collective effort and can thus drive formal leaders to impose uniform information, policy positions, and practices on staff and students in an effort to hold the collective effort together (Blase & Blase, 1994). In this respect, the natural communication and opinion-setting channels of the faculty can become obstacles or even threats to the principal or teacher leader.

THE BIGGER, THE BULKIER

The sheer number of faculty and staff fundamentally determines the number and type of opportunities to lead. The larger the group, the fewer opportunities a principal or teacher leader has for individual relationship-building or problem-solving. The larger the group, the more complex the interaction and decisional process at formal meetings (and the more difficult it is to have 100% attendance!). Conversely, the smaller the staff, the more opportunities for interaction and the more easily the group can convene. The intimacy and intensity of small units present leaders with different leadership challenges than do large units.

In this regard, the ratio of staff to principals in American schools in 1991 was 37:1 (National Center for Education Statistics, 1994). From the viewpoint of organizational planning, change, or supervision, this ratio paints starkly the leadership challenge faced by the average principal. Simply staying current about faculty activities and about the significant professional challenges faculty face—not to mention supervising and evaluating them—is nigh on impossible for the average principal. By contrast, the ratio of supervisors to supervisees in most American businesses is 15:1, a far more conducive arrangement for the highly engaged leadership model that appears to work in some business settings.

Size also generates important differences in school structure and culture. Large schools are perforce more hierarchical. More students mean bigger facilities and these translate into more externalized policies and rules and more "policing." Large schools tend to have more principals and to have formalized teacher leader positions as department chairs or team leaders with pay and release time. Similarly, policy and procedural decisions are more often made by the formal leadership and simply communicated to the faculty and students. Divergent viewpoints are more apt to surface as micropolitical opposition and faculty dynamics tend to be formalized and more "closed" than "open" (Blase & Anderson, 1995). Smaller schools, on the other hand, function more as tribes or families than as bureaucracies. Roles are not as formal and participation in school-wide communication, decision-making, and initiatives is more fluid and more possible than in larger schools (Coalition of Essential Schools, 1997; Meier, 1995).

School size in U.S. public schools varies widely, presenting an array of leadership environments. In secondary schools alone, the average student enrollments in 1996 ranged by state from 1,333 in Hawaii to 168 in South Dakota. Fifteen states averaged above 850 and 13 averaged below 500 students per school. Taking the national ratio of secondary teachers to students (16:1), average faculty sizes ranged from 53 in some states to 31 in others (*Education Digest,* 1996). When support staff are added, these groups climb to about 70 and 45 respectively. Clearly, leaders saddled with calling these larger staffs together for meaningful deliberations face enormous challenges. Even fostering a collective spirit through social gatherings or regular communications about whole-school developments and issues requires substantial time and effort. Although our elementary schools are smaller and more cohesive institutions than most secondary schools, the trend through this century at all levels of public school has been toward larger, more formally structured institutions and away from smaller, more professionally controlled ones.

Our classical principal-as-leader model was invented to meet the needs of these larger institutions. Deemed too bulky and unruly to be productive learning environments on their own, schools were given bureaucratic leaders to assure the smooth and safe functioning of the apparatus of schooling (Callahan, 1962; Tyack & Hansot, 1982). In contrast, the current reform movement with its emphasis on accountability and student learning has spawned a strong smaller-is-better, less-is-more movement (Meier, 1995; Sizer, 1992). We seem not only to be saddled with a leadership paradigm from the 1920s but with schools whose size and structure make any other leadership paradigm very difficult to develop.

A UNIQUE LEADERSHIP LANDSCAPE

The overriding observation from this brief tour of structural conditions in schools is that they work against the success of classical leadership. To the leader charged by central office with the responsibility of improving teaching and learning practices, teachers are frustratingly beyond reach, busy with students and other primary responsibilities a huge percentage of their total time at work. Even the simplest directive or consultation with a staff person can be difficult to arrange or schedule. Many principals and teacher leaders transact such business "on the fly," often with students or other staff within earshot. Conversations and consultations snatched in the corridors, in a classroom before school, or over lunch tend to be about immediate concerns—the student sent to the office, the problems the team is facing with undone homework, this afternoon's special music program—and not about deeper and more long-range systemic issues. Formal meetings—the staple of classical leadership—are normally viewed as subsidiary to the main work people do at school with children and they are scheduled at difficult times when attendance, energy, and attention are less than optimal. Even in middle-sized schools—say, with enrollments above 300 and staffs above 25—the sheer numbers of staff and the dead weight of institutional rules and schedules make pulling people together for coordination, planning, collaboration, or even regular communication an arduous process. Put simply, schools are organized for teachers to teach students, not for adults to work together in a routine, centrally coordinated fashion.

Ironically, the very unruliness of school life—this conspiracy of busyness—

often convinces classical leaders to become increasingly directive, controlling, and bureaucratic (Cuban, 1988). In response to the frustrations of assembling staff and keeping in touch with them individually, principals' communications become one-way and emphasize mass information, administratively driven meetings, and managerial directives. Those staff who can routinely assemble at faculty, committee, or team meetings determine what the school or team vision will be, how the schedule will be structured, what the policy alternatives are, and even what curriculum and grouping practices will guide the work of all teachers. Those who cannot attend— or choose not to—drift away from leaders' attempts to develop a coordinated, coherent team. Frustrated by seeming unresponsiveness or by overt resistance to their attempts to manage and coordinate, principals and formal teacher leaders find themselves pressing and even requiring new teacher practices, new curriculum standards, and more uniformity (Muncey & McQuillan, 1996). Despite leaders' desires to be transformational, their inability to reach everybody routinely with the same message and to "get everybody on the same page" incline them toward the top-down, transactional leadership relationships and methods that school reform literature declares ineffective (Blase & Anderson, 1995; Darling-Hammond, 1997; Evans, 1996; Fullan & Hargreaves, 1991).

My review of work-life realities, however, discloses vital informal opportunities for leadership upon which, I will argue later, we can build a new conception of school leadership. More effective teacher leaders and principals conduct much of their business—and form the heart of their relationships with staff—"on the fly" and "by walking around" (Barth, 1990; Little, 1988; Sergiovanni, 1996). Unable to be everywhere to attend to all the important business of their schools or teams, leaders engage in the issues and decisions of teachers, students, counselors, and parents by dropping in and out of them. The many informal conversations and encounters among these core participants offer formal leaders untold opportunities to form relationships, make decisions, and take actions that shape the school's direction and performance. As important, it is in the milieu of these conversations and encounters that *informal leaders* emerge from the faculty and staff. This is where thinking is done and decisions are made that most directly influence how and what children are taught and how they are treated each day. In some schools, team and committee structures encompass and legitimize this work, even providing planning time for it during the day and week. More often, this organizational action is not channeled into the formal structure and culture of the school. As we see in later chapters, this informal network of relationships, communication, and engagement in practice is a vital and energetic asset to the leadership of schools.

Schools, then, bear little resemblance to the bureaucratic images that we often use to describe them and their leaders (Shedd & Bacharach, 1991). They are, instead, loosely coupled (Weick, 1976). In John Goodlad's (1984) words, they are "little villages" of teachers and students that exist within the "constrained and confining environment" of the school as a whole (p.113). The harsh reality is that the "busyness" of people in these little villages operates in constant tension with the rules and policies of the constrained environment. Principals and other appointed leaders come to be seen as people with position power whose job it is to direct, confine, and monitor rather than to support, entrust, and collaborate. The world of teaching and learning polarizes in the minds of students, staff, and parents from the world of administration and management.

Our challenge—and the central purpose of this book—is to see beyond these classical notions of leadership-as-administration a new conception of leadership that capitalizes on the professional tribalism of educators. Schools have strong cultures and teachers have a powerful sense of professional community that shape their practice and their relationships to one another. The informal social architecture, as I point out in Chapter 3, brings them together beyond the reach of principals and often teacher leaders. A model of leadership that works for the schoolhouse must draw on assets found in this fundamental reality. Only then will schools become environments that support productive work and learning for *both* children and adults.

The Planetary Culture of Schools
The Social Context of Leadership

The rule of privacy governs peer interactions in a school. . . . It is not acceptable to discuss instruction and what happens in classrooms with colleagues.
—Lieberman & Miller, (1992), p. 11

Chapter 2 makes the case that school schedules and structures restrict opportunities for classical leadership, helping to explain the frustrations many school leaders experience. This chapter observes that the culture and social norms of most schools also conspire against conventional forms and styles of leadership. Teacher leaders and principals not only must find times and means for leading busy teachers and staff; they also must face the constant challenge of engaging faculty in school-wide, long-range issues—issues that often seem distant, secondary, and even irrelevant to those who work directly with children. Simply in the act of assembling teachers and staff in a faculty, a team, or a committee, leaders are assuming that the social and political relationships among adults can be interrupted or suspended and a new working relationship imposed. As many leaders have discovered, individuals and groups turn out to "have a mind of their own"; collective decisions do not always mean collective support; many policies and program changes agreed to in writing are just as agreeably never practiced.

Teachers in many schools operate like planets in a galactic subsystem, maintaining their own orbit and unique classroom spin. They revolve around a common mission and a centralized management system. In most schools, their orbits can be tight or loose, their periodic encounters with either school purposes or the office rare or frequent. It is other staff that influence these orbits most, however, not the central gravitational pull. The literature exploring the sociocultural system of schools has, to our good fortune, blossomed in the past 30 years to help us understand this planetary culture. Since Philip Jackson's *Life in Classrooms* (1968), scholars and practitioners have filled books and journals with a rich array of description and analysis of teachers' work lives, attitudes, beliefs, and skills. In this chapter, I note five themes from this literature that mark the cultural context of school leadership:

- Teacher rewards are intrinsic and student-focused.
- The ethos is individualistic.
- Collegiality is voluntary and permissive.
- The teacherhood is a semiprofession: It is undervalued and peripheral.
- Organizational issues are the domain of administrators.

THE REWARDS COME FROM STUDENTS AND CLASSROOMS

Most teachers—and importantly, our most effective teachers—draw their greatest professional satisfaction and personal fulfillment from the immediacy of their work with children (Johnson, 1990). When teachers and other staff say, "It's the kids that keep me in this work," they make plain their central motive: Despite the many hours at low pay, it is the stimulation, the human contact, the unpredictability of and feedback from working with children that rewards them (Jackson, 1968; Johnson, 1990; Lieberman & Miller, 1992; Lortie, 1975). Work with children is, after all, the fundamental mission of the American teacher. David Tyack (1974) and Larry Cuban (1984) richly describe the "evangelical" fervor of early proponents of public school teaching that has sustained the efforts of many teachers over the past two centuries. Teachers have seen themselves as agents of democracy, as civilizing forces in the frontier and immigrant neighborhoods alike, and as carriers of a "moral mission" (Fraser, 1989; Johnson, 1989; Tyack & Hansot, 1982). Teaching, for the many who stay with it for a career, is truly a calling and, as with all callings, the sustaining rewards are intrinsic ones.

At the heart of teachers' satisfaction is, for many, their almost total control over what they do with their students. The classroom is the teacher's professional empire. Strong norms of privacy often make the walls around each empire impenetrable even to longtime colleagues (Lieberman & Miller, 1992). Goodlad's (1984) study of American schooling, the largest ever undertaken, concluded that "teachers controlled rather firmly the central role of deciding what, where, when, and how their students were to learn" (p. 109). He and his colleagues found, as well, an "implicit curriculum" of passivity, rote learning, and 70% teacher-talk in the classrooms of the country. Historical evidence emphasizes that teachers have tended toward conventional teaching methods and materials because, in part, these methods have established track records as mechanisms for student control (Tyack, 1989).

Educators value the intrinsic rewards of working with children in part because the "indemic uncertainties" of their work make extrinsic rewards problematic (Lortie, 1975). Teachers' work, with its "absence of concrete models for emulation, unclear lines of influence, multiple and controversial criteria, ambiguity about assessment timing, and instability in the product" (Lortie, 1975, p. 136), makes it very difficult to specify evidence of success. Surrounded by these uncertainties, teachers view their effectiveness as contingent on exercising control over classroom factors, including children. The belief that "I can make a difference" hinges on the assumption that "I can control enough of the important factors" in the educational equation to have students learn and learn to behave. In this regard, the ability to control is essential to feeling rewarded as a teacher (Bandura, 1997).

Teachers' attentions, then, are riveted within their classrooms. From the standpoint of school leadership, Lortie (1975) observed that "it is likely that [teachers] will care deeply about working conditions which they believe increase the flow of work rewards" (p. 101) and not so deeply about most other school-wide business. Each teacher's classroom, shaped as it is by his or her group of students and professional career stage, gives that teacher's work life a unique planetary spin. When principals, department chairs, or team leaders knock on teachers' doors with an important school-wide issue, most teachers will ask, "How will all of 'that' affect my success with 'this'?" Their willingness to become engaged in leadership's agendas will hinge on the answer to this question.

AN INDIVIDUALISTIC ETHOS

Despite its apparent uniformity, teachers' work is valued by teachers for the autonomy and individuality it allows them (Jackson, 1968; Lortie, 1975; Reyes, 1990). Their ability to serve their students requires flexibility, responsiveness, and the opportunity to get to know students well (Darling-Hammond, 1997; Johnson, 1990). As with all professions, the competence of the teacher hinges on his or her ability to make correct decisions on the spot and to calculate the many factors presented by the busy classroom environment. Individual discretion and autonomy are, most believe, essential to this competence (Cuban, 1984; Rosenholtz, 1986).

Over the years, the individualistic quality of teaching has been reinforced from several directions. The inability of scholars or practitioners to develop "any resilient scientific or other paradigm for teaching" has consistently encouraged teachers to follow their experience, not books—to trust "clinical knowledge" or "craft knowledge," not "theoretical knowledge" (Johnson, 1989, p. 250). The diversity among students and their unpredictability require of teachers constant reassessing, recalibrating, and decision-making about individuals and appropriate methods for them. Further, growth and diversification of learning theory, pedagogical methods, and the effects of environment on learning have continually reinforced the importance of teachers' judgment, intuition, and ability to use their own individual talents creatively.

The femininization of the teaching force has, especially of late, stimulated individuality, highlighting women's particular qualities and talents (Biklen, 1995). To some degree, women have always resisted the standardization of the profession, stressing the nurturant qualities of the role under a "domestic ideology" characterized by patience, affection, moral power, and piety (Clifford, 1989, p. 315). These affective qualities stand in counterpoint to efforts, induced largely by men, to govern teaching through rigorous science or administrative rule (Noddings, 1984). Women teachers put their whole beings into "reading" their students on many levels at once and are adept at responding to the quixotic learning conditions in classrooms. Teaching, as Sari Biklen (1995) puts it, calls upon teachers to "give up some of their personal needs, [their plans, and even the formal curriculum at times] in order to be present for children" (p. 181).

As this quality of the "women's true profession" has gradually emerged and been celebrated, so has teaching as a career choice been recognized as a vital avenue for women and minorities to establish their individuality and economic independence (Biklen, 1995; Clifford, 1989; Hoffman, 1981; Urban, 1989). Beginning in the mid-19th century, teaching was one of a very few options for women to support themselves and to sustain intellectual independence and moral autonomy. Expanding this theme through this century, women and minorities have led movements to protect the teacher's voice in decision-making and policy and to maintain a buffer around the teacher's ability to employ her individual professional judgment over classroom and student matters (Urban, 1989).

The tendency toward individuality in teaching thus sets up a counterforce to classical leadership. Attempts by principals and formally appointed teacher leaders to organize, coordinate, restructure, and monitor have understandably met with curiosity, doubt, and even resistance from teachers who proudly guard their professional knowledge, prerogative, and integrity (Evans, 1996; Lieberman, 1988b). District and state initiatives often squeeze a school's titular leaders between a hierarchical, top-down mode of leadership and an individualistic and increasingly activist profession. When issues of gender and race overlap these organizational tensions— as they often can—the potential for resistance and conflict multiplies.

COLLEGIAL WORK IS VOLUNTARY AND PERMISSIVE

Much has been written in recent years about the isolation and loneliness of teachers (Darling-Hammond, 1997; Lieberman & Miller, 1992; Rosenholtz, 1986). Teachers spend the vast majority of their days with children, not with colleagues or parents. Spending on average 47 hours per week at their work (Carnegie Foundation, 1990), many teachers find that the emotional and physical investments of teaching leave them too exhausted for other activities beyond those 47 hours. Even when they recognize the need for collegial support or for collaborative planning and action, teachers find it very difficult to muster the energy or budget the time for these activities (Little, 1982; Louis & Kruse, 1995).

On one hand, coping with isolation is practically a rite of passage for many public school teachers. Schoolmarms and schoolmasters of the past served in isolation, winning their spurs by persevering when argumentative parents, unruly students, and bureaucratic interference threatened their effectiveness and very survival (Cuban, 1984). Isolation, still today, comes hand-in-hand with individualism: New teachers prove their worth by surviving the hours each day "alone" with children (Donaldson & Poon, 1999). It is the teacher's choice to collaborate with another teacher or to join in a school-wide initiative, not an obligation. Dan Lortie (1975) observed from his studies of teachers that "norms [that shape collegial interaction and cooperation] are permissive rather than mandatory. The subculture . . . defines the degree of cooperation as a matter of individual choice" (p. 194).

Isolation, on the other hand, leaves teachers out of touch with professional and emotional resources that can make their work both more effective and more rewarding. Goodlad (1984) found that American teachers felt that their work was more satisfying when they were involved in school problem-solving, influencing teaching and school-wide decisions, and feeling staff cohesiveness (p. 259). Reflective practice groups, mentorships, and team structures have in recent decades demonstrated the power of collegial networks and partnerships (Darling-Hammond, 1997; Lieberman & Miller, 1992; McLaughlin & Yee, 1988). Studies of collective teacher efficacy and professional culture have begun to make the case for interdependent working relationships (Bandura, 1997; Bascia, 1994).

Collegiality as a value, however, remains secondary to one's classroom obligation. Lortie (1975), Rosenholtz (1986), and Reyes (1990) found that teachers valued collegial contacts primarily as a source of useful ideas for their teaching and as a source of personal support. To the extent that a teacher needed such external resources, he or she sought out and sustained relationships with colleagues. The result is a complex interplanetary relationship, characterized by "somewhat arbitrary" natural groupings: "smokers, nonsmokers, men, women, academic teachers, vocational teachers, [those thrown together] by the vicissitudes of scheduling" (Lieberman & Miller, 1992, p. 47). Ann Lieberman and Lynne Miller (1992) typify these faculty groups as

> families where unspoken understandings dominate. There are strong characters, strong personalities, leaders, those to be tolerated. There are ways of being open or being closed . . . people who are listened to and people who are ignored . . . endless tensions that one learns to tolerate . . . endless shibboleths about doing it all for the children while ignoring the adults and the interaction between them. (p. 94)

Each individual planet, then, finds its own place in the gravitational fields of the galaxy. Some are pulled more strongly together and affect one another's orbits while others are repelled. Still others seem nearly unaffected by the presence of other teachers, staff, and administrators. For leaders in the classic mold, leadership involves exerting stronger central gravitational pull, tightening up orbits, and overpowering teacher-to-teacher counterforces. In their efforts, they threaten to violate the "permissive association" norm; and this can provoke outright protest and passive resistance. In the end, as we have seen in recent studies of school reform, the culture that has naturally grown up in a school is almost always more powerful and more resilient than the formal structures, rules, and press from leadership (Evans, 1996; Muncey & McQuillan, 1996).

THE SEMIPROFESSION: UNDERVALUED AND PERIPHERAL

The school galaxy does have an order, however. Their professional training and values provide core patterns for educators' work and beliefs. So, too, does the bureaucratic organization of U.S. schooling. And these two usually conflict, giving rise to a pattern of life in public schools where the "profession" and the "bureaucracy" define the order. The unfortunate result of this tense marriage is that public educators have come to be seen as "semiprofessionals" (Biklen, 1995; Carter, 1989). Teachers live an ambiguous existence, revered and rewarded by their individual work but increasingly "undervalued" by their pay and their social status, particularly in comparison to the other professions (Rury, 1989). The ironies of their condition have led some to view teaching as "alienated" work (Clifford, 1989). Both the uncertainty of their status and their alienation contribute to the difficulties leaders face organizing and mobilizing staff.

A number of factors reinforce this condition. Schoolteaching historically was transient work; communities recruited anybody they could to conduct a 10-week session and turnover was high. Teachers were often only one generation away from blue-collar work and life styles. According to Carter (1989), teaching was a first step from blue-collar status toward white collar as "schools . . . made use of the services of educated white women and educated black men and women whose alternative employment opportunities were quite limited" (p.54). Despite attempts by universities and states to "train" and certify only the best teachers, in the 1990s our public schools are still forced to employ uncertified and poorly performing teachers (Darling-Hammond, 1997). Educators themselves—and especially men—reinforced the "undervaluing" of classroom teaching by using it as a stepping stone to more highly valued work as lawyers, businessmen, and administrators (Clifford, 1989; Herbst, 1989).

The growth of school districts, school size, and bureaucratic regulation contributed mightily to the definition of teachers as underlings: "By 1925, schools were firmly controlled by their administrators, and teachers were incorporated in the developing hierarchies at the lower-rung levels" (Urban, 1989, p. 195). Efficiency and standardization of practice redefined teachers' work by declaring that satisfactory teaching was that which met certification standards, state-approved curriculum and classroom practices, and the school district's performance checklist (Cuban, 1984; Meyer & Rowan, 1978). Although progressive arguments and attempts to organize teachers strived repeatedly to keep individual discretion and voice alive in the teacherhood, the power of states, school boards, and administration held the growth of professional autonomy at bay (Bascia, 1994; Urban, 1989). Here, the roots of our classical model of leadership were planted: School success was to be assured by executive educators (superintendents and principals) imposing enlightened practices and policies upon their guileless, semiprofessional staffs.

The subservience of teaching is inextricably wrapped in issues of women's place in our society and in the workplace. The successful campaign to establish common schools between 1840 and 1900 drew primarily women into the teacherhood except when wage-earning alternatives were scarce for men (Labaree, 1989). By 1940, 80% of all American teachers were women (Fraser, 1989). As schools grew in size, the corresponding development of school administration pulled men almost exclusively toward the principalship and superintendency. An analysis of mobility patterns within public education (Labaree, 1989) demonstrates a historical career path for upwardly mobile American educators that leads from elementary teaching to secondary teaching and eventually to administration or higher education. Labaree documents that this path "selects" for men and for Whites (p. 177). Clifford (1989), who examined cultural gender norms surrounding the creation of school administration and the elevation of teachers to administration, claims that the American system demonstrates "an aversion to women administrators" (p. 327), a conclusion supported by Shakeshaft (1989), Rusch and Marshall (1995), and others. Similar patterns have been documented for teachers from racial minorities (Clifford, 1989; Urban, 1989).

The result is well established: Many female teachers serve under the direction—and often at the discretion—of male administrators. Many African American and Latino teachers serve similarly under White direction. Issues of gender and race, whether individual or societal in origin, can thus overlie teachers' relationships with their principals, superintendents, board members, and chief state school officers, reinforcing the likelihood that teachers will feel—or in fact be—undervalued (Biklen, 1995). For many principals and teacher leaders, initiating leadership will thus engage in others a subtext of feelings and doubts about power, respect, and professional value. Their attempts at organization, coordination, and quality control in these circumstances can appear to be dominating and oppressing and can smell of sexism and racism. Classical bureaucratic leadership, which assumes that greater expertise and superior judgment reside in higher offices, can thus unwittingly barricade a school's formal leaders from its "semiprofessional" staff. Indeed, the unionization of public school resulted largely from this relational dynamic (Bascia, 1994).

SCHOOL-WIDE MATTERS ARE FOR ADMINSTRATORS

School staff often are content to have someone else deal with the sometimes contentious and frequently mundane organizational work of the school. This work ranges widely from upset parents to a school board or central office initiative to a scheduling or disciplinary challenge. Although teachers may feel marginalized and subservient, they can also be thankful that somebody else—typically the principal—buffers them from matters important but nevertheless secondary to their teaching. Especially as discontent with public schools has increased, the tendency for teachers to retreat to their classrooms and department meetings has left principals alone holding the fort. Dan Lortie's (1975) study of teachers found that most wanted their principal to "use his authority to facilitate their work. He should support the teachers . . . keep them well supplied [and] . . . ensure an atmosphere favorable to teaching by 'providing good administration'" (p. 199).

This buffering-and-support function is vital for teachers. It permits their individualism to flourish while it saves them from being engulfed by the ambiguities and conflicts that often rage at the school-district and community level. In the last 20 years alone, public schools have been swamped by demands for special education, vocational education, court-mandated integration, gifted/talented education, charter schools, and outcome-based state testing and embroiled in "school wars" over values, religious freedoms, and sexual preferences. Individual teachers could not respond to each of these waves of change.

Lortie (1975) saw this phenomenon contributing to an overall conservatism among American teachers. Faced with public debate over the direction of their schools and with uncertainties over resources and outcomes, teachers seek "'more of the same'; they believe the best program of improvement removes obstacles and provides for more teaching with better support" (p. 209). In this respect, public school teachers tend to blame the environment for insufficiently supporting their past and current teaching rather than to conclude, as outsiders have, that their teaching is flawed (Public Agenda, 1996). Although Linda Darling-Hammond (1997) is not so fatalistic, she similarly finds that teachers feel vulnerable and that seeking protection by administrators from the political winds only makes common sense.

The net effect of this "leave that to the administration" phenomenon is that many teachers and other school staff remain reticent to engage in organizational decisions or challenges. They will do so insofar as they believe that, by participating, their own work with children will be enhanced. In this light, teachers have clear expectations for their principals, believing that they should use their authority "to serve teacher interests: parents should be buffered, troublesome students dealt with, and chore-avoiding colleagues brought to heel" (Lortie, 1975, p. 200). In this respect, the planetary motion of staff around a central principal functions as a stabilizing and protective system and permits teachers to do the important work of teaching without being dragged into organizational and community chaos. In the world of leadership studies, this is a vital dynamic as it works against heavy collective involvement in decision-making and organizational change. Indeed, this dynamic has severely hampered efforts at participatory decision-making, site-based reform, and collaborative leadership (Blase & Anderson, 1995; Evans, 1996; Geisert, 1988).

THE LEADERSHIP PICTURE: HERDING CATS, PUSHING ROPE

Many principals and formally appointed teacher leaders find their work colored by the language and assumptions of the hierarchy. Central office, school boards, and the public approach them assuming that they have control over most if not all personnel and activities. They are expected to resolve problems through administrative or collegial authority, to ensure student performance and faculty accountability, and to govern the activities of school efficiently. Staff, too, want their principals, department heads, and team leaders to make their working environments orderly and to remove hurdles and problems with aplomb. The observations of this chapter, however, suggest that the culture and social norms of most schools make delivery on this classical model of leadership very difficult (Cuban, 1988). Leading educators is more like herding cats or pushing rope than it is like running a well-oiled machine. The frustrations of principals and teacher leaders who have attempted to lead in the bureaucratic-rational framework are now driving able educators away from formal leadership positions altogether (Evans, 1995).

The five attributes of school culture in this chapter help, however, to articulate the challenges that leaders face in mobilizing school staffs to improve. Each attribute points, as well, to a quality that a more fitting model of school leadership should include. To involve staff meaningfully in organizational matters, leaders must grapple with the enormous gravitational pull of staff's attention and energy toward students and the classroom, conference table, gym, or stage. Students are the lifeblood of teachers' professional beings. The reward and the meaning they derive from being teachers resides with students, not with school-wide management issues, long-range questions and goals, or even another teacher's pressing problems. Classical leadership relies on authority and charisma to attract or coopt teacher energies for such organizational work; these tools are plainly insufficient for that task. The challenge for leaders is to integrate into the school-wide work they propose the constant opportunity for teachers and staff to enhance their professional efficacy in their primary roles. *A new leadership model must construe school leadership as being about students, learning, and teaching.*

Making this task more complicated is the individualistic quality that predominates in teacher work and teacher cultures. Effective teaching requires teachers to seal off their time and space with students and to turn their whole beings toward the intricate art of educating. Teachers learn to teach in isolation, and the identities they develop both as professionals and, especially for women and minorities, as independent, autonomous adults, often accentuate their self-sufficiency. Having survived the initial years, many are not eager to make themselves vulnerable to others by sharing what they do or by admitting deficiencies (Lieberman & Miller, 1992). To the lead teacher with a new plan for assessment or to the principal with a new regulation, teachers ask, "Will this jeopardize my successful ways of working with students? Will it compromise my professional autonomy?" The challenge for leaders is to approach staff in ways that legitimize their hard-won knowledge and skills while inviting them to examine the significant challenges facing the school's success with all children. *A model for school leadership must both honor teachers and support frank critique and creative improvement.*

Fortunately, the isolation of teaching can provide a powerful impetus to connect with other staff. This impetus does not mean that all staff want to gather around school-wide challenges. Isolation generates a need for affiliation, not for more work, more assignments, or more task-oriented meetings. It means, more often than not, that when teachers do meet, they need to connect, they need social and personal time to be with other adults and permission NOT to talk shop. Most importantly, the norm in schools supports *permissive* collegiality; collaboration is by individual choice. Leaders who try mandating collective decisions, teamwork, mentorships, or collegiality are apt to find some staff who comply, others who resist, and still others who simply ignore their efforts to "force us to work together." For the principal with a tight agenda or the team leader with a deadline, teachers' needs—their stories, jokes, complaints, and off-task behavior—can be maddening. They can be, as well, for the teacher who is anxious to have a meeting over with so she or he can get home or get on to practice or rehearsal. The challenge, then, is to strike a balance between faculty needs for affiliation and for physical and emotional replenishment and the school's need for coordination, planning, and improvement. *A new model of leadership must respect the human needs of school staff even as it seeks to mobilize them to meet school challenges.*

Complicating the leadership picture even more, the historical subservience of teachers has created a culture in school districts where distrust and the abuse of power lie just beneath the surface of leadership work. If teachers feel undervalued and alienated to start with, leaders can with little provocation be seen as dominating and power-hungry. The leader–follower relationship can quickly polarize, putting leaders in the position of constantly seeking to heal broken trusts and clarify mistaken messages. And when the leader is male and the staff member is female or when the leader is White and the staff member's race is in the minority, the potential for power and trust issues to muddy the leadership process is even greater. The challenge for leaders is to establish relationships with staff that are authentic and robust enough to sustain open communication about issues of equity, power, trust, and performance. *A new model of school leadership must honor relationships as an integral dimension of leadership.*

Given these realities, it comes as no surprise that school staff develop the attitude that administrators are hired to handle the school-wide "leadership stuff" and, by implication, they themselves should be freed of this responsibility. Principals and formally appointed teacher leaders often feel mired in a catch-22: They are intent on building collaboration for projects they initiate, assuming that teachers and staff will see the merit in the idea and "buy in"; yet they are greeted by apathy and exhaustion and increasingly by staff who say, "Just tell me what you want me to do." Their challenge is to differentiate their roles and responsibilities so that everyone can be appropriately engaged in improving student learning. *A new model of school leadership must expect and enable each person to enhance her or his contributions to student learning both individually and as a member of the school community.*

In the culture described by these five themes faculties and appointed leaders engage in a dance around whose authority, expertise, and priorities will determine the work they enter into together. The staff member legitimately asks, "What is it about your agenda that is so vital to my work that I should change my schedule, my beliefs and values, and my practices?" At the core of this dance is the leader's professional and personal relationship with staff members. How principals and sometimes teacher leaders respond to this question establishes whether trust, openness, and personal affirmation will be the rule in their relationship or whether it will be marked by domination, required compliance, and fear. How the leader deals with the sensitive interpersonal dimensions of this dance, as we see in future chapters, determines his or her success as a leader.

CLASSICAL LEADERSHIP FOR SCHOOLS: SQUARE PEG, ROUND HOLE

The landscape of school life realities depicted in this chapter and the preceding one is familiar to most American teachers and principals—and often depressingly so. When principals, department heads, team leaders, or a "steering committee" turn to colleagues with a plan or even the nugget of an idea for improvement, these realities loom. They often force changes of strategy, timetable, and even personnel. They have eventually defeated well-intentioned leadership efforts altogether. No time to meet, much less to do ongoing planning. Insufficient information to understand the challenges or to plan knowledgeably. Meager energies remain after a day spent with students and duties. Few opportunities to consult and collaborate with colleagues either for their expert opinions or their moral support. The culture of autonomy and individualism feed divisions and even hostilities between administration and teachers and within the faculty. Uncertainty about outcomes worms its way into conversations, weakening resolve and solidarity around the new idea. Staff question administrators' commitment, trust, and support: If we get behind this, will they fund it? Will this mean we can try what *we* believe will work best? And there is the problem of scope which intensifies in larger and larger schools: Are we trying to reform the whole school? How can we reach every student through every teacher tucked away in the nooks and crannies of the building and the curriculum?

One principal, upon reading a draft of these two chapters, cautioned me to "lighten up," pointing out that this depiction of the school landscape, although accurate, was downright discouraging for any school leader to behold. But that is exactly my point. We need to stop framing reform as "the leader's problem." We need to reframe leadership itself so that our square-peg notions of how leaders should function no longer violate deeply embedded round-hole realities of school life. If we do not, we will continue to count an alarming number of communities and faculties who have become critical and even cynical about their formal school leaders. Tragically, we will count as well a growing number of principals and teacher leaders who give up on leadership and a similar trend among capable teachers to eschew a future in school leadership altogether.

Numerous observers have noted the long-standing incompatibility between our classical approach to leading schools and the natural features of schools and the teacherhood (Darling-Hammond, 1997; Evans, 1996; Fullan, 1997; Sergiovanni, 1996). America's infatuation with the "rational-structural" approach to organizing its institutions led by 1940 to an "education bureaucracy" that sought to routinize and control idiosyncratic, human activities of learning and teaching. The tenets of leadership that are deeply embedded in this bureaucratic paradigm are reinforced by our governmental and business institutions and cultural values (Bacharach & Mundell, 1995; Bolman & Deal, 1991). In brief, they are:

1. Leadership is invested in individuals occupying formally appointed roles. Authority is ascribed to those who hold these roles by law, by policy, and by past practice. School boards, superintendents, and principals determine policies for others, establish purposes for others' work, and identify priorities to focus that work in order to accomplish high-quality outcomes.

2. Leaders have greater knowledge and can make better judgments than those they lead. They are privy to the most vital information and expertise and should control the flow of this important information through the communication system. They are rightfully responsible for school-wide planning, quality control, and "the truly important" decisions.

3. Leaders manage a rationally organized system for production that will maximize outputs by running with maximum efficiency. In schools, this system has five major elements:
   a. a stable system for the control of student behavior
   b. a uniform curriculum structure and implementation system
   c. a single model for "best" teaching and learning, often based on behaviorist principles
   d. specialization of staff to meet specialized needs of the student population
   e. measurement of products against prescribed standards

4. Leaders optimize the production of student results by this system through a command-and-control pyramid structure. This enables the school to (a) be responsive to emerging needs and community preferences and (b) change its practices to meet these needs and preferences.

These principles of leadership for schools mirror closely the corporate para-digm (Callahan, 1962; Tyack & Hansot, 1982). We invented principals when schools became so large that we needed someone besides the teachers to handle the spillover and the coordination of facilities, bodies, and time. Coincidentally, in the 1920s and 1930s, state governments and universities teamed up to standardize "best practice"—best curriculum, best tests, best libraries, best school organization, best teacher qualifications. The principal's job—defining our original conception of school leadership—was to see that his or her school conformed to this "one best system" (Tyack, 1974). Principals called faculties together to hand out the new city curriculum, to read the latest memorandum from the central office, to teach the teachers what they should be testing for and how they needed to be disciplining their children (Spring, 1997).

Leadership, in a word, was administration—the administration of the plans and policies developed by wiser and more powerful people in the central office, the university, and the state capital. To a considerable extent, the imposition of this model of "leader as administrator" was intended to bring order, uniformly high performance standards, and assured outputs to a system of schooling that has always been viewed by policymakers and organization planners as chaotic, overly indepen-dent, and subject to slip-shod performance. That is, the square-peg model of classi-cal leadership's very purpose was to bring "squareness" to the round-hole qualities of teachers' lives and schools' performance.

David Tyack and Elisabeth Hansot (1982) argue that this system seemed to work well for America until the 1950s and 1960s when the promise of affluence provoked previously silenced people to recognize that it had not worked for them. Poor and minority parents demanded that the public schools serve their children as well as they served children of the affluent. Schools suddenly found themselves pressed to teach all students, not just the 40% they had typically graduated from high school prior to 1950. And among the "other 60%," they found children of color, children with behavioral and learning challenges, children of poor urban and rural origins, children from cultures that heretofore had seen no practical value to a formal education. With the 1960s and 1970s came a level of political activism that insisted that public schools serve "all children"; advocates saw to it that federal and state lawmakers changed statutes to compel schools to provide a free and equal education to all. The outcomes-and-accountability movement of the 1980s and 1990s turned up the pressure by publicly condemning schools for their past perfor-mance and insisting on public tests to determine which schools were failing and which were succeeding with all their children.

The incompatibilities between the classical leadership model and school reali-ties have been noted in this and the preceding chapter. I have represented them in Figure 3.1 and summarize them in the following paragraphs. First, classical leader-ship gives formal authority to people appointed to specified leader roles. They are, by policy and even law, presumed to determine and promulgate goals, standards,

FIGURE 3.1 Classical Leadership and the Realities of School Life

Tenets of Classical Leadership	*Work-life Realities of Schools*
Leaders have formal authority and school-wide roles • Appointed by superintendent/board • Set school-wide policies to accomplish quality outcomes • Determine purposes, standards, & priorities	Educators earn authority from peers; roles are separate & equal • Informal leaders strongly influence faculty/practice • Teachers treasure autonomy and individualism; feel marginalized (reinforced by gender/ethnicity) • Teachers control classroom policy and practice • Administrators "do" school-wide management for us
Leaders have superior expertise and information • Judge school needs and priorities • Manage communication system/information • Determine planning/decision-making • Are responsible for quality control	Teachers/staff possess most valued expertise & information about students, learning, & teaching • Formal communications are sporadic; unheeded if irrelevant to staff • Teachers share information and affiliate informally; informal norms shape teacher practice • Teacher decisions and professionalism "make" the school
Leaders manage a rational production system that: • Structures curriculum • Routinizes teaching and learning • Measures outcomes • Controls behavior • Assigns personnel and distributes resources	Professionals flex in response to student/school needs • Students/learning are dynamic, idiosyncratic • Teachers adapt curriculum & instruction to students & available resources • Staff protect style differences & professional autonomy; school is complex and planetary • Outcomes vary with student, goals, community
Leaders control students, staff, and activities • Adhere to chain-of-command structure • Make practices conform to policies and procedures to attain organizational goals • Direct system to respond to emerging needs, preferences, and events	Control over core work resides with staff • "No time and no way" to tightly coordinate action • Formal leaders' control of management & resources seen as obstacle to effective work with children • Teams & individual relationships most powerful influence on staff • Collaboration is voluntary and permissive, not subject to mandate

and organizational priorities in order to fulfill the school district's and state's mission. *The classical leader's appointed authority, however, runs up against the earned authority of teachers and other staff,* an authority that grows from the respect of their colleagues and, frequently, their recognized competence with children. Here, the individualism, professional judgment, and student-centered mission of teachers stands in counterpoint to the policies, the school-wide management issues, and the priorities of central office, school board, and government. At its most extreme, these differences boil down to contests of power and will between "the administration" or school board and "the teachers."

The second incompatibility revolves around where the expertise lies for the school's success. In the classical system, people are appointed to leadership posts because they have demonstrated top-of-the-line expertise. Their superior expertise qualifies them to make decisions, set policies, evaluate personnel, and control the flow of information. In schools, however, expertise with children and instruction is most highly valued. Talents, information, and individual discretion reside with teachers, counselors, parents, coaches, and aids, not in centralized offices. Here, *the classical leader's need to be expert and to be informed runs up against the fact that the staff are the most informed and the most expert with the children they teach.* Information is shared and decisions are made informally among people when the opportunity or need arises, not when formal meetings compel them or system-wide planning schedules permit them. The pace of this "real work" moves much faster than the formal system can move, making quality control very difficult to exercise.

The third area of incompatibility lies more deeply in the assumption that the business of the organization can and should be structured into a rational system. The classical system structures the work process, the worker's talents, and resources so that good products are produced. The leader manages this system and is responsible for its overall performance. The rub in schools stems from the fact that the core work—learning and teaching—has proven resistant to rational, one-size-fits-all formulas. Put another way, good teaching requires professionals to be responsive to children, flexible in their planning and teaching, and supported by a system that also can flex. Here, *the classical leader's need to organize and to make the work of schools predictable and uniform butts up against the constant variation of student learning needs, teacher styles, and surrounding conditions.* The best-laid plans of classical leaders always face the exception—the student who clearly needs a different program or assignment, the teacher whose current teaching unit requires a double class period this week, the team that wants to try a discipline system different from that of the entire school.

Finally, the classical leadership model is incompatible with public school realities because it assumes that leaders control the organization sufficiently to be able to change it. The bureaucratic-rational system typically relies on chain-of-command authority to assure the organization's responsiveness to external pressures or internal needs and preferences. Leaders, in consultation with whomever they choose or at the behest of the governing board, can turn the organization, if not on a dime, quickly enough to permit it to continue functioning well. Schools, as we have amply seen in these two chapters, do not operate in such a tightly coordinated fashion. Staff are scattered, transactions occur on the fly, opinions and attitudes are heavily influenced by individual and small-group preferences, and individuals, by and large, control their own work. Here, *the classical leader's assumed capacity to change the organization runs up against the fact that many people control the work in schools that is most essential to success.* Formal leaders can control structures and management systems; they can even change them single-handedly. But such restructuring will not substantially change how teachers work with students. And it is very likely to create such hostility and resistance among those who object to being treated as semiprofessionals that the outcomes will in fact be very different from those sought by the leaders. The culture of permissive collegiality, the decentralization of the work, and the physical impossibilities of lock-stepped action throughout a school make bureaucratic control unfeasible for all but the simplest management requirement.

Given the apparent misfit between the classical leadership paradigm and work-life realities, we should not be surprised that our public schools have not responded to that leadership. The classical paradigm worked when larger schools were being created and public school advocates believed that learning could be made into a rational process. It continues to serve a function in establishing a safe environment and orderly appearing routine in the school. But as a means to lead our public schools into more effective teaching and learning—that is, mobilizing people to more fully reach the school's goals—the bureaucratic-structural model leaves much to be desired.

Our leadership paradigm has failed in another, more pernicious sense. Principals and formally appointed teacher leaders have found themselves caught increasingly in the collision between the square peg and the round hole. Principals, in uncommon numbers, are leaving their positions in search of more fulfilling and personally healthful work. Burnout and "finding balance" are hot topics on professional meeting agendas. Every state now faces a crisis as applicant pools for administrative and formal teacher leadership roles are drying up. In short, the harder those in leadership positions try to lead in this classical model, the greater the personal (and perhaps professional) price they risk paying.

The now widespread assumption that public schools need to change has thankfully brought our classical notions about leadership fully under the microscope. As schools have explored empowerment, participatory decision-making, teacher leadership, reculturing, and "improving from within," we seem now to be able to appreciate fully the limitations of our past notions of leadership-as-administration. It is past time that we create a model of leadership that will help our best educators to succeed. Such a model must both mobilize schools toward demonstrable improvement in student learning and make the work of leading manageable and personally fulfilling. It must, that is, permit educators and citizens to change the conditions for children and adults that have stifled both leadership *and* learning. In the remaining chapters of this book, I develop a leadership model that, I believe, meets these challenges.

CHAPTER 4

A More Fitting Model of Leadership for Schools

We need to develop our own theories and practices [of leadership]—theories and practices that emerge from and are central to what schools are like, what schools are trying to do, and what kinds of people schools serve.

—Sergiovanni (1996), p. xiii

Our attempts at leadership for school improvement have failed to mobilize the autonomous and dispersed work forces of our schools as rapidly and as widely as many would like. I have suggested that the fault for this lies more with our conception of leadership than it does with the realities of schools. American public schools are unusual types of organization. They function more on moral conviction and professional judgment than they do on tightly prescribed goals and technical rationality; their power is distributed, and the citizen can potentially influence policy more than the educator. The evidence suggests that trying to lead such organizations using the classical model has failed to meet the two standards of leadership I established at the beginning of this book: that true leadership mobilize the school to new, more effective levels of performance demanded by its environment and that true leaders thrive as they participate in leadership rather than merely cope or, worse, become personally and professionally depleted.

We have in the United States grown up with a concept of school leadership-as-administration that has dangerously polarized our assumptions about who is responsible for and capable of providing leadership for schools. Particularly now that American society is expecting higher performance from its public schools, the pressures on principals to act as classical leaders, to "deliver the goods," are enormous. Ironically, as Sergiovanni (1996) argues, these leaders will hit the same wall of school realities that has frustrated past attempts at reform and restructuring: "In true North American fashion these changes are expected to be implemented quickly. This quick-fix pressure leads many school leaders to look for easy answers that do not result in meaningful change" (p. xiii). Most tragically, it is experiences of this sort that have convinced some of our most talented leader-educators to step back from formal leadership positions or never to seek them in the first place. The result of attempting leadership in ways that do not fit the realities of school has been, in

Robert Evans' (1995) words, that "we are disempowering and burning out the people who must lead reform" (p. 36).

This chapter proposes a model of school leadership that honors the longstanding structures and culture of our public schools. My goal is to create a way of thinking about school leadership that can mobilize members of the school community to improve the school's service to children and families—even changing the structure and culture of the school if members believe that they are thwarting student growth and learning. To attain this goal, the model of leadership must address the five challenges laid out in Chapter 3:

- Give busy educators continuous opportunities to enhance their efficacy in their primary roles through engaging in school-wide leadership work.
- Honor educators' hard-won knowledge and skills while inviting them to examine the significant challenges facing them and the school's effectiveness.
- Strike a balance between faculty needs for affiliation and replenishment and the school's need for coordination, planning, and improvement.
- Nurture relationships that are authentic and robust enough to sustain open communication about issues of equity, power, trust, and performance.
- Welcome all willing partners in taking leadership responsibility, differentiating roles and responsibilities so every person who wants to can appropriately participate.

My second goal is to foster a way to be a leader that makes leadership a personally desirable and manageable activity. The model of the administrator-as-leader makes succeeding as a principal increasingly difficult. The broader notion, rampant in our culture, that leaders are individuals with "heroic" qualities violates, when applied to public schools, the democratic value system and distributed power arrangements we find there. As I have been developing this fresh model, one of the driving motivations for me is to create a way to lead in schools that entices and propels the very best and most committed teachers to participate.

The chapter begins with an introduction to the model's core premise: that leadership is not a quality with which individuals are imbued or a process that selected individuals conduct with followers; rather it is a form of relationship among people that has the effect of mobilizing them to accomplish purposes they value. Following this first section, I discuss in greater detail the three main "streams" of activity that play into the creation of leadership: a relationship of mutual openness, trust, and affirmation; commitment to valued purposes; and a shared belief in action-in-common. The chapter concludes with a brief discussion of how these three streams blend to promote school mobilization. Building upon this theoretical groundwork, the next six chapters explore the implications of this model for leadership practice and for principals and teacher leaders.

THE BASIC CONCEPT: A RELATIONSHIP THAT MOBILIZES PEOPLE FOR MORAL PURPOSE

The vast majority of writing and thinking on leadership places the leader himself (and more recently, herself) in the foreground. As John Gardner put it in his 1990 book, *On Leadership,* "People who have not thought much about it are likely to believe that all influence originates with the leader, that the leader is the shaper, never the object of shaping by followers" (p. 31). In this section, I introduce a model that views leadership residing in a collective relationship where participants are both "shapers of" and "shaped by" one another. In its simplest form, the model argues that *leadership is a relationship that mobilizes people to fulfill the purposes of education.* It has three integral dimensions: the relational, the purposive, and the mobilizing.

A Relationship, Not a Person or a Process

Leadership has long been viewed as a function of the relationships between leader and follower; usually leaders use that relationship to influence followers to believe, think, or act. This notion is central to our classical, bureaucratic models of leadership. It works best in hierarchically organized organizations where the work is technical and can be routinized (Rost, 1993). In public schools, however, where egalitarian, professional values are the espoused norm and authority is distributed, leadership resides in the relationships among people. When the relationship among teachers, principals, staff, and others permits, it can mobilize them to share in actions, beliefs, and values. Leadership, then, requires not one person but at least two, and preferably many.

A relationship that fosters leadership is characterized by mutual openness, trust, and affirmation. People enter into it freely and consensually; if they are coerced, the relationship is not leadership but a bureaucratic contract or authoritarianism. Rather than freezing the leader and follower in an essentially unequal, I-influence-you relationship, this model views all members of the adult school community as essential partners. Given the importance of all adult roles in the school—teacher, counselor, principal, parent, band director, coach, staff member—the school's capacity to fulfill its collective purpose through the mobilization of all is maximized when leaders emerge from any and all of those roles. In a school where every adult is both "shaper and shaped," each person owns a share of influence and responsibility not just over her individual job but over school-wide concerns as well. Such an approach multiplies exponentially the possibilities for making leadership work. It is an approach that encourages participation, ownership, and commitment.

Strong support for the relational view of leadership exists. From Joseph Rost's (1993) notion of leadership as "an influence relationship among leaders and their collaborators who intend real changes that reflect their mutual purposes" (p. 7) to Linda Darling-Hammond's (1997) stress on a new professionalism in schools, a collective relationship is replacing the person as the kernel of leadership. Additionally important, a relational approach provides not only for more diverse participants and styles but more specifically for women's proclivities for egalitarian-collaborative ways of working (Helgesen, 1995). In Nel Nodding's (1984) view, the relationship *is* the essential feature of how any two people work together; she writes, "how good *I* can be is partly a function of how *you*—the other—receive and respond to me" (p. 6).

Most conventional views of leadership, founded on the premise that the leader makes leadership happen, present few opportunities for anyone but the leader to shoulder the power, authority, and responsibility for the group's success. Most critical, when the group is not going so well—an accusation often leveled at public schools—it is the leader alone who assumes most blame. To change, the leader needs either to change others ("It's really their inability to respond to my leadership that's at fault") or to change himself ("But I've already staked my claim on this approach. I can't change now!"). The result, in the public education world, has been that teachers blame administrators—and administrators blame teachers—for their inability to turn the ship on a dime. Such blaming can magnify differences of gender, ideology, and power, driving school staffs toward paralysis rather than mobilization. By contrast, viewing leadership as a relationship provides many more entry points for all members of the group to take responsibility and action for helping the school in its vital work.

To summarize, the relational element of leadership occupies the central place in the model. *Leaders foster a relationship that permits those who share in it to mobilize when the need arises.* The relationship is of such a character that the people who are webbed together by it can act collectively. What the group does as a result of the leadership relationship is of utmost importance; simply moving or acting in concert does not constitute the exercise of leadership. Leadership occurs when the action fulfills the school's fundamental purposes.

The Fulfillment of Moral Purpose

Educators have long approached their work as a calling rooted not just in passing on knowledge but in nurturing the good in children:

> Our schools do much more than pass along requisite knowledge to the students attending them. . . . They also influence the way those students look upon themselves and others. They affect the way learning is valued and sought after and lay the foundations of lifelong habits of thought and action. They shape opinion and develop taste . . . contribute to the growth of character and, in some instances, they may even be a factor in its corruption. (Jackson, Boostrom, & Hansen 1993, p. xii)

The educator's calling has a moral dimension: When all is said and done, he or she seeks to make individual lives and society in general better; teachers enlighten and empower their students and they ameliorate the human condition (Palmer, 1997). The American public sponsors public schools in the belief that benefits will accrue not only to individual children and their families but to our society, economy, and democratic system of self-governance (Gutmann, 1987; Tyack and Hansot, 1982).

To a large degree, our faith in educators' sense of moral purpose sustains the planetary, individualistic culture of our public schools. We have structured schools to maximize each teacher's contact with students under the assumption that, with minimal guidance from district curriculum, textbooks, and supervision, the teacher's devotion, sensitivity, and talents make for the best learning. We have always—and we continue even now—to endorse the principle that parent and teacher can and should be the ultimate judges of what is good for our children. Particularly as government agencies, school boards, pressure groups, and administrators have pressed teachers to change, teachers have steadfastly refused to cede responsibility and control over their work with children—the heart of their moral contract with American society.

The model of leadership we pursue in schools must accommodate this fundamental moral reality. If the leadership relationship is to mobilize many, it must strike a chord with their deepest sense of calling. As we saw in Chapter 2, teachers and other staff who devote their days and their lives to educating children find it difficult even in the best of circumstances to invest energy in agendas that seem only tangential to their primary purpose. The adult membership of the school, if their relationship is to result in professional action, must find that relationship a clear path for the fulfillment of their own calling. Investment in it must, especially for busy teachers and administrators, promise professional fulfillment. The challenge faced by people who aspire to lead, then, is to understand school-wide work in terms that resonate with teachers' moral purpose.

Leadership can be said to exist in a school only insofar as it contributes demonstrably to growing healthy, skilled, and well-adjusted children. This "purposive" dimension (Vaill, 1998) taps into both educators' and parents' deepest motives for investing their lives and their children in our public schools. It gives their relationship, then, not only moral energy but a direction, goals, and a way to judge how well their work is benefiting children. A relationship among educators, parents, or others without this sense of purpose and commitment is not leadership.

Mobilization

The third dimension of the model posits that the leadership relationship results in action that serves moral purpose. That is, leadership mobilizes people to action that serves the learning and development of children. People joined in a leadership relationship *will* engage in working together to improve their effectiveness both individually and collectively. Ronald Heifetz (1994) views this mobilization as "tackling tough problems—problems that often require an evolution of values. . . . [This] is the end of leadership; getting that work done is its essence" (p. 26). Purposive action is an essential ingredient in the leadership relationship.

Leadership, then, takes a school full of people already in motion and enables them to alter their patterns of motion to improve their collective impact on children's learning. Mobilization, as I will describe it later, does not mean uniform or clockwork action (although this form of action is not ruled out). Instead, it means that most people, through their engagement with each other around the "tackling of a tough problem," learn to adapt what they believe and perhaps what they value in order to *behave* differently in their work. I view this as action-in-common, to distinguish it from common or uniform action. The staff are *acting in common reference to their collective relationship and its purposes.*

This notion fits schools much more comfortably than do more heavily synchronized concepts of the action that leadership is supposed to create. As we have seen, schools in their present form offer only rare opportunities to convene, coordinate, and carry out master plans that positively shape student learning. Instead, the informal culture and social structure provide a resilient and often energetic system for communication, affiliation, and professional sharing. This system is marked by its "voluntariness": Collegiality cannot be mandated but is permissive; teachers, within the confines of their schedules, choose to associate with some and not with others; they seek out opportunities to share professionally and do not take kindly to "enforced collaboration." Teachers' actions in the classroom are shaped, most importantly, by what they believe and what they have found to work in the past. They change those actions—that is, they are mobilized to improve—when they are able to believe an alternative might work better, to try it out, and to integrate into their repertoire what does work better (Darling-Hammond, 1997; Lortie, 1975). A prime force in this process is the opportunity to examine the challenges they face in their own practice and to learn, with the support of trusted colleagues, what might work better (Lieberman & Miller, 1992).

The mobilization of a school, then, is at once an individual choice and a collective process. In forming a leadership relationship that mobilizes them to improve, respect for the individuality of each teacher's work is of paramount importance. Leading, in this regard, is more like herding cats or pushing rope than it is like changing the gears in a well-oiled machine or giving orders to dutiful corporals. The collective ethos and culture fostered within the leadership relationship must affirm, support, and challenge each individual within his or her own planetary orbit to rise to the occasion of improving his or her work individually and, if necessary or desired, together (Barth, 1990; Evans, 1996; McDonald, 1996; Sergiovanni, 1996).

Leadership contributes to this action-in-common more by helping the school's dispersed staff to connect with one another around the "tough problems" they individually and jointly face than by telling them how to reform or what standards to attain. The action that results from leadership is very likely to lack uniformity, to occur in far-flung corners of the school's life, and, most important, to be situated in the interaction of adults with children where it is very difficult to detect. *The effects of these actions manifested in the achievements and behaviors of children, however, are detectable and remain the ultimate measure of leadership itself.*

In the remaining three sections of the chapter, I describe in more detail the three dimensions in order to establish their special character prior to examining their implications for principal and teacher leaders in Chapters 5 through 10. I think of these elements as streams that play into the larger current of school leadership that courses through schools. That is, people are in relationships already that shape their knowledge, beliefs, attitudes, and actions. These relationships bring some people together regularly, keep others polarized in opposing camps, and in larger schools may completely separate others. They dictate who pursues what purposes and which staff can have a hand in improving their own or the school's overall performance. Individuals, small groups, the faculty, citizen groups, and students mingle, each bringing their more focused purposes and issues to the busyness of school. In this fluid environment, *those who aspire to purposeful leadership seek to feed, channel, or perhaps even divert the streams of relationships, purposes, and action toward mobilization for improvement.* That is, they work for the following:

1. Relationships of mutual openness, trust, and affirmation sufficient for the players to influence and be influenced willingly by one another.
2. Commitments to deep purposes—to purposes that educators and citizens regard as morally good.
3. A shared belief that together the group or school can accomplish their purposes better than individuals can.

THE FIRST STREAM: AN OPEN, TRUSTING, AFFIRMATIVE RELATIONSHIP

The best way to deal with change is to improve relationships.

—Fullan (1997), p. 17

Fundamental to the concept of a mobilizing relationship is the ability of individuals and groups to influence one another. In John Gardner's terms, this is the willingness to "shape" and "be shaped." Such a relationship forms around interpersonal and professional trust. Adults are drawn together when they feel sufficiently that "I can trust you" to care about me and to contribute to our collective purpose. Trust leads to openness and to affirming in one another positive talents and resources that can contribute to the fulfillment of our purposes (Barth, 1990; Cooperrider, 1998; Helgesen, 1995; Noddings, 1984). This fundamental cement in the leadership relationship permits people to hear one another clearly and to form a consensus, however crude or unarticulated, about the direction the school must take.

Relationships of this kind flourish in organizations where the culture is egalitarian and structures are not highly formalized and hierarchical (Gardner, 1990; Senge, 1990). They grow in organizations that are not heavily bureaucratic and governed by "technical" or "legal" rules and work processes (Darling-Hammond, 1997; Rost, 1993). Where people work in teams and are interdependent, they form familylike or tribal bonds that are marked by trust, openness, and affirmation (Block, 1996; Senge, 1990). Professional organizations (as opposed to wage-rate organizations) tend to promote strong relationships through a fluid, highly interactive, often social process; such relationships promote trust, personal affirmation, empowerment, and efficacy (Weick & McDaniel, 1989). These qualities characterize public schools, although not universally or uniformly. Although these qualities often conflict with classical leadership models, they are patently more compatible with a model that places a relationship founded on trust, openness, and affirmation at its center.

What sorts of conditions help to develop this type of mobilizing relationship? A *common ethical ideal*, supported by a common set of beliefs and values, provides a center around which the relational circle can form (Helgesen, 1995; Noddings, 1984). *Ease of communication is vital*: It flows easily back and forth among members, including formal leaders; people share information and their personal contacts are sufficient for them to judge the trustworthiness of both the information and their colleagues (Argyris, 1993; Senge, 1990). Further, relationships grow when *the work itself depends for its success on coordinated efforts*. When success is enhanced by interdependence, members see reasons to seek out others and build sound relationships with them (Bandura, 1997). Finally, relationships can grow *best when people can interact directly with one another* (Cooperrider, 1998; Gardner, 1990; Schein, 1985). Space, time, schedules, and informal opportunities to affiliate have enormous impacts on the growth of the leadership relationship.

What does this relational stream imply for the leader him or herself? It presents an immediate and even profound challenge to us as individuals. How might I lead when it is the relationship that creates the leadership and its resulting action? Indeed, can I alone be the leader? Clearly not. It takes two to form a relationship. No individual, whether he or she is appointed by a governing body or is self-anointed, can constitute the leadership relationship alone. A person can *seek to lead,* committing himself to cultivating open, trusting, and affirming relationships with others to serve the school's mission. But unless he finds partners to reciprocate in forming that relationship, he will not lead. Leadership, in this relational model, lies in the eyes of those who experience the mobilizing relationship, not merely in the eyes of those who want to lead or are appointed to lead.

Public schools, given the contexts described earlier, are likely to have many leaders, most of whom carry no formal title: teacher colleagues in a grade-level team; a standing committee responsible for monitoring at-risk kids; the principal's steering committee; an informal group of teachers and parents who share a philosophy. These relationships are marked in their minds and hearts by trust, openness, and affirmation. Together, these clusters of people have the capacity to lead. Teachers, principals, or other staff who foster these relationships more visibly and pervasively among staff, students, and community are often more recognizable as leaders. But they could not be leaders without the others who make the relationship possible. Every person who shares the trust, openness, and affirmation that mobilizes is, to some degree, a leader. Importantly, the many leaders in a healthy school do not look and act identically; rather, their different styles, talents, roles, and contributions are apt to complement one another (Heifetz, 1994; Senge, 1990). Although the part played by each person may ebb and flow, the contributions and commitments she or he makes to others sustain the relationship and thus permit—if the purposive and action streams are also present—the school's mobilization toward improvement.

Leaders nurture trust, openness, and affirmation in relationships when they themselves value interpersonal connections and caring in their own right (Evans, 1996; Noddings, 1984; Sernak, 1998). Those who contribute to the stream of affirmative, trusting, respectful relationships in a school do so through four types of activity. They *value relational matters in the affairs of the faculty and staff.* They give attention to people's feeling and to how they are behaving toward one another. Second, they *talk about roles and responsibilities, actively negotiating clear and productive agreements.* Leaders help others to know where they stand and how they can contribute. Third, *they gather people to address common issues and simply to foster working relationships.* Leaders see value in linking and connecting their colleagues. Finally, *they demonstrate in their personal and professional conduct trustworthiness, openness, and affirmation.* Leaders grow leadership relationships through being themselves people in whom others can feel trust, respect, and faith. These will be examined in Chapters 5 and 8.

Growing support for this relational stream of leadership comes from some of America's most prominent school reform writers. Roland Barth's *Improving Schools from Within* (1990) illustrates how opening the leadership relationship to all and focusing collective work on learning generate broad, collective leadership. Ann Lieberman (1995) and Sharon Rallis (1994) highlight the essential roles of teachers and teams with strong working relationships to the success of schools where instruction and learning have improved. Other studies of school reform point to the *absence* of healthy relational norms as a prime obstacle to successful change (Darling-Hammond, 1997; Fullan, 1997; Muncey & McQuillan, 1996). Robert Evans, in *The Human Side of School Change* (1996), found that honesty and integrity in leadership—what he refers to as "authenticity"—are essential to leadership largely because they foster openness, trust, and interpersonal affirmation. Finally, the emerging literature on women's leadership, which is so vital to schools' success, is deepening our understanding of the centrality of relational skills and values to nourishing organizational mobilization and meaning (Buchanan, 1996; Helgesen, 1995; Rusch & Marshall, 1995; Sernak, 1998).

THE SECOND STREAM: COMMITMENT TO MUTUAL
PURPOSES WITH MORAL BENEFIT

The true work of leadership is in marshalling commitment to end-values, such as liberty, justice, equality . . . that raise [members] up through levels of morality.
—Burns (1978), p. 426

A mobilizing relationship molds itself around commitment to a shared purpose. Our organizational and school improvement literatures call it a common mission, a collective vision, a set of core beliefs. Absent this "magnetic North," an organization has no means to determine its direction much less plan its forward progress or judge its success. In identifying this as the second essential element in leadership, I am proposing that leadership does not exist—cannot exist—when commitment to common purposes is shallow or fragmented. Thus a fundamental function of the leadership relationship is that it articulates and invigorates a sense of purpose and, in the process, strengthens members' commitments to both purposes and each other. The streams of relationships flow together with the streams of purposes in a school to help form a river of leadership.

Leadership enables the alignment of individuals' thoughts and values with one another around grand goals that, if met, will assure individual and organizational success. Peter Vaill (1989) calls this active process "purposing." As people are drawn together in a working relationship, this purposing dimension permits them to say, "This is what we are working for here and this is why" with the confidence that there will be personal and collective meaning in that work that will lead to action. Margaret Wheatley (1992) labels this the "formative power of meaning: . . . the leaders we cherish and to whom we return gift for gift" are those partners among us who "give voice and form to our search for meaning, and who help us make our work purposeful" (p. 135).

How does leadership provide this direction-keeping function in organizations? It does so in two basic ways. First, the leadership relationship *convenes and focuses the attention of members on purpose.* With leadership, purposes are everpresent as core beliefs and as a collective responsibility rooted in the fundamental question, "Are we succeeding at why we are here?" Second, it *engages members in examining questions about purposes, including their appropriateness in current conditions.* Leadership assures the organization's direction and performance by ensuring that its purposes are current and practical and that the members feel committed to them (Burns, 1978; Heifetz, 1994; Sergiovanni, 1992). The first of these "purpose" functions calls on leaders to be keepers of the flame and to help each other stay centered in the midst of their action together. Somewhat in tension with this, the second function asks leaders to facilitate inquiry into current purposes and practices and to foster new understandings of the school's function in society when the old purposes fall out of currency.

A leadership model that emphasizes active "purposing" among members suits public schools. As we saw in earlier chapters, schools' mixed purposes and teacher autonomy frequently leave staff isolated and potentially rudderless. Leadership, then, provides relationships through which people can draw meaning from the mission, vision, and goals of the school to give direction to their individual work. There is a "hitching my wagon to these stars" element to the process that is the stuff of mobilization. Feeling joined to others through a purposive relationship, teachers, principals, and others can see how their daily work is both personally and morally tied to the school's mission. This squaring of one's own beliefs and values with the espoused purposes of the organization is fundamentally an individual, voluntary act; leaders cannot will employees to commit. It matches, that is, the norms of permissive collaboration that pertain in many public schools. Finally, a model of leadership that values professional choice and voice as this one does celebrates the autonomy, intelligence, and collaborative instincts of public educators. Nothing could be more important among people who feel treated like "semiprofessionals" and who are at risk of alienation.

The extent to which that commitment—the virtual "contract" the individual makes to hitch her or his wagon to the school's star—is regularly revisited and renewed plays a huge part in its vitality. Personal contact and dialogue are essential to this process. Peter Block (1996) views this as a process of forming "partnership" through an "exchange of purposes" that melds individual goals with institutional mission:

> Each party has to struggle with defining purpose, and then engage in dialogue with others about what we are trying to create. . . . Partnership means each of us at every level is responsible for defining vision and values. Purpose gets defined through dialogue. (p. 29)

Barth (1990), Heifetz (1994), and Sergiovanni (1996) similarly argue that leadership may be found more in the dialogue, open questioning, and constant invention of better practice among practitioners than in the speeches, directives, or closed-door meetings of titular leaders. That is, it happens in the many informal, on-the-fly conversations that typify communications in public schools. Leaders constantly engage with their colleagues in a process of inquiry about individual and collective performance: Are we meeting the literacy needs of our minority students? Is the portfolio assessment system satisfying parents as well as teachers? How might I use more demonstrations and hands-on activities to augment my teaching of these concepts? Supporting this process is a strong working relationship and a commitment to dig deeper and reach further to fulfill the school's mission.

A leadership model that incorporates purposing serves public schools because they are so constantly exposed to what John Gardner (1990) calls "pluralistic pressures" (p. 32). These pressures and cross-pressures stem from constituencies' projecting their desires and moral imperatives onto the school, each from their own angle (Gutmann, 1987; Jackson et. al., 1993). As agents of a "free, appropriate education" for every American child, schools have welcomed increasingly diverse student needs and increasingly demanding societal needs. Correspondingly, the moral outrage of educators and citizens alike has grown at schools' inability to meet all those rising needs. These circumstances present leaders in school an extraordinary leadership challenge. As public, democratically governed institutions with professional employees, schools can tackle questions of purpose successfully *only* through a model of leadership that, through attention to relationships, values each voice and each person's responsibility to contribute to school success (Barth, 1990; Darling-Hammond, 1997; Glickman, 1993).

Those who aspire to leadership often engage in three sorts of activities in this regard. (These will be explored further in Chapters 6 and 9.) They assist the school community *to articulate purposes that staff and constituents view as morally good.* This is fundamentally a process of articulating mission and core values and helping members attend to them in their individual roles and work. Second, leaders are constantly at work *mingling the practical, daily work of staff, students, and parents with the ideals of the school's purposes.* They help their colleagues and constituents to understand more deeply how their efforts contribute—or do not contribute—to the school's mission. In the process, they foster a heightened sense of personal and professional purpose and reward. Third, leaders *seek out challenges by questioning incongruities in their work and asking, "What can we do about this?"* Whether it be about their own performance, the performance of others, the school's structure and procedures, or the performance of students, leaders invite tough questions and test the appropriateness of current practice against the school's ideals. In these opportunities lies the essence of commitment to purpose, the vital chance to reaffirm or disconfirm that "our purposes are ones which permit me to find meaning in my work."

THE THIRD STREAM: SHARED BELIEF IN ACTION-IN-COMMON

> *Each component of change [is] cultivated by those who* do *reform.*
> —Berry (1995), p. 132

The first two streams—a trusting and affirming relationship and commitment to common purposes—require a third element if they are to constitute leadership. The third stream is a shared belief that the collective effects of individual actions are greater than their sum. It is a faith in action-in-common—where individual actions integrate to support *everybody's* success. This belief is in collective effects, not merely in coordinated action. Action-in-common for some tasks may require tight coordination and uniformity; for example, four teachers planning an integrated teaching unit or the assistant principals tightening student security. For others it might require very little of either; for example, coaching teachers in communication skills to use with parents or providing non-language-arts teachers with strategies for assisting students with writing. This leadership stream carries a strong relationship and a sense of transcending purpose not just to the edge of action but into action. It enables the leadership relationship to mobilize the group to enact new practices, new policies, and new learning. It is what makes the organization, when the occasion and need arise, "mobilizable."

Belief in action-in-common derives from two group phenomena: (1) a conviction that organizational purposes will be met better by action-in-common than by unlinked individual effort and (2) sufficient evidence from action-in-common to reinforce this conviction. The leadership relationship gives members confidence that their efforts together will transform ideals to reality, that their "theories and planning" will convert to "action" and fulfill valued purposes (Argyris & Schön, 1974; Vaill, 1998). The principle is that success breeds success by building faith in the group's collective work. Albert Bandura (1997) and others, in their work with the concept of collective efficacy, find in higher function organizations that members' belief in their collective capacity to succeed is higher than in lower functioning organizations. When people feel appreciated and a vital part of their school or company, their willingness to participate beyond their classroom or job assignment and to devote personal assets to collective success increases (Cooperrider, 1998; Louis, Kruse, & Bryk, 1995; Smith, 1999).

Conviction in action-in-common and actual action-in-common reinforce one another, spiraling together to move the organization. Each aspect—the group's belief that "together we can do more than I can do alone" and the actual work involved—is both chicken and egg. Leaders cultivate this collective belief by coalescing attention on issues vital to the school's success and focusing the available energies of members on this important adaptive work. That is, they do not use scarce collective time and attention to force institutional uniformity on members. Rather, they *help people to address together the challenges that are demonstrably "distressing" their ability to reach their goals* (Heifetz, 1994). Leaders help teachers, counselors, staff, and parents confront issues and evidence that trouble them because they reveal obstacles to effective performance. From confronting the challenges, leaders *facilitate problem-solving, planning, retraining, and team-building that support new action* in classrooms, corridors, offices, and playing fields. The relationships leaders foster are strong enough and the sense of purpose robust enough to make the commitment to learning, trying, and sticking with new methods of teaching worth the investment in personal time and effort. Leadership that fosters belief in action-in-common does so by stimulating a *bias for action and the will to try.*

These leadership activities suit the public school context. Every adult is knee-deep in children and the challenges they present. There is a premium on actionable solutions to practical problems, particularly as they promise to enhance work with children and thus the educator's personal and professional sense of accomplishment. Conditions vary so much that routine, authoritative solutions from the boss or a manual do not fully work. So mobilizing members to attend to their important problems and to create their own solutions is a value that leadership must add if teachers, counselors, coaches, principals, and parents are to invest in leadership. This kind of work often involves "changes in people's values, attitudes, or habits of behavior" (Heifetz, 1994, pp. 87–88). That is, it involves marshaling members' commitment, energy, and creative powers to generate positive solutions to major issues, thereby empowering them to act on those solutions.

How do those who aspire to lead contribute to belief in action-in-common? In Chapters 7 and 10, I examine further four leader activities. Leaders *highlight the interdependent aspects of their colleagues' and constituents' work.* They look for opportunities to connect adults who share students or who have complementary talents so those adults can multiply their effectiveness rather than work in isolation. Second, leaders *feed others a steady diet of feedback on their collective work and its effects.* Engaging in leadership means facing the evidence that can help staff and parents know how well their efforts with children are working. These activities build relationships among adults around their common objective: to do the best they can by the children they share. Ironically, the leadership relationship will be most important to them when the feedback shows that they are facing significant challenges. Third, leaders *demonstrate in their conduct the value of collective learning and action.* They articulate and model values and norms that exude confidence in the school and its members. Their actions as well as their words say to others, "The whole *is* greater than the sum of the parts." Finally, leadership activities *enable people to act on the information they have about their effectiveness and to feel supported in seeking new and different practices.* Leaders not only encourage, problem-solve, and plan with those around them; they form partnership with others for implementation and action. Their own activities reveal a bias for action and a commitment to learn from it.

MERGING THE THREE STREAMS INTO LEADERSHIP

The three dimensions of leadership I have begun to describe in this chapter—the relational, the purposive, and the action—are inseparable in the experience of leadership. It helps to separate them intellectually as we analyze how leadership is functioning in a school or for a group and especially as we think about cultivating stronger leadership. But their power stems from how they function together. I view them as three streams converging, intertwining, and even conflicting in the life of a river. Once in the river, we cannot really separate the water droplets of one stream from the other. Altogether, they constitute the flow, the shape, the health, and the power of the river, intermingling in ways that we need constantly to study but which we are unlikely ever to reduce to a simple and accurate model.

The three streams converge in the life of a school to shape the character of leadership there. Running most deeply is the relational stream. It determines most profoundly whether and how people will join together when leadership must be exercised. The relational stream carries emotional and interpersonal connections toward—or away from—collective effort. The purposive stream bears peoples' intellectual and philosophical predilections: beliefs, values, theories of learning and teaching, models of human development, management paradigms. This stream flows with ideals and aspirations, so I see it playing above and even beyond the reach of the relational stream. Finally, belief in action-in-common relies heavily upon the other two streams. It engages members in learning, planning, and acting for improvement, supported by strong relationships and a robust purpose. So I visualize it at the center of the leadership river, flowing forward on the strength of relationships toward goals inspired by purpose. Leaders' work lies in the interweaving of these streams into one strong current.

As I elaborate on these three streams in the following chapters, I offer a developmental scheme for each. Staff relationships, for example, can be examined at any point in time; we can evaluate them and explore their capacity to support leadership for the school. Similarly, a faculty's understanding of and commitment to mutual purposes and their belief in their capacity to act-in-common can be assessed. The quality of a school's leadership is a function of the health of each leadership stream.

For example, a staff can be robustly purposive and proudly refer to their mission, vision, and curriculum. At the same time, however, relationships among members and the collective sense of faculty efficacy can be much less well developed or even conflictual. Such a school is likely to be driven by philosophy and intellect to perform at a level that cannot be supported by its relationships. Where the purposive stream dominates the relational and action streams, a school is apt to be frustrated by unfulfilled goals and possibly dispirited staff and disappointed leaders. Leadership there is not likely to come to fruition until those who lead attend to the group's relationship issues and questions about their ability to act productively together.

The health of each stream determines the flow of healthy leadership in a school. As staffs develop themselves with the essential facilitation of their leaders, they grow their capacity for strong relationships, for clearer and more actionable purposes, and for faith that "together we are more effective than we are singly." At the point where all three streams reach critical levels of health, they begin to interact in more mutually reinforcing ways. Their forces and currents join into a larger and more powerful flow which generates systemic action—the product of leadership.

THE MERITS OF THE MODEL

In our search for a more appropriate model of leadership for schools, the three-stream concept I have begun to describe has much to recommend it. First, *it makes leadership something that all vested members of the school community can participate in.* The relationship welcomes the many people who share a basic faith in the value of education and democracy. It inherently honors their talents, their passions, and their will to act on that faith. It recognizes the many dedicated teachers, administrators, secretaries, parents, and others who, largely through informal networks, do join as communities of leaders to share the challenges, the joys, the responsibilities, and the rewards of making their schools better for children. In this regard, the model reinforces the "public" in public education, it respects the independence and individualism of teachers' work with children, and it taps into resources much more widely than more constrained and structured models of leadership.

Second, the three-stream model *removes the burden of solitary leadership—though not the responsibility for developing leadership—from appointed leaders.* It frees principals, team leaders, and department heads from thinking that it is their job alone to "lead the followers" toward improved school outcomes. For principals, especially, the burden of feeling that "I need to be all things to all people" falls away when members of the school community share a common responsibility for meeting the major challenges to their success with children. Although the work of redefining the leadership relationship will take time and trust in most schools, a new model that fits the social architecture and planetary culture of schools has obvious appeal.

Third, the three-stream model *conceives of leadership work as organizational improvement; it is about mobilization and about action that benefits children.* As I will explain in more detail in coming chapters, the leadership relationship permits members of the school community to come together for problem-solving, learning, and action-planning when the school is facing serious challenges to its success. The leadership relationship is enduring; although the group cannot and need not be constantly engaged in change, its relationship enables the group to do significant collective work when conditions call for it. Every school-wide decision and action are not the group's responsibility; schools, classrooms, offices, and co-curricular programs require individual planning, action, and management from those primarily assigned to them. But when the school or its members find themselves facing evidence of failure, conflict, and distress over their success with children, their relationship, their sense of purpose, and their will to act enable them to readily convene, devise better practices together, and carry them into action.

Finally, the three-stream model *acknowledges the existing regularities and social architecture of school life and invites—possibly obligates—all members of the community to join in meeting common challenges.* Teachers, counselors, other staff, and parents can find in this model a way to express their moral purpose and the challenges they face as they educate children. It offers them a relationship that they may use to "grow" their individual and collective competencies and, with them, their belief in their own action-in-common. Vital to this is the compatibility of this model with women's ways of participating in collective life and of leading. With its emphasis on action-in-common instead of uniform action, the model legitimizes the independence, autonomous judgment, and orbital patterns of educators' work without compromising common purpose.

Although the three-stream model has promise, I hasten to add that it is only a model, a way of thinking anew about how leadership does and could work in schools. Chapters 2 through 4 have articulated the need for a new model and the basic logic of the three-stream conception. Lessons emerging from reform efforts in American schools emphasize the power of relationships in successful efforts to mobilize educators, communities, and students toward more effective learning and teaching. In the next three chapters, I examine some basic leadership activities that feed each stream and explore the challenges principals and teacher leaders face in taking them on. As will become clear, educators will encounter both prospects and pitfalls as they approach the central work of relationship-building, nurturing commitment and purpose, and fostering belief in action-in-common.

CHAPTER 5

Relationship-Building

Prospects and Pitfalls

*Acts of leadership occur not simply in presidential mansions and parliamentary assemblies
but far more widely and powerfully in the day-to-day pursuit of collective goals through the
mutual tapping of leaders' and followers' motive bases and in the achievement of intended
change. It is an affair of parents, teachers, and peers as well as of preachers and politicians.*
—Burns (1978), pp. 426–427

This chapter and the two that follow shift the focus from leadership to leaders. I
invite the reader to consider what leaders do as they contribute to the three streams
that mobilize schools to be their best. This chapter explores the first of the three
streams and asks, "What challenges do principals and teacher leaders face in fostering strong working relationships?" Chapters 6 and 7 take up the purposive
and action-in-common streams with a similar focus on principal and teacher
leaders.

These chapters are not detailed "how-to" manuals for leaders. Rather, they
depict clusters of leader activities that contribute to each leadership stream and then
revisit the school realities of Chapters 2 and 3, asking, "How is it that schools are—
or are not—places where leaders can lead in this way?" I then address how principals and teacher leaders are uniquely positioned to play different but complementary parts in the facilitation of relationships, the generation of commitment to
purpose, and the belief in action-in-common. In regard to some functions, principals are more appropriately positioned to advance the cause of leadership; in others,
teachers are. In all cases, the partnership of principals and teachers leaders is the
central force in the flow of school leadership.

Before beginning, a cautionary note: Addressing leadership by discussing what
individuals "must" or "can" do can be deeply misleading. From the standpoint of
the relational model developed in this book, it takes at least two to lead. The aspiring leader's first thought and first step is for relationship-building, the forming of
an "us," not a "me and you." As you read these chapters, then, challenge yourself
(as I have had to challenge myself) to understand leaders' activities as collective and
facilitative, not as unilateral and causal. Remind yourself, as I do, that the proof of

a person's leadership is not in her or his lone actions but in the contribution to the group's mobilization—to the stimulation of purposeful action with fellow leaders.

GROWING HEALTHY WORKING RELATIONSHIPS: WHAT LEADERS DO

The best way to deal with change is to improve relationships.

Fullan (1997), p. 13

Working relationships marked by trust, openness, and affirmation require invest-ments of care, time, and interpersonal talent. If leadership is to thrive, the relation-ships among the school's members must be sufficiently strong to withstand the stresses and to seize the opportunities the school will encounter. Creating such rela-tionships among people who come to the school with no previous personal connec-tions and sustaining them through many intense days with children and community is hard work. The heart of this work lies in four fundamental ways leaders interact with others.

First and foremost, *leaders give attention and importance to interpersonal matters among faculty and staff.* In many schools, gatherings of teachers and staff are "all busi-ness." In the interest of speed and efficiency, we avoid or suppress issues about how people are working with one another, who feels "counted" and who does not, or how decisions are made. The pervading spirit is, "That's the way things are done here; live with it." As we know all too well, this attitude drives relationship issues underground where they fester and dominate teachers' room talk, carpool conver-sation, and teachers' association and administrative team time. Leaders attend to these matters. They acknowledge the frustrations, anger, and disappointment as well as the successes, celebrations, and interpersonal connections that staff feel as they work with one another. Fullan and Hargreaves (1998) describe this leadership work as "emotional management," arguing that "[school] structures are only as good as the relationships and know-how of the people who occupy them. Emotional man-agement is ultimately about attending to these relationships properly" (p. 119).

In attending to relationships, though a huge and complex endeavor, leaders validate others' feelings about the staff and their place in it (and, sometimes, in the larger context of district, community, and profession as well). They make room in conversations, dialogues, and meetings for others to give voice to their concerns about working relationships and to celebrate their productive collaborations. Val-uing this dimension of educators' work lives in this fashion asserts the importance of behavioral norms and work values; it says to all, "How we function with one another is important to each person's effectiveness and serves as a model for our students." In this respect, leaders set the agendas and model the values that become standards for the group. For those who aspire to lead, committing time, explicit attention, and "emotional attention" to how colleagues feel and how they are working with one another is an absolute essential.

Second, relationship-building involves what David Sanderson and I (1996) have termed "contracting": *Leaders help everyone be clear about roles and responsibilities with regard to each other's work.* At the heart of the leadership contract is a mutual willingness to "shape and be shaped" by one another (Burns, 1978). Typically, faculty and staff are concerned about responsibility, support, justice, and power: What am I responsible for? How will I be cared for and treated justly? And who will have power over me and my decisions? Leaders put these issues—often considered publicly unmentionable in schools—out in the open for the group to discuss and clarify. Their goal is not necessarily to create an egalitarian working relationship (although the egalitarian ideal is very dear to American public educators). More important than whether the relationship is structured in one manner or another is that it has been openly and voluntarily contracted—and that it can be renegotiated on an as-needed basis.

Leaders surface with others these sometimes delicate issues of responsibility, power, and authority. Instead of avoiding a conflict between departments or staff members where one criticizes the other for dropping the ball with students or being wrong-headed about curriculum, leaders help staff identify the nature of their differences and clarify responsibilities for children. Where teachers, counselors, administrators, and parents need regularly to coordinate their treatment, assessment, and planning for students, leaders help articulate their goals and their views of their roles and responsibilities. Where individuals or groups feel constrained or minimized by the authority or behavior of others and these dynamics are hampering the work of the school, they help people confront such relationally destructive matters and work toward professional solutions. Sernak (1998) and Evans (1996) offer detailed examples of this important relational work.

Third, relationships characterized by trust, openness, and affirmation grow strong when *leaders sponsor and facilitate continuous, authentic connections among colleagues.* There is no substitute for direct experience with others if the goal is to build a working relationship in the group. Trust grows from repeated contacts with another person. We learn that we can be open with others and that others will openly share with us through working together on issues that matter, that require our active participation, and that demand we hear one another. We learn the affirmative qualities of colleagues by being with them—in business and social contexts both—and experiencing their optimism, humor, and buoyancy.

Leaders support the development of healthy working relationships every time they arrange for staff to convene and participate with one another around issues significant to them. This is not simply a matter of identifying an agenda and throwing people into a meeting. Providing for the time, protecting the group environment so that the group's work can be done, and facilitating the group to draw out trust, openness, and affirmation are essential (Donaldson & Sanderson, 1996; Evans, 1996; Senge, Kleiner, Roberts, Ross, & Smith, 1994). In this regard, the leader of meetings and work sessions is well served by a cluster of important interpersonal skills that are explored in Chapters 8 through 10.

Finally, strong working relationships grow when *leaders themselves demonstrate trustworthiness, openness, and affirmation.* People look to leaders to define what is normative for the group. Leaders' actions are frequently more powerful in this respect than are their words (Argyris & Schön, 1974; Barth, 1990; Schein, 1985). The staff's ability to feel trusted and to develop trust in one another is greatly enhanced when their leaders are trustworthy and affirming rather than suspicious and critical. Knowing that "what we see is what we get" (even if that does not totally match "what we want") goes a long way toward establishing the predictability necessary for people to trust the entire working relationship (Bennis & Nanus, 1985). Similarly, seeing that the leader is confident enough personally in her place in the relationship to share openly information, ideas, and feelings gives permission and encouragement to others to do the same. Finally, faculty confidence and hope grow as they see in the leader's actions clear evidence of optimism about the school's work and his or her own confidence in them (Cooperrider, 1998; Fullan, 1997).

Sometimes cynicism overtakes public educators, particularly when members of the public deride them for the failure of schools. Low public confidence can erode teachers' and principals' already tenuous sense of progress and professional efficacy. It can easily play on their low pay and their semiprofessional status and breed hopelessness, powerlessness, and defeat. Schools where these sensibilities permeate the atmosphere sometimes foster healthy working relationships through fighting together against those groups they believe threaten their professional ideals. If appointed leaders do not demonstrate in their actions trust, openness, and affirmation, the only option left to those who care is to fill this leadership void by silent resistance to or open defiance of those in authority. Ronald Heifetz (1994) terms this rather common form of leadership in public schools as "leadership without authority." Although such leadership is constructive, it can as well develop into a standoff with administration that can paralyze a school.

These four clusters of leader activities begin to paint an image of the school leader that contrasts with the classical principal profile. On the other hand, it is reminiscent of many teachers who have informally won the admiration and respect of colleagues, students, and community. Their validation of relational issues, their facilitation of roles and responsibilities, their "being there" face-to-face, and their personal trustworthiness and optimism literally grow trust, openness, and affirmation among those around them. The concept seems simple, even obvious. But the realities of school life make it quite difficult for some—especially those who carry formal authority—to perform these activities. In the next section, I explore how these realities present opportunities and hurdles in this regard.

SCHOOLS AS PLACES FOR STRONG
WORKING RELATIONSHIPS

Most educators have been members of faculties, departments, teams, or professional groups in which the relationship was strong and resilient enough to foster true leadership—leadership that mobilized them to productive action. Indeed, the current reform movement is generating rich examples of how adult relationships can create and sustain improvement in this way (Darling-Hammond, 1997; Lieberman, 1995; Meier, 1995). What is it about schools as places for leadership that permits the development of such relationships? What hinders that development?

Conditions That Fragment Relationships

Four of the conditions typical of U.S. public schools highlighted in Chapters 2 and 3 clearly militate against relationship-building. The first is the *size of school staffs*. With staffs often numbering upward of 60 (and above 100 in many urban and secondary schools), the human dynamics are simply too complex for safety, trust, and affirmation to grow naturally among most adults. Collective responsibility and influence will not flower without intense and talented cultivation in such unwieldy workplaces. On the contrary, the numbers of staff and often the geography of large school buildings encourage informal small group affiliations. These, particularly where they are reinforced by formal roles such as high school departments or grade-level teams, can paradoxically undercut the development of a whole-school relationship by developing strong relationships in these smaller units.

Second, the *isolation and individualistic culture of teachers* in classrooms all day leaves scarce opportunity for a strong collective relationship to grow. Teachers have no time, no energy, and sometimes no interest in connecting with the whole group. Their focus remains with their students, their teaching activities, their co-curricular passions. The individualistic culture of the teacherhood disposes few teachers, from their entry into the profession, to expect that their relationships with one another will play a large role in their career success. To a large extent, their professional obligations are individual: to teach the assigned students as well as they can; to carry out basic duties; to engage with parents as necessary. For many, the classroom presents enough responsibilities and challenges that they would not willingly seek out any more beyond their classroom walls. As we have seen in many attempts at reform where school-wide affairs become conflictual or seemingly irrelevant to learning and teaching, teachers turn away and close their doors on leadership efforts.

Third, the *history of hierarchical relationships* in our schools can undercut the development of openness, trust, and affirmation and the sharing of responsibility and decisions. It is not so much the division of tasks and responsibilities among teachers, staff, and administration that inhibits strong relationships as it is the way power and authority have crept into the roles. Amplified by the semiprofessional, subservient self-image of the American public teacherhood, issues of respect and safety pester school faculty relationships. Teachers feel underappreciated by principals. Principals feel frustrated and resisted by teachers. Teachers and staff are divided by affiliations and animosities that grow up around departments, grade levels, length of experience, genders, and personal and micropolitical affiliations. The leadership relationship cannot readily develop where "status-grading" stratifies access to information, to decision-making, and to resources and teaching assignments.

A final inhibiting factor is *the formality of most occasions when the whole faculty come together.* As I note in Chapter 2, well-meaning administrators and teacher leaders tightly structure the tasks and time when teachers and staff are called together. The result is that people often have woefully little opportunity either to get to know one another or to explore freely issues important to them and their primary work. Relationships remain superficial as the formal processes for discussing and deciding on issues keeps people at arm's length from one another. Responsibilities, instead of being shared, are too often assigned to the principal, to a committee, or to nobody at all. In such environments, the relationship can become politicized; decisions occur through the negotiation of interest groups and power-wielders because trust, openness, and affirmation are insufficient to encourage people to "shape and be shaped."

These four aspects of life in schools are familiar sources of frustration for many school leaders (Evans, 1996; Fullan & Hargreaves, 1994). The challenge they face is to recognize how these and other conditions shape the existing relationships among faculty and staff and then to devise ways to cultivate openness, trust, and shared responsibility. Fortunately, four qualities of school life work to make schools places where such relationships can thrive.

Conditions That Unify Relationships

The first is the reality that *staff have power, responsibility, and the autonomy to act* in most of our public schools. The fact that teachers and parents, coaches and counselors, and students themselves exercise the greatest influence over student learning establishes an essential equality among these important players. Despite our hierarchies, curricula, and rules, Janey and Jimmy learn best when their parents, teachers, and other significant adults are in synch—when the relationship among them is open and trusting, communication is clear, and the goals for Janey and Jimmy are shared. Most parents and educators intuitively understand this; the shared relationship remains the ideal in many homes, schools, and communities. As one Maine teacher put it to me recently, "If we could just cut through all these words and all these mandates and agree that we're here for the kids, the parents and we [teachers] would do fine." Recognition of this basic equality among the key players and of the significant role each must play is a very powerful common ground for leadership relationships.

A second quality that encourages strong relationships is the *very human, personal need for affiliation.* This need, often heightened by the isolation and demands of schoolwork, causes teachers, principals, and other staff to form deep and lasting relationships at work. Often the strongest of these relationships stem from commonalities among people: They share a room, they teach the same students, they have the same free period, they started teaching at the same time, they agree on basic issues, their own children are the same age. At the root of many relationships is the need to share and enjoy time with others, the need to connect and befriend, and the need to seek professional assistance and camaraderie. Schools, although they do not provide many opportunities to connect, over time become webbed by the bonds that grow up among adults. The informal, on-the-fly contacts over coffee, in the corridor, at lunch, or commuting to work are a rich medium for the gradual growth of these relationships. These naturally formed relationships are a fertile soil for growing the permissive collaboration that is so central to shared leadership among educators.

A third factor pulling people at school together is *their commonness of purpose and mission.* To the extent that all staff feel a sense of calling about their work, they share an image of themselves as an important and consequential force in the lives of the students they share. Their common mission, vague and unspoken though it may be, provides the basis for the development of more explicit purposes and norms of professional behavior that characterize a group with shared responsibilities, mutual influence, and trust. The personal philosophy, moral passion, and calling that brings many educators into the profession can feed the core of this relationship, providing a good-faith assumption of solidarity and shared responsibility even before actual interpersonal relationships have had a chance to build deeper trust. The historical roots of the teacherhood as a means for women and minorities to achieve self-determination can contribute to this passion and sense of professional identity and efficacy.

Finally, the *challenges of the work itself* can pull people together professionally and personally. Especially as school improvement efforts include structures for professional sharing and collaboration, the old norms of isolation and self-reliance weaken, making it permissible (if not desirable) to seek help and support from others. The teacher confronted by a student who will not behave or cannot learn fractions, the counselor caught between an irate parent and a rueful child, the principal balancing staff requests with the community's budget all benefit by reaching out. Although regular, formal opportunities for professional support and problem-solving remain hard to come by, the legitimacy of sharing problems and asking for help from colleagues encourages openness, trust, and affirmation. Where these have been supported, norms of shared responsibility and decision-making grow and schools make progress (Darling-Hammond, 1997; Little, 1982; Louis & Kruse, 1995).

In summary, the portrait of schools as places where the leadership relationship can grow is a mixed one. Although all-too-familiar conditions like the size of facul-

FIGURE 5.1   Staff Relationships: A Range of Readiness for Strong Working Relationships

FRAGMENTED ⟵―――――――――――――――――⟶ UNIFIED

• No trust • Staff closed to one another's views • Staff seldom affirm one another • Independence is the preeminent value • Staff too large for personal connections • History of conflict and staff turnover	• Small groups formed around personal needs and purposes • Trust and affirmation within these groups • Little trust/affirmation between groups or with administration • Formal structures and rules dominate the culture	• Small groups formed around professional (and perhaps personal) purposes • Trust, openness, and affirmation within these groups • Groups/teams able to mobilize for change when team conditions require • Trust and affirmation with formal leaders of school	• Most faculty and staff feel connected to many others • Trust, openness, and affirmation characterize school-wide interactions • Staff mobilize to meet school-wide challenges • Continuity of leadership and staff • Strong working relationships exist among formal and informal leaders

ties and the divisions between administration and teachers and among teachers themselves militate against the formation of such relationships in the whole school, strong informal relationships "just happen" in small, informal groupings. These often become robust social units, but they do not necessarily become professionally productive or contribute to a whole-staff relationship that mobilizes people. These pairings and small clusters of staff, however, are the most vital tributaries to the larger stream of relationships in schools.

READINESS FOR STRONG WORKING RELATIONSHIPS

Clearly, staff relationships in American schools come in an array of conditions: Some schools are blessed with faculties that have developed healthy trust, openness, and affirmation among them; others struggle simply to have a civil faculty meeting. Leaders who seek to grow strong relationships among their colleagues inherit existing relationships. Their leadership work begins with evaluating those relationships, the existing norms that shape interpersonal conditions among teachers, between faculty and administration, and within the whole adult working environment. Figure 5.1 illustrates on a continuum from "fragmented" to "unifed" staff readiness for a leadership relationship. It touches upon the eight factors discussed here and provides a rudimentary way to diagnose the relationship-building work that leaders and staff face.

Leaders' work in this relational dimension involves engaging in the staff relationship in ways that will "grow" it along this range from "fragmented" to "unified." At a given moment in time, a school's leadership potential might reside in only a few people or a few groups where the relationship is healthy enough to support professional commitments and action-in-common. In some schools, the sheer size of the staff will suggest that leadership needs to be diffused to teams small enough for working relationships to thrive. In still others, a history of bitter contract negotiations dividing faculty and administration and perhaps even the faculty itself suggest that leadership needs to start simply with healing and connecting.

Whatever the challenge in this relational stream of leadership, leaders will need to emerge from both administrative and teacher ranks. Indeed, it is difficult to imagine a strong working faculty where leadership is not present among principals and leaders. In the next two sections, I explore how principal and teacher leaders are positioned, by virtue of their roles, to contribute to the growth of this relationship.

PRINCIPALS AS PARTNERS IN THE LEADERSHIP RELATIONSHIP

The relationship between principal and teacher is frequently an elephant in the school's living room: It is talked about daily in teachers' rooms, offices, carpools, and kitchen debriefings but seldom discussed openly within the faculty group itself. The principal (and here I include both principals and assistant principals) brings to this relationship the formal baggage of the administrative role: hierarchical, historical, authoritative, political, and legal constraints that often contribute to the fragmentation of relationships. But principals also can powerfully shape the professional and personal relationships that make a school rewarding for educators and students (Barth, 1997; Blasé & Kirby, 1992; Sernak, 1998).

Four characteristics of the principal's role shape their success in cultivating open and affirmative relationships. For each characteristic, however, I identify a corresponding leadership challenge for the principal.

You're Different

Principals aren't teachers or staff. They have formal authority in hiring, supervising, and firing and presumptive power to decide schedules, duties, assignments, and many other details central to staff work lives. They are sometimes made principal because they are "good management material," not because they were superb teachers. Once hired, they become part of the hierarchy, part of "management"; they have, as a principal once said to me, "crossed the big divide where old teacher colleagues no longer talk to me in the same way or about the same things." In many schools, the principal is a man, whereas most teachers are women. Often, the principal is hired from another school entirely and brings to his or her work understandings unknown or possibly quite different from those the staff is used to.

Differentness, particularly when it is overlaid with power, status, and gender differentials, is a rich breeding ground for distrust, miscommunication, and the compartmentalization of responsibilities. It can, if left alone, fragment rather than unify relationships in a school. These differentials can interfere with the development of openness and the fundamental equality so important to mutual respect. The size of most schools and the heritage of hierarchy, reinforced as it is in many districts by union–management tensions, leave many principals poorly positioned to form open, trusting relationships with and among staff. I know principals who, faced with this challenge, have retreated to a primarily managerial role where they guide the school safely and smoothly through the year by good-humored regulation. Given the enormity of the challenge to build strong, affirmative relationships while running a school, I cannot say that I blame them.

The differentness of principals, then, tends to make building leadership relationships more difficult. *The challenge principals face is to overcome through the chemistry of their own personalities and interpersonal skills the tendency for this differentness to distance and divide.* Their differentness needs to be acknowledged and made to serve the collective relationship, just as each other member's unique assets should be integrated in a unified relationship. In this respect, all four relationship-building activities contribute vitally to principals' capacity to lead: attending to interpersonal issues that will crop up with staff, clarifying authority and power in roles and responsibilities, maximizing personal contacts, and demonstrating trustworthiness, openness, and affirmation. These will be taken up in Chapters 8 through 10.

You Have Access

Counteracting the principal's differentness is the relative freedom to set her or his the own schedule and access to faculty and staff. Principals, if they have sufficient staff to cover the daily management demands, can be with teachers, counselors, and other key personnel who work with students. They can also be with parents. Their contacts can take a variety of forms; most will be "on the fly" during prep periods, at lunch, or before and after school; but some can be in small groups, in teams, and with committees. These contacts are, from the standpoint of building leadership relationships, superb opportunities to unify and to counteract fragmentation. Teachers are isolated. Many of them want regular opportunities to discuss their work or simply to pass time in mature conversation about topics important to their work. Principals, by attending to these affilliative and professional needs of staff, can generate significant beyond-the-classroom relationships and action.

Importantly, the relationships a principal builds with individual and small-group conversations can foster trust and clarify responsibilities because these encounters can be face-to-face, personal, and informal. The obstacles raised by the differentness of the principal can be overcome by strong interpersonal skills and a commitment to strong relationships in these face-to-face contacts. Principals who are successful in this respect live by the maxim "put people first." They acknowledge the importance of staff feelings and what they say about how well the group is working together. They set their daily agendas not only by lists of tasks to be done but also by whom they need to converse with, whom they need to offer feedback, or whom they have not touched base with in a while.

The principal's relative freedom of movement, then, is an important asset in developing leadership relationships. *The challenge for principals is to understand the significance of putting relationships first and to cultivate in themselves the skills and sensibilities to succeed at relationship-building.*

You Can Enable

Principals are in a unique position to make some things happen in the school. They can influence funds, supporting some ideas and activities and leaving others strapped. They can influence agendas at meetings and in conversations, shaping what others talk about, think about, and do to some degree. They often have the most direct line to central office and, sometimes, to power brokers in the community. In short, principals can wield the power and influence to enable some people, some projects, and some agendas; conversely, they can use this power and influence to disable others.

The presence of this power—and sometimes merely the possibility of it—creates important sensitivities in the principal's relationships. If she or he uses this power unilaterally, faculty and staff can easily conclude that it is the principal's priorities, preferences, and desires that govern what is nurtured and what is not. Dependencies and counterdependencies can develop. In-groups and out-groups can spring up. Enablement, in this sense, can feed some and cripple others; it strengthens and affirms the principal's relationship with some staff but can weaken and undermine that with others. It can fragment or it can unify. The principal needs to use this power very sensitively, bringing resources and attention to bear on the priorities and projects of the group. If it nourishes the collective agenda, it can unify people who are often engaged in separate and different activities. Such activity builds an affirmative collective relationship. Through the principal's enabling of the group's agenda, she or he uses the position in a manner that subjects her or his power to the needs of the group rather than to create dependencies on the principal and the principal's agenda.

Principals' power to make things happen complicates, often detrimentally, their role in building leadership relationships. *Their challenge is to understand what their power and authority are, how they effect principal-staff relationships, and how to behave so that their power and authority enhance the leadership relationship.*

You Alone Are Not Enough

Inevitably, most principals are frustrated with their inability to reach as many staff as often as they need to. This aspect of the principalship has two important variations: the physical and the interpersonal. First, the principal simply has too many adults to establish relationships with and among. The typical ratio of administrators to staff in American public schools is over 37:1. School buildings are too spread out. Teacher schedules are too much of a hodge-podge. Nobody has time after school. It is particularly difficult to assemble committees or teams for important communication, deliberation, and interpersonal maintenance functions with the principal. Even in schools with assistant principals, the complexity of attending to each staff member makes this aspect of administration more than full-time work.

Second, numerous interpersonal factors make it difficult for any one principal to form effective relationships with all staff. It is easier, for example, to form strong relationships with the willing than with the unwilling staff member. The principal's personality simply rubs some people the wrong way or his or her past history in the school has left a trail of doubts and mistrust. The personal issues some staff are facing undercut their ability to attend, much less commit, to the collective relationship the principal is attempting to build.

Both physical and interpersonal factors leave most principals feeling personally and professionally challenged by the task of forming trusting, affirming, professional relationships with every staff person. Most principals resort to mass communication or mass meetings in an effort to frame and nurture a collective relationship (indeed, this is the major means principals use to relate to staff in some schools). Although faculty meetings, memoranda, and public address announcements are efficient ways of reaching many people at once, they are hardly mediums in which the give-and-take and the authenticity of mature, professional communication can occur. Principals facing these realities have only one option: to enlist other leaders in generating a cohesive school-wide relationship. A well-functioning administrative team of the principal, assistant principals, and other school-wide personnel is a fruitful way to counteract physical and interpersonal distance. More important, building a robust working relationship with formal and informal teacher leaders who themselves have strong connections throughout the school is vital. Leaders can unify a school simply by having resilient relationships among themselves.

Principals' supervisory loads, physical limitations, and personal styles and personalities deter them from establishing universally strong relationships with every person they must lead. *The challenge they face is to disabuse themselves and others of the expectation that they must be "the leader" for each person and, in the place of it, to entrust and enable all staff to grow meaningful relationships with one another.*

In summary, this brief assessment of principals' opportunities to lead in the relational stream begins to explain why leadership can be so difficult for principals. Their administrative mantle, the sheer size and number of interpersonal tasks they face, and the intractability of existing relationships between staff and administration clearly constrain even the most talented and optimistic relationship-builders. Working through others such as assistant principals, formal teacher leaders, and especially informal teacher leaders to unify relationships is practically essential for principals in larger schools. No matter what the circumstances, the four leader activities covered in this chapter appear critical to principals' success both forming authentic relationships themselves and encouraging them among others.

TEACHER LEADERS AS PARTNERS IN THE LEADERSHIP RELATIONSHIP

Teacher leaders are positioned quite differently from principals to contribute to strong working relationships. Their membership in the faculty establishes a foundation of equality and assumed mutuality upon which teacher leaders can build. In this section (and in subsequent chapters), I distinguish between two types of teacher leaders: *formally appointed leaders* such as department chairs, team leaders, association officers, and standing committee chairs and *informal leaders* who naturally emerge among their colleagues as trusted and respected catalysts. While some teacher leaders fit both categories, formally appointed leaders practically always encounter in their relationships with colleagues some of the same baggage that principals do. Informal teacher leaders have no administrative duties and they often avoid the hazards of power and privilege that sometimes (and even unintentionally) confuse formal teacher leaders' relationships with colleagues (Moller & Katzenmeyer, 1996; Wasley, 1991).

What, then, do teacher leaders carry as assets and liabilities in the building of leadership relationships? In my analysis, their assets tend to be greater than their liabilities. Particularly when compared with many principals, teacher leaders have tremendous potential—and responsibility—to grow strong, productive relationship among their colleagues.

You're a Member

The greatest asset a teacher brings to the leadership relationship is comembership in the teacherhood. Teacher leaders are teachers! They pull in the same harness as others; the focus of their days is on students and instruction; they are members of the association; they share the burdens of low status but also the fellowship of common purposes and the teacher's calling. In many instances, teacher leaders have an established history of contribution to the school, to students, to the community, and to colleagues. They often bring to the leadership relationship, then, trustworthiness, a fluid and open relationship with many teachers, and a record of interaction that affirms their ability to collaborate with others and build unifying relationships.

They can also participate naturally in the informal life of the staff and faculty. Here, the need for camaraderie and adult affiliation in the moments between classes and assignments pulls teachers magnetically together, creating an ethos and running dialogues that affect the school. Informal teacher leaders, especially, are both a part of this culture and potent players in the staff relationships that shape it. In the corridor, in the teachers' room, and at meetings, they occupy a more powerful strategic location within the social fabric of the school than do administrators. (Indeed, Wasley's 1991 case studies reveal that formally appointed teacher leaders can readily lose access and open communication with colleagues because of their affiliation with administration.) They are, if they are sensitive to these important social and cultural dynamics, able to shape and be shaped by colleagues in a continuous give-and-take that can have major impacts on faculty attitudes, beliefs, and even behaviors.

An asset that many women teacher leaders can bring to relationship-building is, in the view of a growing number of writers, a natural leadership style that emphasizes the interpersonal and emotional dimensions (Crosby, 1988; Helgesen, 1995; Regan & Brooks, 1995; Sernak, 1998). Sally Helgesen (1995) found that "women's ways of leading . . . rely on the value of interconnectedness" (p. 224). Echoing Nel Noddings' (1984) observation that women see themselves working toward an ethical ideal in "circles and chains" of relationship (p. 198), Helgesen argues that women see leadership as "strengthening oneself by strengthening others" through "webs of inclusion" rather than hierarchies that distance people (p. 233). Relationships are not merely a system for interacting for many women; they are the root of their pedagogical and personal philosophies as educators (Titone & Maloney, 1999). Women who naturally foster connectedness are likely, in this view, to be leaders if their inclination toward relationship-building feeds into purposeful action. In my experience, the clusters of informal teacher leaders that have grown naturally among women (and that often include men) have exceptional and largely untapped power to improve our schools.

Teacher leaders' comembership in the society of teachers gives them a foundation that can readily be grown into a leadership relationship. *Their greatest challenge is to understand the vast potential of their roles and to approach their activities as leaders with this in mind.*

You Share the Work

A special part of this comembership is the teacher leader's ongoing work as a teacher. Not only does her daily engagement with students and instruction demonstrate a sharing of the work, but also it validates her base of knowledge and revalidates her credibility. The teacher leader shares the challenges of reluctant students and new lessons and the rewards of a child's success or a parent's collaboration. Her immersion in teaching gives her a currency in the issues of the team's or department's work. She brings to her relationships both the credibility as an educator and the student-centered, instructional focus that are necessary in facilitating decisions among colleagues about planning the next unit, revising assessment procedures, introducing a new learning activity, or diagnosing a student's learning or behavior difficulties. In contrast to those of the principal and some formal teacher leaders such as department heads, many teacher leaders' values, norms, and allegiances are aligned with those whom they seek to lead rather than fragmented by administrative allegiances.

A teacher's leadership, then, holds the promise for his or her colleagues that their real work issues will inform the improvement of the school. This quality of the role provides for an important reciprocity in the relationship teacher leaders can cultivate with colleagues (a quality that was viewed by Lambert et al. in 1995 as the *sine qua non* of leadership itself). Fellow teachers and even staff and parents seek out teacher leaders because of their expertise about teaching and students, their craft knowledge in the very issues that most trouble teachers, staff, and parents. They know many instructional techniques. They are skilled with a wide range of children and often with parents. They are able problem-solvers and sensitive listeners. Teacher leaders generate unified relationships by spawning productive work. Their authority is not—at least in the case of informal leaders—hierarchical. It is, instead, earned. Their usefulness to others is not dictated, scheduled, or imposed. It is, instead, acknowledged and demonstrated through their natural contributions, their modeling of the characteristics and values of a superior educator.

Teachers' leadership relationships, because these leaders continue to share the work of teachers and staff, can be among the most influential forces in the school. *Their challenge is to protect the focus on teaching and learning that has given rise to their strong collegial bonds to others and to resist replacing this "classroom" view with a "management" view.*

Your Group Is Small and Manageable

One of the greatest assets of teacher leadership, particularly in contrast to principal leadership, is that teacher leaders often work in small, manageable groups. Teams and committees frequently number fewer than 10 members, well under the 16 to 20 that many group experts consider maximum for effective teams (Johnson & Johnson, 1995). If these groups have a specified mission and meet regularly, they are particularly conducive to relationship-building and, from there, to mobilization for action. In such groups, teacher leaders can meet face-to-face either in team meetings or individually with group members on a daily, if not more frequent, basis. Communication about shared work—students, a joint lesson, a proposal to the administration, a meeting with parents—can occur naturally and more easily than in larger units. The teacher intent on exerting teacher leadership, by stressing her own trust of others through openness and affirmation, can shape group norms in such a way that others feel excited and trusted to pick up a share of the group's responsibilities.

Most important, teams and committees that have enduring lives in the school can become opportunities for affiliation, a critical antidote to the isolation of teaching. Leadership that recognizes this fundamental need by making room for social and personal connection helps build relationships that are apt to run deeper than those fostered by merely working on tasks together. Trust, openness, and affirmation are rooted in these more personal *and* professional relationships, making them strong enough for members to feel comfortable both shaping others' thinking and actions and "being shaped" by them. Teacher leadership can thus invite authenticity from the group's members and, whether through harmony or conflict, can build a strong new consensus for group beliefs, meanings, and action (Lambert et al., 1995; Moller & Katzenmeyer, 1996). These qualities, it is important to note, are not always put to work supporting school-wide or even positive initiatives for students. They can fragment whole-school relationships even as they unify relationships in these working groups (Evans, 1996).

Teacher leadership, operating as it often does in smaller groups, has great potential for building trust, openness, and affirmation in those small groups. *The challenge to teacher leaders is to foster and celebrate the success of such teams and to help them nourish, not undercut, institutional mission and whole-school relationships.*

You're Out of Circulation

Despite the vast potential of the teacher leader in the circle of staff relationships, these teacher leaders often have great difficulty simply maintaining access to those with whom they work. Especially if they teach full time, teacher leaders do not have the time or freedom of movement regularly or purposefully to maintain strong working relationships with many other teachers or staff. Neither do they have access to information about events and issues arising throughout the school, except through the informal network. So teacher leaders must rely on the administration and on colleagues' willingness to share information, needs, and ideas. They are, in this sense, dependent on their colleagues for their success (a characteristic of their leadership that is in fact a great asset).

In many schools, teacher leaders have been formally appointed and given release time from teaching specifically so they can keep in touch. They are team leaders, grade level coordinators, department heads, or head teachers. Importantly, they are assigned to work with a small enough group of teachers and staff so they can build a relationship with them and maintain it. They can call meetings and expect teachers to respond to their initiatives and requests. Often, it appears from studies of teacher leadership (Wasley, 1991), there is a trade-off in these arrangements between an enhanced ability to organize and coordinate and a loss of com-embership that can result from the quasi-administrative nature of formal appoint-ments.

Access to teachers and to opportunities to form strong leadership relationships is a problem for many teacher leaders. *Their challenge is to create professional and personal connections among others so that information moves freely and decisions and actions are taken by those with direct responsibility for children.*

TENDING THE FLOW OF RELATIONSHIPS

Leadership relationships grow from a foundation of trust, openness, and affirmation. Where leaders demonstrate those qualities in themselves and nurture them in oth-ers, the relationships among members of the school grow stronger and, as they do, they give the school the capacity to mobilize itself for improvement. This chapter has examined factors that shape the flow of this vital leadership stream. Although the interpersonal realm of leadership is complex and underappreciated, my analysis suggests its potential. Schools are places where unified relationships can and do evolve among teachers. They are, as well, places where fragmentation can easily occur. Leaders shape the healthy evolution of purposive relationships and do so most powerfully through natural, informal, and even incidental interactions that connect and respect people.

The relational stream of leadership is the most fundamental and important of the three streams. *The litmus test for leadership is whether working relationships are suffi-ciently strong to support commitments to a common purpose that lead to action-in-common.* I have made a case for the vital role that teacher leaders play in meeting this litmus test. (The skills and qualities needed are taken up in Chapter 8.) In comparison to principals, teacher leaders begin from a relationship that assumes trust, comrade-ship, and common purpose. The hurdles that teachers must clear as they tend to the flow of relationships are considerably lower than those that principals face. Prin-cipals have a special responsibility, however, to honor the relational domain even as they face the challenges of staff size, hierarchical cultures, and the real and perceived differences between themselves and teachers that can so easily erode trust, openness, and affirmation. At the same time, principals have access to people, to resources, to information, and to power that makes their place in the leadership relationship vital in a different way.

The challenge, then, is for principals and teacher leaders to invest together in building unifying relationships. Teachers and administrators who seek to mobilize their schools to improve need one another. They are complements. They are, as well, a vital leadership medium for the school—people of position, stature, respect, and thus influence. In this regard, they are a microcosm of the larger school com-munity; their own relationships with one another are apt to be mirrored in the larger faculty and staff and even beyond the school. Their habits of interaction, their levels of trust and openness, and the interpersonal norms that govern the way this cadre of leaders functions echoes throughout the larger unit. In this regard, the relational stream of leadership begins with those who aspire to lead. For every leader, the seminal question is, "Will I trust others, be open with others with the information and concerns I have, and affirm the worth of others?"

CHAPTER 6

Stewardship of Commitment to Purpose
Prospects and Pitfalls

> *Essentially the leader's task is consciousness-raising on a wide plane. . . . The leader's funda-*
> *mental act is to induce people to be aware or conscious of what they feel—to feel their true needs*
> *so strongly, to define their values so meaningfully, that they can be moved to purposeful action.*
> —Burns (1978), pp. 44–45

Strong relationships lie at the core of effective leadership. People who lead generate trust, openness, and mutual affirmation that grow shared responsibility and mutual influence. But the relationship, although it is the most essential and core current in the school leadership river, is itself not enough. Leadership is, as well, purposive and it leads to action. This chapter identifies the prospects and pitfalls that principals and teacher leaders are likely to encounter in the second or purposive stream of leadership.

I first present an overview of three core activities that constitute the stewardship of mutual commitments to common purposes. I then return to the school realities depicted in Chapters 2 and 3 to ask, "How are schools places where mutual commitment to common purposes can grow?" On the basis of that discussion, I then examine challenges and opportunities that principals and teacher leaders usually face as they seek to be stewards of purpose and commitment.

MARRYING PURPOSE AND COMMITMENT: WHAT LEADERS DO

Schools now customarily post their vision statements and publish their missions for all to see and, presumably, understand and support. They are expressing a basic aspiration for their school community: that everyone will both "get" the purposes of the school and "give" their personal and professional commitments to those purposes. Indeed, if students, parents, teachers, staff, and administration are to avoid working at cross-purposes and to merge their efforts with one another, the coherence brought to the entire school through common mission and mutual commitment is a most desirable goal. A substantial literature, spanning organizational performance studies, task group research, and school reform, reinforces the significance of the marriage of purpose with commitment (Darling-Hammond, 1997; Hesselbein & Cohen, 1999; Rees, 1991; Senge, 1990). Peter Vaill (1989) describes this "purposing" function of leadership as "that continuous stream of actions . . . that has the effect of inducing clarity, consensus, and commitment regarding the organization's basic purposes" (p. 52). Leaders infuse the leadership relationship with purpose through their actions in three ways.

First, *leaders articulate a vision and a value system for the school that staff and constituents recognize as good and as consonant with their own purposes.* This leader activity has a long record in the leadership literature (Burns, 1978; Nanus, 1992; Rost, 1993). Leaders make public the purposes of the organization: the core goals of the organization, the reasons it was formed, and the effects it seeks to produce. Whether through written mission statements, strategies, and policies or through oral transmission, leaders function as reminders of the philosophical direction of the school. Such statements are unabashedly idealistic and even unattainable; in fact, that is part of the magic they perform in drawing effort and energy from people. As keepers of the organization's raison d'etre, leaders in their actions convey a vision for the school that "is expressive of the feelings [they hold] for [it] and its work. It is the basis on which the [school] acquires and maintains personal meaning for all those associated with it" (Vaill, 1998, p. 95).

Central to this activity is giving voice to the moral benefit of the mission. Burns (1978), Glickman (1993), Noddings (1984), Sergiovanni (1992), and Rost (1993) all connect the growth of commitment to members' personal judgment that moral benefit will result from joining their own efforts with those of the organization. Burns' (1978) analysis of the moral element draws on both philosophy and psychology; his conclusion is that values "become an expression of the *conscience* and *consciousness.* Hence holders of values will often follow the dictates of those values in the absence of incentives, sanctions, or even witnesses" (p. 75). Leaders' efforts to articulate what the organization's values are need to appeal to members' consciences and to infuse their consciousness as they go about their work lives. Leaders work, then, to realize these purposes and values in the rules, roles, and daily activities of the school. Goals and ground rules do not remain empty words but come alive in the operations of the school.

Here, the second leadership activity enters the mix. *Leaders are constantly at work "bridging" the practical, daily work of members with the ideals of the school's purpose.* Peter Vaill (1998) emphasizes how "purposing" stems from a "continuous stream of actions" by all those in the leadership relationship. It is not simply a matter of words and symbols. Leaders bridge the space between the "espoused" and the "enacted," between theory and practice (Argyris & Schön, 1974). Their understanding of teaching and learning and of students and teachers is detailed and concrete. They talk with colleagues, parents, and students both about goals for student learning and about how today's activities and decisions will impact the child's progress toward those goals. Leaders, as they bridge the ideal with the practical, help people see how their own labors contribute to their goals, quite literally aiding busy educators and citizens to see their work as purposeful.

The leader's success in this respect breeds in staff, students, and parents a sense of efficacy that in turn deepens their commitment to their work and the school. This deeper commitment grows from the realization that "what I find meaningful about my work is also meaningful to the organization I work within." Coherence between "my work" and "my school's work" generates a sense of confluence that is both rewarding and motivating (Barth, 1990; Helgesen, 1995). The leader's ability to help others see the greater purposes in their daily work thus fuses within the group loyalty, commitment, and hard work to fulfill both individual and organizational interests. Faculty meetings, team planning sessions, and conversations are not "just busy work"; they are opportunities to participate in problem-solving and decisions that are important to students and to the school's mission.

Although these first two leader activities establish basic predictability and stability in the school's direction and culture, the third activity revolves around *testing purposes and questioning the appropriateness of current commitments and practices*. Here, leaders help the school confirm its purposes by inviting examinations of practices and results, by opening the school to critical evidence, and, if necessary, by changing practices and values in order to help the school fulfill its grand function (Fullan & Miles, 1992; Noddings, 1984; Senge, 1999; Vaill, 1998). Leaders convene staff and parents to address evidence that students are *not* learning, behaving, and developing as they hope. In doing so, they foster a spirit of inquiry and healthy self-criticism, encouraging people to face, not avoid, difficult questions and conflicts that arise. Leaders thus cultivate members' independent authority as "critic colleagues" to one another and to the organization as a whole. In members' self-examination, debates, data collection, and invention of new alternatives, they can both advance the organization and strengthen their commitment to work for its purposes (Block, 1996; Glickman, 1993).

Engaging in this work means, for leaders, encouraging what I call "counterfluence"—voices that differ and that seek to change dominant patterns of influence. Counterfluent voices typically raise questions of value: Should we divert resources from this program to educate that group of underserved students? Should we elevate the cooperative learning curriculum to equal status with reading, writing, and arithmetic? Should we punish more and sympathize less? As leaders skillfully facilitate participation in such questions of purpose and priority, they summon a yet deeper level of commitment—a commitment not merely to stand behind today's mission statement or practice but to seek better ones and a yet more impactful future.

Such important adaptive work requires a strong staff relationship and talented facilitation. Especially in public schools, where competing value systems among constituents can tear apart coherent mission statements and give rise to evidence of failure, the melding of stakeholders' voices is essential to organizational strength.

The reaffirmation of the core values that bind people together and shape each person's autonomous work hinges paradoxically on the encouragement of counter fluent voices and open differences rather than on tight compliance to curriculum guides, routine practices, or the party line (Fullan & Hargreaves, 1998; Glickman, 1993; Sizer, 1986). If leaders facilitate the process well, staff and parents emerge with renewed commitment to a newly invigorated professional mission and a heightened sense of comradeship in the service of their purposes (Sergiovanni, 1992).

In public schools, this purposive dimension of leadership has ample opportunity to flourish. Although basic agreement exists about the purposes of schools, these purposes often conflict in the particular case of a school (see, e.g., the drive for equity of educational attainment for all students versus the drive for optimizing learning for the most able). We can agree at the most general levels that schools exist "to do the best for every child," but our specific understandings of what "best" means will differ, particularly in the case of any single child or classroom of children. The leadership relationship provides a forum for staff, parents, and even students to engage together in the often messy work of thinking through the difficult choices presented by these challenges. School leadership works with these "tensions" rather than ignoring or suppressing them (Ackerman, Donaldson, & van der Bogert, 1996; Fullan & Hargreaves, 1991). By attending to this purposing stream, leaders help schools revitalize their role in assuring the survival of the organization by adapting it to serve better the community and society that supports it.

SCHOOLS AS PLACES FOR PURPOSE AND COMMITMENT

How does the average American public school stack up as an environment for purposive leadership? Do schools characterized by the patterns of work life described in Chapters 2 and 3 seem like places where leadership can draw people into a covenant of commitment and purpose? What challenges face principals and teachers as they strive to keep a healthy stream of purpose and commitment alive and flowing through the school's work?

Conditions That Weaken Common Purpose

The typical public school offers both challenges and assets to leaders attempting to actualize purposes and build collective commitment. The first of three challenges lies in *the individualistic "planetary" culture of the teacherhood, the isolated and autonomous work, and the lack of time for collective activity that divert people from understanding their purposes as institutional purposes.* We hear constantly that planning, evaluation, and innovation cannot happen in schools because "you can't change a jetliner while it's in flight." Teachers, counselors, advisors, and even principals do "parallel work"— a polite term for "your own thing"—and, despite their need to connect, have neither the time nor the energy to do so. Scholars point to the "loose coupling" in schools between the work of different teachers, between teaching and management, between school and community, and most seriously between the work educators do and the goals, purposes, and results of that work (Meyer & Rowan, 1978; Weick, 1976). Indeed, schools are often characterized as having "moderate interdependence" among parts and people in contrast to corporations and industrial production lines (Bacharach & Mundell, 1995; Bandura, 1997).

Perhaps more corrosive of collective capacity, educators too often see little purpose to their work beyond the goals and challenges of their daily work with students. Indeed, we know that their satisfactions and rewards flow almost wholly from their work with kids. In contrast to the often abstract and lofty mission statements that dot our hallways and board meetings, down-to-earth, student-specific, daily objectives dominate the attention and are key to the fulfillment of most people working in schools. For leaders, simply corralling staff attention and turning it to serious school-wide challenges, let alone garnering the commitment to address them, can be extraordinarily difficult.

Second among the challenges, *when school staffs assemble, they are often unable to grapple effectively with serious issues of purpose.* In part, this is due to the hierarchical nature of these gatherings; usually summoned by the administration to a faculty meeting, staff are expected to invest in an agenda of managerial details and short-term plans and issues. Time is often short and low quality (immediately before or after teaching when teachers have other more pressing responsibilities). Hierarchical relationships do not encourage free expression of views, especially counterfluent views. Indeed, if a strong working relationship does not exist, the interpersonal dynamics of these meetings can be more harmful than productive. Collective opportunities for leadership, then, are extremely difficult to come by in many—and particularly in our largest—schools.

A third major challenge to leaders' purposive activities stems from the *diffusion of mission and displacement of goals experienced by our public schools.* Particularly in the last three decades, the pluralistic "publics" in public schools have become more articulate and more demanding. College-bound parents, "parents of the average kids," and special-education advocates vie for attention with soccer parents, band boosters, the state department of education, the church group, and the teachers' association. Booming from the pages of our newspapers and the podiums of our state legislatures are the voices of business, demanding performance and accountability. The wonderful thing about this picture is that each of these different voices has a legitimate place in our democratic system of schooling and each is now being heard. The tragedy is that all too often the professionals who need to respond to these voices cannot readily respond.

School staffs share a value orientation and a commitment to caring, but conditions do not permit them to respond collectively to the challenge of reinventing the American public school. They have little opportunity to assemble and deliberate.

Leaders at the state and district levels impose new purposes, practices, and account-ability measures on them that cannot be adopted or implemented. Funds and pro-fessional development are not sufficient. Hours and energy simply run out. Public schools as they are presently constituted cannot be all things to all people. This familiar spiral toward overburden makes purposing more difficult even as it makes it more necessary.

Conditions That Strengthen Common Purpose

Although busy public schools face challenges maintaining clarity, consensus, and commitment around purposes, they also count three assets. First, *their basic mission is stable and evokes deep, common commitment from most educators, parents, and citizens.* Citizens are especially confident about the performance of their own local schools; they are also convinced of the moral imperative of our public education system (Goodlad, 1984; Tyack & Cuban, 1995). Our case literature on school life and school culture brims with evidence of the faith that many teachers and principals place in the benefits of their work (Johnson, 1990; Lortie, 1975; Rosenholtz, 1986; Sarason, 1982). Teachers, by and large, believe in their own efficacy and are pro-pelled by a long tradition of service and caring (Bandura, 1997; Noddings, 1984). For many, the investment of time, energy, and care in children is a moral mission not only to improve the individual lives of their students but to promote social progress. Such conviction is a deep wellspring for leadership.

A second asset is that *the culture of schools is heavily oriented to small-group affiliations where consensus and commitment can grow.* Although the sense of mission most educa-tors bring to their work might not focus at the institutional level, the personal mean-ing that many teachers derive from their work centers in the connections they feel to immediate colleagues (Lieberman, 1988a; Louis, Kruse, & Bryk, 1995; Rosen-holtz, 1986). Collaboration and teamwork are more likely to occur around students, curriculum, and the improvement of their own teaching than around more global challenges facing the school as a whole. The egalitarian and informal norms in most schools reinforce voluntary connections among faculty and staff. Staff affiliation needs pull busy educators together, if only in spare moments and for social contact. Although these do not necessarily serve institutional or even professional purposes, they can provide a vital relational foundation for taking on larger questions of pur-pose. In this respect, a fundamentally healthy professional culture is necessary for purposive leadership.

A third asset for purposing in schools is *the growing propensity to work in teams and other small professional work and learning groups.* In response to the culture of teacher isolation, American schools are experimenting with grade-level teams, interdisci-plinary teams, reflective practice groups, communities of learners, and the like. De-scriptions of these smaller work groups and their place in larger schools demonstrate that they can build clarity of purpose, collegial support, more effective practice, and

greater commitment (Barth, 1990; Louis & Kruse, 1995). If given enough autonomy and resources, teams of educators working with a discrete group of students
have proven to be powerful environments for leadership. Whether they are teams
within a school or simply small enough schools to retain their team qualities, they
can function as decision-making units for a specific set of students, a coordinated
instructional team, a longer range planning and evaluation group, and a colleague-
critic circle (Meier, 1995; Sizer, 1992). If the team operates supportively for its
members, teams (or, in small schools, the entire faculty) function as the leadership
unit, engaging members in deliberate dialogue about purposes, shaping their daily
actions accordingly, and building both commitment to the unit and an enhanced
sense of personal efficacy in the process.

Readiness for Unified Purpose

These three assets and the three challenges that preceded them depict schools as
places with the capacity for purposing. They draw from a deep tradition of public
service that Americans support. Faculty and staff develop small-group affiliations
that naturally reinforce commitments to purpose. And increasingly, schools are purposefully using teams and small work groups to target staff's energies on specified
students and outcomes. But the typical public school also faces factors such as size,
compartmentalization, and the diffusion of mission. These often blur clear purposes
and erode group solidarity, undercutting a sense of collective commitment. Clearly,
some schools are so fragmented, so torn asunder by their history of failure and poor
support, that "getting it together" to establish purposes that vitalize staff and community commitment seems nearly impossible. However, schools can be turned
around. Each school presents its own challenges to leaders intent on strengthening
the sense of purpose staff feel as well as deepening their commitments to it. Figure
6.1 represents a range of states of readiness for this purposing work.

　　The sense of purpose in a school can be described somewhere in the range
between "faint" and "robust." The leaders' challenge is to engage colleagues and
community in the journey from an entirely individualistic do-your-own-thing culture toward one where clarity, consensus, and commitment to purpose mobilize
members toward common ends. In the next two sections, I explore how principals
and teachers are—and are not—positioned to help their schools on this journey.
As with the creation of healthy relationships among staff, principals and teachers
often have contrasting yet complementary capacities to engage in this stream of
leadership.

PRINCIPALS AS STEWARDS OF PURPOSE AND COMMITMENT

Principals are expected to carry the torch for whole-school concerns—establishing
a vision, assuring smooth management, making the school responsive to school

FIGURE 6.1   Staff Commitment to Purpose: A Range of Readiness for Commitment

WEAK ⟵━━━━━━━━━━━━━━━⟶ ROBUST

• No stated common purposes • Conflict among advocacy groups • Commitment only to individual purposes • Routines and rules dictate activities of staff and students • Criticism and questions about performance provoke defensiveness • Large, geographically diffuse school building • Teaching is viewed mainly as a job	• Publicly stated general purposes; superficial commitment to them • Work characterized by commitment to comply with rules and regulations • Congenial culture masks do-your-own-thing practices • Little collaborative work	• Shared sense of purpose • Commitment to profession and to school has a moral dimension • Collegial affiliations and commitments are strongest in small groups and teams • Team agendas come before school agendas • Teams assist teachers to meet professional goals; membership generates team efficacy	• School-wide purposes are clear, widely shared, and open to question and revision • Individual work and roles clearly contribute to these purposes • Many opportunities to plan, implement, and assess individual, team, and school-wide efforts • Openness to criticism and self-evaluation • Most staff feel professionally rewarded and collectively efficacious

board or state requirements, or even foisting change on unwilling staff and students. They are true middle managers, often caught between a faculty who are intent on their students and their teaching obligations and an outside world that increasingly seeks to change what those teachers do and produce. How are principals positioned to provide purposive leadership? The picture is a mixed but hopeful one. Principals can see the whole school environment and shape how others see it. On the other hand, their knowledge of teachers' work and relationships with teachers can be problematic. Altogether, four qualities shape their opportunities.

You See the Field

Principals, because of their freedom to move throughout the school and its environment, are in a position to keep the overall purposes of the school foremost in their own and others' consciousness. And, vital for the exercise of leadership, they are able to detect issues that will challenge the school and its established purposes. They are contact people for parents and citizens. They have the benefit of central office's district perspectives and access to political and policy signals from beyond the system. Professionally, they often have opportunities through journals, conferences, and professional associations to hear and discuss critically important perspectives that can assist with their schools' self-assessment and planning. Principals thus have ample opportunity to make purposes clear and to monitor and build commitments to them.

This access to broader trends and pressures allows principals, if they use it well, to understand the adaptive challenges facing their schools. Most important, they can sort among all the demands on them and, with the help of staff and others, choose to focus staff and community on challenges that are truly adaptive—challenges that, if addressed, promise to help the school change in ways that will enhance its performance. Although this activity requires considerable discretion, it requires most a willingness to face conflict and to assess performance honestly. Principals are positioned well to do this because they have the assumed authority and responsibility to call together staff and others and to use this collective time for the good of all. By history and cultural expectation, it is what we expect of our formal leaders.

Principals can use their positions to focus attention and energy on those school-level challenges that determine the school's ability to fulfill its purposes. *The challenge is to identify key challenges that bear on student success, thereby engaging adults' commitment to addressing core issues of purpose and performance.*

You Are a Bellwether of Professional Values

Principals also play a major part in shaping staff norms and culture. Principals' opportunities, both symbolic and instrumental, to reinforce core purposes and values can either undercut or solidify collective understanding of mission. If they use their formal authority to assert student-centered, collaborative norms and values among staff, they can be major influences in establishing a culture of hope and safety for adults (and thereby for children). If they visibly support the learning and professional skill development of staff, principals contribute palpably to the school's capacity to fulfill its complex and challenging purposes. Through emphasizing and contributing to core values and skills, principals have more than average impact on the robustness of others' commitment to their school and their work.

Principals do this work by attending to both "ceiling" and "floor" norms and skills. That is, they use their opportunities to communicate and the status of their office to reinforce high standards of professional performance and student attainment. They remind everyone that their mission is to strive for the heights and they bring definition to those heights. Simultaneously, however, they are uniquely positioned to address those individuals whose performance and motives threaten to fall below a "floor" of minimal standards. These standards are often unspoken, yet they are powerful influences on the group's sense of efficacy and safety. They can weaken commitment or make it more robust. The principal carries the hopes of the entire staff when she or he faces an employee whose marginal behavior causes concern or whose performance threatens to drag down the performance of others. Principals' supervisory activities with staff and students symbolize their—and the whole school's—values and their level of commitment to them.

Principals, more than any other single individual in the school, can enliven strong professional values and skills. *Their challenge lies in using their bellwether position sensitively and courageously to encourage and reward the best professional practice in others.*

You Can't Shake History

Stimulating an affirming and confident adult culture does not come without its serious challenges for most principals. In the history of our schools, administrators have not always upheld strong professional values. In fact, principals often must work through a smokescreen of staff doubt, distrust, and weakened commitment to school-wide matters. Power unfairly wielded in the past or simply an anti-authority spirit in the school leaves many principals digging their way out of poor relationships that they have inherited. From this position, principals who attempt to rally staff around purpose and to call up greater commitment to work for them can encounter cynicism, avoidance, and outright resistance.

Other reinforcing staff doubts about the motives of principals is their tendency to lump their principal's views with those held by central office or with mandates from state "bureaucracies" staff that they find fundamentally demeaning. Called to a faculty meeting or asked to read a memo from the principal, staff legitimately wonder whether the principal's words and directives are motivated by the school's espoused purposes and mission or by some more nefarious bureaucratic need to rein in runaway staff or impose someone else's political will. When the agenda is more challenging and adaptive—say, community members' protests about the school's low reading scores—these uncertainties become even more weighty. It takes affirmative and trusting relationships characterized by reciprocal influence for principals to work through these bureaucratic smokescreens. Staff need to trust that principals' decisions and actions are in children's best interests, not driven by politics, power, or ego.

Principals' success at stewarding purpose and commitment is often hampered by a history of staff distrust toward administrative initiatives and motives. *The challenge lies in developing relationships that are characterized by open dialogue between principals and faculty so that staff trust in the principal's motives and purposes.*

Our Purposes Aren't Always Your Purposes

A second obstacle for principals is that they are often isolated from student learning issues and the work of teachers. Principals are frequently so inundated with short-term demands and problems that their work lives become governed by management tasks and decisions. They find little time for "seeing the field," or they end up seeing the field through "management-colored glasses." Their submersion in office and maintenance detail, coupled with their inability to stay engaged with staff regarding their work with students, positions principals poorly to convene their staff around significant student-learning challenges. Goal displacement—the substitution of immediate or expedient goals for longer range educational purposes—is a common malady among principals (Cuban, 1988). When management displaces instruction as the governing purpose of a school—even if it is only in the mind and actions of the principal—the whole school risks losing its focus on children and instruction and commitment weakens.

In short, principals can lose touch with classroom concerns and, thus, weaken their capacity to frame for staff the significant challenges that they need to work on. So goes the coffee-mug saying, "Old principals don't die. They just lose their faculties." Given the difficulty of running a school, often short-handed, many new principals establish their initial identity around managerial competencies and never truly "win over their faculties" as instructional leaders. They never came to know the students and the teaching challenges they present well enough to capture the full attention and commitment of teachers. Without these, principals cannot help teachers, staff, parents, and students to merge their daily work routines with the broader purposes needed to generate a robust commitment to fulfill them.

Principals face the constant drag of managerial purposes and run the risk daily of substituting those purposes for the school's—and teachers'—major purposes. *Their challenge is to stay close enough to the instructional challenges of staff and children to help others see the leadership relationship as a means to improve their effectiveness with students.*

In summary, principals are positioned better to shape the purposing stream of their schools than they are the relationship-building stream. Their formal roles and legal authority give them responsibility for keeping the vision and mission alive. Staff and community usually look to the principal in such matters. How principals execute their responsibilities, then, colors deeply whether commitment is faint or robust. The leader activities described earlier in this chapter—articulating purposes, helping others bridge from ideals to actual practice, and embracing healthy self-criticism—all lie within the principal's reach. As Debbie Meier (1995) describes her own work at Central Park East High School, the principal who leads is deeply engaged in the learning activities of students and the teaching activities of teachers and parents. She or he is the bellwether of professional values for the school and, despite the divisions that can open between principal and teachers, the power of the principal's professional example can help staff forget them.

TEACHER LEADERS AS STEWARDS OF PURPOSE AND COMMITMENT

What assets and liabilities do teacher leaders bring to the leadership of purpose and commitment? Although teachers are not presumed to speak for the school and its purposes as principals are, they nevertheless can as leaders powerfully influence the professional norms and the daily beliefs about "what it is we're doing here." Many argue that teacher leaders are the central players in establishing this "professional authority" through asserting high standards of practice and knowledge (Darling-Hammond, 1997; Lieberman, 1988a; Sergiovanni, 1992). Formal teacher leaders such as department heads and team coordinators represent the faculty in curriculum and policy decisions. Within the faculty itself, informal leaders' stature and affect often powerfully influence how faint or robust is the sense of purpose among their colleagues.

You Too Live the Central Challenges

If principals find themselves distanced from the central challenges of instruction, teacher leaders frequently face them every day in their own teaching and in their conversations with colleagues. Teacher leaders' engagement in the work of teaching positions them both to "see" well this portion of the school's "field" and to shape collegial norms by modeling and advocating. Their conversations with colleagues, team meetings, and immersion in the ambient buzz of corridors and teachers' room keep teacher leaders apprised of issues confronting teachers in their attempts to fulfill the purposes of their curriculum and school. How can I reach this group of boys? What skills should we embed in this unit on Africa? How will we manage all the data from this assessment? When should we invite parents in to review kids' progress? These issues are the stuff of leadership work: Knowing what they are and appreciating how they are affecting the work and spirit of staff are essential to engaging with them in the hard work of adapting skills and strategies to be more effective. Both formal and informal teacher leaders are specially positioned to articulate such challenges.

They are, as well, often influential professional models for their peers. If their relationship with colleagues is strong, their ability to carry themselves with professional dignity and to demonstrate their skills in their work with children can set the standards of the teacher group. Indeed, it is often through their exemplary teaching that many teachers earn informal leadership influence. They know students, parents, and the community. They are skilled with a range of children. They are innovators in their classrooms. They speak up for student and teacher concerns. From their positions in the centers of collegial circles, leaders examine their own classroom activities; they read, experiment, and seek out greater pedagogical expertise. These qualities draw others into the circle and into their own quests for higher professional achievement. Teacher leaders who are comfortable in this norm-setting role can palpably shape a collegial environment that is safe enough to stimulate open discourse and questioning among other teachers, students, parents, and even administrators.

Teacher leaders are uniquely positioned to identify key challenges to the school's instructional improvement and to engage others in examining practice and committing to improvement. *The challenge for them lies in finding the time, energy, and access to colleagues in which to develop such purposive leadership circles.*

Your Group Can Focus Its Purposes

Teacher leaders' capacity for purposing is enhanced by the small size and closeness of the groups with which they work. In contrast to the principal's task of coalescing a large and diverse staff around common purposes, teacher leaders often facilitate small groups that are formed with a common focus and purpose. The seventh-grade team, the humanities faculty, the student assessment committee, or the student assistance team all carry purposes that teachers can attach to their own daily work with students. In this regard, the teacher leader often starts with a group that has already formed around a purpose and whose members feel a commitment to it.

Further, staff teams increasingly have time to confer and plan and may even share common space, promoting the merging of values and skills around shared techniques and goals. The teacher leader's encouragement of professional exchange of this sort, although it faces the obstacle of teacher autonomy and individualism, positions him or her to foster common language, common ideals, and a robust commitment among staff to one another and to their goals. The ninth-grade team in a high school develops a common set of transition activities for September through November. The social studies department creates common rubrics for student assessment throughout the year. The student assistance team generates a diagnostic system for all teachers to use in the early identification of at-risk students.

In working together, teams also offer valuable opportunities for regular adult contact and affiliation, for connecting on a more personal level, and for enjoying colleagueship. They can merge the relationship-building function of leadership with the purposive function; teacher leaders—and particularly informally recognized ones—can through the power of their professional example and their facilitation skills have a major impact on both relationships and sense of purpose. In this regard, informal leaders have an immense advantage over principals and even over formally appointed teacher leaders.

Teacher leaders' greatest asset is that they often work with small groups who share clarity, consensus, and commitment regarding their purposes. *Their challenge is to foster dialogue and coordinate efforts that integrate the team's purposes and commitments with school-wide mission and other groups' purposes.*

Just Don't Try to Make Us!

The most significant hurdle teacher leaders face in purposing is the norm of autonomy that permits some colleagues simply to dismiss them and their efforts to build connections. Under the flags of academic freedom, departmental autonomy, or exhaustion and impoverishment, teachers can ignore even informal attempts to organize them and to cultivate collective action. The norm of autonomy can, then, permit past practice, philosophical divisions, and interpersonal conflicts to rule the staff culture and to undercut widespread commitment to common purpose. School cultures that protect individuality above all other values can permit even unintentionally the persistence of conflicting goals and practices, subpar teaching, inappropriate student practices, and poor adult modeling. Teacher leaders, try as they may to model high professional standards and to inspire their colleagues, simply do not have the authority or collegial agreement to address performances that fall "below the floor" in this fashion. Indeed, teachers who attempt to confront resistant colleagues are often rebuffed and even rebuked for "acting like administrators" (Sernak, 1998; Wasley, 1991).

Teacher leaders' dependence on willing collaboration from colleagues is particularly problematic in schools with divided faculties. It is also a persisting challenge in schools with large numbers of senior or mid-career teachers whose commitment to their work has gone stale. These colleagues, as Robert Evans (1996) convincingly describes them, have legitimate reasons not to respond to a teacher leader's excitement and exhortations to change. Indeed, many reform-minded teachers have been frustrated by colleagues who have "seen it all before" and remain unwilling—and possibly unable—to mobilize themselves. Efforts to "lead from within" can actually divide faculties further, encourage clannishness, and provoke competition for power and resources (Blase & Anderson, 1995).

Teacher leaders can be dismissed or openly resisted by colleagues, often with little apparent consequence for those colleagues but with great consequence to staff commitment and collective purpose. *Their challenge is to build relationships with these colleagues and, simultaneously, to honor and address their doubts and worries about joining in a leadership relationship that embraces change.* In short, teacher leaders' challenge is to make room in the leadership relationship for colleagues who doubt or hold different opinions.

TENDING TO THE VITALITY OF PURPOSES

U.S. public schools have come under fire in recent decades for serving purposes that are out of step with 21st-century social and educational needs. The flurry of treatises about the "new mission" of our schools, however, does little to enliven the daily work of teachers with more relevant purposes or to generate robust commitment to them. That remains the challenge for principals and teachers in each of our schools. Rejuvenating the purposive stream of our schools is a leadership process that extends far beyond handing out treatises and posting fresh school missions. Leaders not only articulate the central purposes but also help others infuse their daily learning and teaching with these purposes. Most important, they invite opposing views and evidence that might reveal weaknesses in the school's performance. Leaders' work lies in adapting the school's performance to the changing needs of its students and community, not simply in maintaining old practices and purposes.

Here is the litmus test for leadership in this second stream: Staff clarity about and commitment to basic purposes fuels greater effort not only for high-quality practices in their own spheres but for reinventing school-wide purposes and practices when necessary. Both principal and teacher leaders are essential to the mobilization of a school around commitment to purpose. Even more essential is that these leaders play complementary, reinforcing roles. The principal has the attention of the school. She must use her position to articulate a compelling vision for all and to include divergent views and criticism in a vibrant and continuing dialogue about how well learning and teaching practices are meeting children's needs. But "imprisonment" by managerial duties and details can limit the principal's credibility and access to the instructional world. On the other hand, teacher leaders carry both interpersonal and professional credibility. Their greatest asset is their ability to coalesce small groups and teams around clearly instructional purposes and, from their successes together, to deepen the individual and collective commitment to their work. Both principals and teacher leaders will face persisting tensions between the "classroom" view, the team view, and the "whole-school" view. This only accentuates the interdependence of these leaders: The school needs them all to function in a single leadership relationship. The skills and qualities leaders need in this stream are described in Chapter 9.

It should be readily apparent that, to succeed, this second stream of leadership needs a firm relational foundation. The stewardship of commitment to purpose needs not only firm core values and beliefs but the strength within the group to question those values and beliefs—and the practices they give rise to—when evidence compels a reassessment. Another tension lies here between leaders' efforts to clarify mission, goals, and standards so everyone's work can cohere around them and the very real possibility that no single set of these will guarantee the successful learning of all children. One of the leaders' greatest challenges is to sustain a hopeful and professionally robust culture that *both* reinforces core values and skills *and* embraces criticism and the search for better ways to serve children and society. School staffs who respect and affirm one another have the collective strength for this challenging, purposing work. They need leaders who successfully blend the relational stream with the purposive stream of the school's life.

CHAPTER 7

Nurturing a Belief in Action-in-Common
Prospects and Pitfalls

Caring leadership [entails] . . . envisioning leadership from the center of the organization, not from the top, and allowing co-workers to work from their own positions of strength in order to contribute effectively to the organization and to take responsibility for their work.
—Sernak (1998), p. 15 *(emphasis in original)*

The first two dimensions of leadership—a relationship of mutual influence and commitment to common purposes—cannot by themselves mobilize people to care for their school. Although they establish the collectivity and the motive to act, they are only staging for the capacity to act. This capacity lies at the heart of the third leadership stream: a belief, reinforced by shared experience and action, that together the group can accomplish goals that would be impossible to accomplish individually. If leadership generates a sufficiently mutual relationship and a commitment to purpose among school members, this capacity for action-in-common is what enables the mobilization of the school to meet its purposes.

The proof of leadership has long been in the action. When teams, countries, armies, companies, or schools perform in demonstrably superior ways, we assume that leadership has played a large part in mobilizing members to achieve. James MacGregor Burns' (1978) ultimate test of leadership is "the degree of production of intended effects . . . actual accomplishment" (p. 22). Peters and Waterman's (1982) "excellent companies" had "a bias for action," a penchant for following the adage "do it, fix it, try it" (p. 132). In public displays of organizational performance such as team sports, we can see in an arena of split-second action the passing of a Magic Johnson or the positioning of a Mia Hamm for a shot as they weave decisions and actions into the game's flow. As with sport, the most productive organizational action is not identical, uniform, and lock-stepped. Action-in-common results from the voluntary choreography of many individual efforts, calling upon the idiosyncratic talents and characters of each person (Senge, 1990; Wheatley, 1992). What prospects and pitfalls do principals and teacher leaders encounter as they attempt to choreograph action in their schools?

GROWING THE CAPACITY FOR ACTION-IN-COMMON: WHAT LEADERS DO

The leadership relationship, in this third stream, engages staff daily in shaping one another's conviction that organizational purposes are better attained by action-in-common than by unlinked individual effort. As is true for our society in general, they must believe that the system they work in is fair and worthy of support. This shaping of beliefs is accomplished indirectly for the most part. Certainly, mission statements and leaders' exhortations will directly shape some staffs' understanding of the work and their role in it. But experiencing success is far more profoundly convincing. Seeing is believing—particularly in highly autonomous work settings like schools where people ultimately determine their own actions and where compliance has meager power. I have identified four ways that leaders shape the group's belief in their action-in-common.

First, leaders *identify the value of interdependent work*. Members of organizations in which the work requires interdependence are more likely to understand the importance of action-in-common. The "quality team" movement in industry, spawned by the thinking of Edward Deming (Fellers, 1992), explicitly brought workers with different skills and tasks together in integrated work units so they could decide how to merge their talents and resources most productively. Importantly, the work done by one worker is not identical to the work done by the next; their action-in-common involves performing different tasks in parallel and in synch with one another to the extent that it creates a whole greater than the sum of each person's part. The leadership relationship allows members to see opportunities for interdependent work to enhance their individual work and to help colleagues to see and appreciate these as well.

Valuing the interdependence of people's work means that leaders facilitate ways to accomplish that work. This means fostering connections among colleagues who share responsibility for a phase of production, a group of students, the quality of an outcome. Leaders, then, intervene on behalf of interdependent work in the schedule, the arrangement of space, the flow of resources, and the examination of problems. Their activities enable colleagues to connect and to collaborate. The result of their activities is that those colleagues experience greater success and their belief in their work-in-common is strengthened.

Second, leaders *ensure a steady diet of feedback on work and its effects*. Through their relationships, leaders offer ways to examine results continuously, sharing data with everyone and fostering an environment that supports problem-solving and ownership (Heifetz; 1994; Senge, 1990; Wheatley, 1992). The professional culture fostered by leaders helps members in groups and in the whole to understand the results of their labors and the extent to which they match the goals they aspire to achieve. Chris Argyris and Donald Schön (1974) captured this process in their description of double-loop learning. Here, evidence of performance is shared within the staff group and, nurtured by a strong leadership relationship, strengthens the group's belief in its own action-in-common:

> As individuals come to feel more psychological success . . . they are likely to manifest higher self-awareness and acceptance [of others], which leads to offering [others] valid information, which again leads to feelings of psychological success. As groups manifest higher degrees of openness, experimentation, and emphasis on individuality, individuals in them will feel freer to provide valid information that will tend, in turn, to enhance these group characteristics. (p. 91)

To fulfill this feedback function, leaders themselves are constantly seeking valid and reliable information about the organization's performance. This activity is not limited to traditional supervision of personnel and organization. It is much broader and considerably more focused on evidence of products and outcomes and follows the principles of action research (Elliott, 1991). The leader's activity concentrates not so much on collecting evidence as on creating ways for the group to share it, make sense of it, and ultimately act upon what they learn. Leaders thus nurture "communities of learners" and an organizational life for all colleagues that centers around learning (Barth 1990; Senge, 1990). As educators come to see themselves as learners and as sense-makers, their belief in their own individual efficacy and, as important, their collective efficacy grows (Bandura, 1997).

Third, leaders build a belief in action-in-common through *demonstrating values that reinforce the importance of collective responsibility and collaborative work*. Just as the leadership relationship forms around clear common purposes, it models and stresses values and behaviors that say, "The whole *is* greater than the sum of the parts." Those in leadership live and work in collaboration, asserting norms that communicate trust in others both to resolve important issues and to do excellent work. In place of solely individualistic goals and independent work, they seek advice, feedback, and assistance in their own work with students, parents, and colleagues. They respect others' responsibilities and offer colleagueship, feedback, and assistance. Leaders choose to work through collaborative partnerships for tasks that are too complex for one person or that require the buy-in of many, such as how staff, parents, and students judge what students need to learn and how the school will respond to threats to its safety and civility (Louis, Kruse, & Bryk, 1995; Schein, 1985).

The authority and power traditionally vested in formal leaders must unambiguously support these collective norms (Argyris, 1993; Heifetz, 1994). That is, if leaders' deeds say, "I must make the final decision; I am ultimately in charge," others will feel that their own responsibility, accountability, and authority are finite and secondary to the leaders'. The whole is not greater than the sum of the parts; the whole is "theirs, not ours." J. M. Burns (1978) observed that leadership can be accomplished through "inaction and nondecision"—by leaders' stepping back and facilitating authority and action in others—as well as through direct action

(p. 22). Whatever the course of action, the leadership relationship assures everyone that working together, sharing the load and the successes, is a "lived belief" in the school, not merely rhetoric.

Finally, leaders, as they feed the organization's hunger for feedback, *enable people to act on these data to solve not just their own problems but to meet organizational challenges.* Leadership encompasses those people who have a bias for action, whose commitment to the organization compels them to "fix their own wagon" when it needs it. Writers distinguish two types of work in this regard: alterations to existing work patterns and more profound shifts in the nature and types of work the organization does. Ronald Heifetz (1994) labels the former "technical work" or work where existing practices and resources can address the presenting problem; it is work that calls on "mastery and ingenuity" of skills and processes that we already have in our repertoires (pp. 71–72). When teachers realize they are losing student interest, they alter their delivery or content. When a school realizes that the schedule interferes with a group's learning, the school adjusts it. The solutions to such technical breakdowns are often more training, changing work routines, and importing new techniques into the existing work process. These steps, when they work, reward people with higher success and, in this respect, contribute to belief in the benefits of collaboration.

The second type of collaborative action—adaptive work—can have a far more profound impact on the group's belief in their collective power. This deeper adaptive work responds to an "adaptive challenge" characterized by evidence that current ways of teaching and running schools no longer satisfy student or societal needs. Such work succeeds when the school "adapts" its practices, beliefs, and values to the circumstances that have changed around it. For example, a school recognizes that it has consistently failed to give 30% of its students the practical literacy skills required for jobs. Or the culture that has grown among students makes it difficult for minority students to feel safe and thus to focus on learning. Or a group of taxpayers persists in their demand for programs that will prepare graduates better for full political and economic participation in society. Leaders convene others so they can address the complex factors that have caused the school to be—or appear to be—out of step with its mission in these respects. This "adaptive work," according to Heifetz (1994), enables colleagues to realign their *beliefs, their behaviors, and their relationships* to respond to the school's challenge to meet new needs arising within and around it (p. 26). Although technical improvements can often be accomplished through management, a number of theorists hold that facilitating this more complex adaptive work and mobilizing the organization for this more profound type of change is the heart of leadership (Burns, 1978; Heifetz, 1994; Helgesen, 1995; Sergiovanni, 1992).

Leaders who facilitate the resolution of such deeper adaptive issues give people a reason to believe in their collective action. When those problems are deep-seated, persistent, and divisive, they have immense potential to sap the energies and psyches of staff. These are the sorts of organizational challenges that call for leaders. Leaders, in Heifetz's analysis (1994), engage in five types of activity:

1. Identifying these deeper adaptive challenges.
2. Keeping the "level of distress" among staff and others within a tolerable range so that the group can focus on its challenges, not degenerate into blaming and avoidance.
3. Focusing others' attention on "ripening the issues" into actionable strategies and not on "stress-reducing distractions" that do not lead to action.
4. "Giving the work back to the people" in the organization rather than closeting themselves with all the responsibility and power.
5. "Protecting the voices of leaders" who do not have formal authority, honoring and including these informal or natural leaders whether they agree with formal leadership or not.

Leaders help their groups "face problems," not avoid them or accommodate them with technical Band-Aids (Fullan & Miles, 1992; Glickman, 1993). The leadership relationship invites all members to feel responsible for the organization's challenge and to share in the work of inventing better ways of thinking about it and doing it together. Engagement in this more fundamental adaptive work summons from people a much more profound level of action-in-common and commitment to the organization and to one another than does the work of technical adjustment. Leaders who succeed in mobilizing colleagues in this deeper way have forever deepened the collective conviction that they can influence their own fate (Bandura, 1997).

In summary, this third leadership stream involves leaders in clarifying and emphasizing the ways in which people's work is interdependent with the work of others. By establishing norms that highlight the principle that "together we can attain more than we can in isolation," leaders provide ways of sharing feedback on performance and of enabling the group to resolve issues they see in that feedback. Leaders unabashedly trust collective decision-making and model their faith in the school to solve its own significant challenges. Finally, leaders nurture a widespread sense of collective efficacy through putting before the staff the dilemmas and challenges arising out of their own work, both internally with children and each other and externally with their constituents and community. Leaders, in this last sense, do not shelter members from the hard facts as patriarchal leadership does; instead, they "ask us to be deeply accountable for the outcomes of our institution, without acting to define purpose for others, control others, or take care of others" (Block, 1996, p. 18). Through extending this leadership partnership among members, everyone can put a shoulder to the school's wheel and bask in the satisfactions of their combined effort and achievement.

SCHOOLS AS PLACES THAT NURTURE ACTION-IN-COMMON

Over the past 30 years, American schools have repeatedly been asked to "fix them-selves." As curriculum reform yielded to restructuring, as restructuring yielded to state-mandated policies, and as these in turn yielded to "reculturing," schools have proven notoriously resilient. Action-in-common, even when schools have been under considerable attack from the outside, comes hard for all but the most tightly knit schools. Three conditions tend to paralyze action-in-common in schools, whereas three others propel it forward.

Conditions That Paralyze Action-in-Common

First, our *schools are not conceived or organized so that the work of teachers and others is interdependent.* What one teacher does is not directly dependent upon what another teacher does, day in and day out. Mr. Franklin's success at teaching fractions today to 90 seventh graders does not influence directly any other teacher's work teaching English, democratic principles, or cooperation skills to those same seventh graders. Indeed, American schools have frequently been described as "loosely coupled"— one person's work is not directly linked to another's, and daily teaching activities are only circuitously linked to the production of long-term outcomes. Even man-agerial directives do not evoke 100% compliance in many schools. Educators' dis-cretion and control over their work, reinforced by a culture of individualism, make interdependence largely a social phenomenon, not a professional one, in many schools.

Action-in-common in schools, if it exists at all, looks more like parallel play than voluntary collaboration. School-wide policies, curricula, and regulations are translated through each teacher, each counselor, and each coach, enacted in the isolation of a classroom, an office, or a playing field. A good deal of this action takes place on faith that it is, indeed, "in common." But the common plan or policy becomes enormously varied as it is fit into existing practice by different people in different classrooms and offices (Jennings, 1996). Even when a team, a department, or a faculty plan a specific treatment for a child (as in the case of a special education Individual Educational Plan) or a well-structured innovation, the plan inevitably diversifies and even unravels as it is carried into practice (Elmore & McLaughlin, 1988; Fuhrman, 1993). The closest our schools have come to interdependent work is in the case of teacher teams or small schools where the educational process is constructed around collaborative adult efforts and where time and schedules are adapted to these priorities (Darling-Hammond, 1997; Meier, 1995).

A second condition inhibiting action-in-common is the *absence of feedback on practice around which staff can engage in problem-solving and improvement.* Make no mistake: teachers are expert problem-solvers and they are constantly using self-observation and professional reflection in their decision-making. They, however, are by most accounts so busy teaching that their opportunities for feedback and reflection are sorely curtailed. Studies of effective teachers show that they feel deprived of good feedback; when given the opportunity to have an observer and to discuss with observers their most pressing student issues, they not only feel more efficacious, they are more effective with their students (Darling-Hammond, 1997; Johnson, 1990; Little, 1982; Rosenholtz, 1986). And at the school-wide level, extraordinarily little valid data is available to whole staffs for their collective feedback. Hence many schools operate on collective faith: No news is good news; "if complaints are down, we must be doing something right."

In the absence of useful feedback on practice, our schools understandably continue to do what appears to work. Thus we come to revere the "grammar of schooling," a pattern of activity that induces in students appropriate behavior and that creates, for student, parent, and teacher, a documentary record of "learning achievement" that can be summed, averaged, and reported on a periodic basis as evidence of learning (Tyack & Cuban, 1995). A "logic of confidence" takes over: In the absence of demonstrable evidence that discipline, parent satisfaction, or achievement is a problem, we "keep on keeping on" (Meyer & Rowan, 1978). Bacharach and Mundell (1995) conclude that, in the typical school, participants hold so many "diverse logics of action" for their work with children that it is impossible to engage in dialogue about action-in-common without generating conflict in the group (p. 397). So, many of our public schools have become places where individual efficacy rather than collective effectiveness rules. The cult of individuality and isolated control over the processes of teaching and learning make leadership in this arena daunting indeed.

If schools have insufficient feedback to give them valid institutional confidence in their action-in-common, have they nevertheless been able to address major adaptive challenges when they arise? The evidence from the history of educational reform suggests that *few schools and communities can stop the action long enough to understand central adaptive challenges well enough to meet them*. For example, schools now face deep pressures to address the basic educational needs of growing numbers of underserved and minority children; equipped with information-age learning systems, schools have yet to assimilate them into new concepts of schooling or new structures for learning; and alienation among students now presents school staffs with daily— and sometimes lethal—crises. These challenges persist. Citizens grow frustrated and angry. Staff share this distress but also grow defensive. If leadership is inadequate, staff often have few choices but to avoid these major issues or become militant; sometimes they turn their anger and frustration on one another and on the community.

Even when staff and community agree on the need for change, staff typically have insufficient time for collective problem-solving and for learning new ways of working with students and with one another. The conspiracy of busyness is not only time-consuming; it is exhausting. The grammar of schooling is so embedded in the structure and culture of our schools and the minds of our publics, our students, and our staffs that new behaviors do not follow easily from new goals, new beliefs, or new values. Public schools cannot seem to convince their publics of what private industry learned ages ago: that to take on the major adaptive challenges that thwart schools' success requires investments of money, time, expertise, and staff in problem-solving and learning new behaviors, beliefs, and values (Evans, 1996; Glickman, 1993).

So, in most schools in our country, conditions do not exist for these organizations of learning to function as learning organizations. Tragically, educators are deprived of an activity that lies at the very core of their collective efficacy: facing the challenges that impair their effectiveness and devising together ways to do better by children. The great challenge for leadership as it nurtures a staff's belief in action-in-common is to grow "hybridized [reforms], adapted by educators working together to take advantage of their knowledge of their own students and communities and supporting each other in new ways of teaching" (Tyack & Cuban, 1995, p. 136–137).

Conditions That Propel Action-in-Common

The picture emerging here of our schools as places where belief in action-in-common can thrive looks bleak. Quite surprisingly, however, *the culture of many American schools continues to value solidarity of effort, faith in the goodness of the cause, and a sense of community.* Administrators and school board members publicly declare ambitious school-wide goals and visions and attest to the effort and care going into them. The professional ethic, with its history of evangelical fervor for public service, magnetically pulls many who work in public schools toward an image of action-in-common. This creates cultures that are village-like in nature (Goodlad, 1984). It leads to general agreement about goals and to an ethos of congeniality and professional confidence among educators (Lortie, 1975; McLaughlin, Talbert, & Bascia, 1990; Rosenholtz, 1986). The informal organization of school faculties documented in Chapter 2 serves to reinforce the image of schools as extended families that stay vibrant more through social interchanges and on-the-fly connections than through formal, public forms of organization. Many public educators draw from their daily work with children an abiding faith in the value of their service. Where principals and respected teachers have developed a strong working relationship, staff, students, and community confidence in the school's collective ability to respond to challenges builds from this faith into a broader belief in action-in-common.

Successful public school educators have a bias for action that can feed this belief as well. They are pragmatic. Every day they are immersed in a caldron of young minds and bodies, making decisions and directing, cajoling, structuring, and supporting learning activity. Where conditions permit, such as in smaller schools and teams, issues and experiences bubble up into staff conversations and decision-making.

Here, authentic collaboration has a chance to grow around challenges that are real to teachers, students, and parents because it can be converted readily into new action (Darling-Hammond, 1997).

Leadership, then, benefits from the normally high agreement within staffs around purpose and mission, bringing with it an important level of espoused commitment to action-in-common. The challenge is to grow this philosophical commitment into a belief that acting in concert can help a staff live up to those commitments. *Individual schools, now supported by a reform literature that honors "improving from within" and by state and district leadership in some cases, are investing in reform.* Partnerships such as the Coalition of Essential Schools, the League of Professional Schools, and the International Network of Principals' Center have created networks to support staffs and community groups to perform the important relationship-building and purposing work that will lead to a capacity for action. Although this work can generate conflict, threaten the culture of congeniality, and exact new costs on individuals and schools, its emphasis on creating new practices that match each school's history and unique challenges makes it both attractive and successful (Darling-Hammond, 1997; Lieberman, 1995; McDonald, 1996; Muncey and McQuillan, 1996). Indeed, the past decade has taught us rich lessons about how schools can mobilize and the critical role that experimentation, incremental change, and staff learning play in developing risk-taking and a belief in collective progress.

READINESS FOR ACTION-IN-COMMON

In the next sections, I explore principal and teacher leaders' capacity to nurture a belief in action-in-common. As in Chapters 5 and 6, it will help to think of this work as moving schools along a developmental continuum (See Figure 7.1). In some schools, where past events have grown a culture that leaves "every man for himself," the staff can be paralyzed when confronted with the need for action-in-common. Whole-school events and issues are the administrators' job; staff come to see them as obstacles to their own goals, not enhancements. Little or no belief in the benefits of action-in-common tends to negate the value of the organization altogether.

At the other end of the continuum, a school can propel itself toward such action. Here, staff members feel that their own individual actions and those of the organization are synergistically linked. They freely identify adaptive challenges that effect their success with children. They feel engaged in the solution of problems and thus are propelled toward action-in-common. The result is enhanced collective efficacy that spirals the school's performance upward.

Staff cultures most likely blend features that paralyze and features that propel. Again, leaders need to work with the cards dealt them. Their challenge lies in moving colleagues, one by one and as a whole, toward that point where they freely and

FIGURE 7.1   Staff Beliefs in Action-in-Common: A Range of Readiness to Act

PARALYZED ◄━━━━━━━━━━━━━━━━━━━━━━━━━► PROPELLED

• Staff feel alone • Staff see work as independent and disconnected • Staff see the institution and school-wide matters as obstacles to personal efficacy • Value other staff largely for friendship • School-wide issues are for administrators to resolve • Little faith in formal leaders	• Staff communicate to stay informed about personal obligations • Follow administrative guidelines and directives; compliance is a duty • Solidarity for action-in-common is largely for self-protection (union; advocacy) • View collective action as political and transactional	• Widespread belief in common goals, curriculum, and student learning results • Teams evaluate, plan, and innovate together • Communication and collaboration extend mainly to team members • Believe school policies and curriculum will assure consistency and common outcomes	• Widespread belief that the major individual challenges are best met together • Open problem-solving and planning lead to productive action • Sharing performance data is commonplace • Whole-school communication and interaction are commonplace • A climate of active innovation is pervasive

wholeheartedly take action. In the next two sections, I explore how principals and teachers are distinctly positioned to perform this important work.

PRINCIPALS AS NURTURERS OF THE BELIEF

Principals, by tradition and job description, are expected to create collective action in order to assure uniformity in practices, presumably to bring uniformly good results throughout the school. In many, largely managerial respects, principals have succeeded. School environments are mostly predictable and safe. Students and personnel follow master schedules and they generally conform to approved guidelines and curricula. About 80% of American children progress through the public education system and graduate "on time." Principals accomplish this moderate level of action-in-common through a combination of planning, scheduling, and regulation–making on one hand and, on the other, a great deal of often hot-footed monitoring and enforcing. Their positions give them great influence in this regard. These principal activities, however, do not by themselves propel staff toward a belief in action-in-common. They are apt to generate a belief in the need for management and, perhaps, in the action of the principal, not in the contributions of each staff member to the successful learning of all children. What, then, are the particular assets and liabilities that principals bring to nurturing belief in action-in-common?

They Assume That You Can; Therefore, You Can

By tradition and authority, people look to the appointed leader to promote school-wide effectiveness. The principal is *the* person with a whole-school view. The principal's work is about how the parts of the school work interdependently, consistently, and coherently. She or he can call faculty meetings, speak for the school publicly, draw up schedules, encourage restructuring of curriculum, evaluate personnel. The principal who persistently brings core decisions to the faculty so they all can deliberate on issues of learning, climate, and performance affirms the value of each member to the collective. The principal who bases decisions about resources, personnel, and curriculum on the common vision rather than on who speaks the loudest for his or her own program similarly reinforces action-in-common. In short, one of the principal's greatest assets as a leader is the expectation that she or he can coalesce people around a plan or an idea, foster meaningful interdependence, and help them propel themselves into action.

The principal, however, walks a delicate tightrope in this respect. His or her unambiguous belief in collaborative action can easily be interpreted as heavy-handed and overly controlling; it can thus stifle a sense of collective efficacy. In districts with very "union-minded" staff, the principal needs to establish clear professional motives and values or risk being written off as "just management." In schools where faculty are under public attack or are divided over deep issues, the principal's attempts to provide feedback and to engage people in adaptive change can spawn fearfulness, blaming, and even paralysis. This dilemma points out the importance of a strong working relationship to the growth of action-in-common. Principals need clearly to express their belief in the staff's capacity to address the core challenges of the school—those challenges that deal with children, their care, and their learning. Staff need to feel certain that their principals not only believe that "together, we can lick problems that we cannot lick alone" but also that they will be there when the going gets tough.

Equipped with the mantle of authority, the principal has the choice to use it to demonstrate belief in action-in-common—or not. *The challenge lies in sustaining this belief in action-in-common and in sensitively but firmly placing her or his authority behind collaborative action.*

Your Belief in Us Is Important

Principals demonstrate their faith in the collective in some clear ways. The principal, speaking publicly or individually, talks of "our responsibility" and of "what *we* are doing." She or he expresses confidence that "we can do it" while not obscuring real problems with idealized aspirations. Even more forceful, what the principal *does* signals to all her or his belief in action-in-common. Does she or he turn to others with tough problems and trust them to help resolve them? Do her or his decisions indicate faith that staff, students, and community can carry their responsibility—not perfectly or according to an intricate plan, but fundamentally in the spirit of the plan's goals and the school's mission? The principal exhibits trust in the judgment, skills, and energies of her or his faculty and staff by sharing major challenges, no matter how messy they are. Trust propels staff toward action.

Principals also demonstrate belief in action-in-common by facilitating the staff's problem-solving and inventive work. That is, the principal does not declare, "This is your problem," deserting the staff to wrestle with it alone. He or she meets with small groups and devotes faculty meeting time to those issues that effect the staff's success with children. He or she facilitates a process that draws on people's experience, information, and judgment first to "ripen the issue" by clarifying causes and characteristics of the challenge. The principal then channels time, resources, and group energies to solutions and supports action on them. Usually through trial-and-error and "tinkering," staff discover whether new methods work with children. The principal, by virtue of giving priority and organizational and personal resources to issues considered vital by staff, plays a facilitative role in adapting practices that few others can play.

The principal exhibits his or her own belief in staff action-in-common by declaring it, by sharing vital decisions and dilemmas with the staff, and especially by facilitating their collective work on these decisions and dilemmas. *The challenge lies in sharing in his or her many daily interactions the attitude that, "Your challenge is our challenge; together we will improve."*

You Know the School as a Whole

The principal's relatively unfettered access to the life of the school gives her or him special information and therefore special responsibilities. Belief in collective action-in-common requires a steady flow of accurate feedback on practice so that staff can know when their efforts are working and adjust when they are not. Among the many adults who work in and around schools, principals are best positioned to serve as institutional data gatherers (in fact, active principals cannot help but do this!). In this regard, they are absolutely instrumental to the school's learning about itself—and hence to its ability to grow both in performance and in collective efficacy.

Information of all sorts bubbles up in schools, from student attitudes overheard in the hall to group tensions expressed on the playground to a teacher's energetic new unit on agrarian societies spilling over into the lunchroom. Other data need to be systematically gathered—such as test scores, school climate indicators, the performance of graduates, and parent evaluations. The principal, by seeing to the collection of these indicators of the school's performance and by sharing them widely with staff, students, and parents, communicates confidence that the school as a whole can learn from them. His or her effective facilitation of analysis and planning from these data builds directly the staff's competence as a problem-solving team. Action propelled by such professional inquiry, whether it be a new school-wide practice or each staff person's individual adjustment of practice, is the very essence of lasting school change (Darling-Hammond, 1997; Newmann & Wehlage, 1995; Tyack & Cuban, 1995).

The principal's role in collecting accurate, useful information and in sharing this feedback widely establishes a core of authenticity crucial to the staff's belief in itself and its ability to act. *The challenge lies in gathering accurate data and in protecting the time and fostering the collective confidence to learn from them.*

You Are the Boss

Although the principal's greatest asset is her or his formal position and, with it, the expectation that she or he will nurture collective efficacy, the principal's greatest liability stems from that formal position as well. The principal is the presumed leader, but sometimes also the feared boss. She or he is almost always the person with statutory power over staff employment and with live contacts in the power hierarchy. Indeed, central office and community often expect decisive, executive action by the "head man." This paradox is most discomfiting to many principals; whether they seek to be collaborative or not, principals find that they are viewed as "management," caught in a "top-down" role. Often the sins of principals past—or superintendents and boards present—are visited upon the heads of new principals. Further, principals who try to collaborate can find that staff refuse to accept collective responsibility for whole-school matters, regarding them as the principals' obligations, not theirs. The picture is one where the principal is caught among expectations to tell rather than listen, act singly rather than confer, and do combat rather than collaborate.

In fact, principals have legal and organizational responsibilities that cannot be easily or sometimes wisely shared. Consider the many managerial decisions principals make in a day or week that, individually at least, are so insignificant as not to merit collective consultation. Consider the case where the principal alone must address a staff member's performance that is so weak that it impedes student learning or burdens his or her colleagues. Or consider the case where a community group is wreaking havoc in the press or a central office practice is dismantling working relationships within the school. Principals, in such cases, need as a matter of ethics or expediency to act alone. Within the larger context of their efforts to share leadership, these actions may seem inconsistent and can undercut others' beliefs in the principal as well as in collective participation.

These circumstances make it very challenging for some principals to believe in action-in-common, much less nurture that belief in others. In this respect, all principals must come to terms with their positional authority. They must be comfortable explaining to colleagues why they have made unilateral decisions and reinforce in the process how their decisions are guided by the common vision. And they must remain accountable to staff, just as they are asking all staff to be accountable to one another as a working group. How a principal carries the inevitable mantle of authority spells her or his true belief in the judgment, skills, and action of others.

Principals' formal authority can erode belief in action-in-common and paralyze whole-school change. Hence it must be carried with care and used with great purpose. *The challenge is to address directly staff perceptions of the principal's role and to clarify issues of authority and responsibility that can cloud their trust in her or his motives for collaborative action.*

TEACHER LEADERS AS NURTURERS OF THE BELIEF

Although principals are presumed to cause organizational action, teachers generally are not. The rules of the hierarchy and the culture of individualism relegate teachers' action to the classroom arena. Faculty norms often impose an informal "hands off" policy on intruding into one another's teaching affairs. On the other hand, teachers draw strength and sustenance from one another and their sense of solidarity, equality, and professional calling. In fact, they control most of what occurs in the educational realm of a school. Teacher leaders face substantial challenges in this culture, but they also bring significant assets to it that help them generate belief in action-in-common.

You Are Us

Teacher leaders, by virtue of their membership in the teacherhood, can have vast informal influence within a faculty, staff, and community. As "one of us," their opinions, proposals, and practices can carry unusual power with colleagues. This is particularly true if a teacher's leadership is informal, the product of his or her naturally earned authority and credibility among peers. If the teacher leader has "risen from the ranks" and been appointed to a formal teacher leadership position by administration—even though this is reason enough for some colleagues to question his or her allegiances—the teacher leader carries "the teacher view" into his or her relationships and school-wide activities (Little, 1988; Wasley, 1991).

Simply by expressing and demonstrating belief in the teacher group's ability to work together, teacher leaders can have an immense impact on the staff's belief in itself. In team, committee, and departmental meetings and gatherings, the leader's attitude and confidence can either affirm that "we are all in this together and I believe we're making a difference" or spread doubt about the group's capacity and purpose. Through action strategies developed in such groups and feedback on progress, such affirmative beliefs can literally propel the group into action. This is especially true when the team's action is focused on specific children: A grade-level team, for example, seeking to improve certain practices within the classrooms of its own grade is more likely to develop belief in its own action-in-common than a committee attempting to restructure an entire school.

Teacher leadership can build on the inherent solidarity and credibility that teachers extend to their colleagues, turning it back into affirmation and action for the group. *The challenge lies in creating opportunities to work together so that the group's plans do turn into action.*

You Know the Troubles I See

Teachers who lead have another great asset: They often continue to teach and, thus, their focus, their daily worries, and even the rises and falls of their energies and emotions resemble those of their colleagues. They daily "walk in our shoes." Their proximity to the daily challenges teachers face with students gives teacher leadership a focus on "real action"—action where they and their colleagues can, if they succeed, make a difference for children. Unlike principals, teacher leaders can respond over lunch to a colleague's success with a new unit during the morning. They can listen over coffee or the copy machine to a concern about a child. They can follow up such conversations individually or in team meetings, "ripening the issue" for a solution or simply providing comradeship.

Their capacity to facilitate problem-solving in the immediate instructional worlds of their peers permits teacher leaders to influence directly the teacher group's collective efficacy. The colleagueship of teachers, reinforced as it may be by gender and background similarities, gives teacher leaders a handle both on the tasks facing teachers and on the emotional highs and lows they feel. By listening and consulting, they help colleagues identify challenges and assets. As critical friends, teacher leaders spawn problem-solving circles that give all participants a voice. Here, women's inclination to honor feelings and relational issues can make them powerful facilitators of others' sense of membership and capacity to act (Biklen, 1995; Helgesen, 1995). Despite the difficulties they may face in gaining access to colleagues' practices or meeting as a team, teacher leaders can generate strong connections among colleagues through natural interactions during the school day and week. These, in turn, can not only cultivate a belief that "we are in this together" but also propel them toward informal common actions that enhance their collective effectiveness.

Teachers' focus on students and on the challenges of teaching and learning position them to facilitate learning and planning among their peers that can directly and persuasively lead to new action. *The challenge, again, lies in having sufficient time and energy and strong enough individual and group relationships to make this work. The* natural connections among teachers are among the best opportunities to nurture common values, beliefs, and practices.

Your Team Can Act!

In the growing number of teacher teams and standing committees in schools, teacher leadership has an unusual opportunity to create belief in action-in-common. Team members can plan their own action and propel themselves into implementation. Teachers can personally and directly view the fruits of their labors. The Sixth Grade Team Leader or the Science Department Chair facilitates the planning of a new unit or the analysis of recent assessment data. The scope of the team's work is manageable: the sixth grade, a unit, a set of data, a state requirement. The leader's task is to help the group itself identify specific strategies and carry them into action. This is the stage on which the team's aspirations for students and hopes for their own action-in-common are played out. Formal leaders carry a share of that action, just as others do: They try the new advising protocol; they report their successes and failures at the next team meeting; they are there day-by-day and sometimes moment-by-moment to share their colleagues' successes and struggles.

By the same token teachers in leadership positions who fail to mobilize the team's thinking and planning can just as powerfully undermine a team's belief in its action-in-common. As we witnessed in the era of restructuring, simply assigning teachers to teams and anointing someone "teacher leader" can backfire. Teams, department, and committees require time to form and resources for planning their own new ways of practicing (Donaldson and Sanderson, 1996; Little, 1988). Teacher leaders, as I explain in later chapters, need to be skilled facilitators within their groups as well as articulate advocates for their groups with the administration and faculty. Clearly, their own belief in their team or group plays heavily into the group's ability to act for the benefit of children and the school.

Teacher leadership has, in team and committee settings, a powerful effect on teacher beliefs about their abilities to act-in-common. *The challenge lies in nurturing the group's development into an effective team even as the team and its members are busy making decisions and taking action.*

But You're Still "Just a Teacher"

The fact that teacher leaders often have little or no formal control over organizational factors creates tension in their work. They often cannot without great effort assist their teams and colleagues to obtain necessary resources, schedule changes, administrative blessings, or simply the support of other teachers. They often do not have a budget to work with or sufficient autonomy to make decisions about space, time, teaching materials, or instructional practices. Or they simply haven't the time and energy to do these things on top of the teaching they do each day. Ironically, teacher leaders are sometimes expected to function as "mini-administrators," to carry teacher causes "up" into the administration, and to carry administrators' wishes "down." This combination of constraints can frustrate teacher leaders, making them feel neither fish nor fowl and leaving their colleagues thinking that "things are no better than before" teacher leadership positions were invented.

Complicating the picture are issues of gender and overall administrative philosophy. Women leaders find themselves advocating on behalf of their colleagues to a male principal or superintendent. Teacher leaders take proposals for change from their teams and colleagues to administrators and school boards only to be told why the district cannot carry them out. These situations often place women leaders in unfamiliar and even hostile surroundings where, perhaps, they find themselves arguing in public with their bosses. Returning to their teams after doing battle for the team's proposal, uncertain colleagues might wonder about the teacher leader's allegiances as she explains the principal's rationale for not supporting the proposal (Wasley, 1991). In many respects, the female teacher leader who ventures forth on behalf of her team into a school, district, or community dominated by masculine leadership metaphors can be squeezed from all sides into a mission impossible. Her inability to "deliver" for her team then tests her and her colleagues' belief in teacher leadership in general and can undercut their belief in their action-in-common. Principals insensitive to this dynamic can, as well, tragically conclude that "teacher leadership doesn't work."

Teacher leaders, lacking formal authority, access to resources, and experience in often gendered managerial cultures frequently find they have a weak voice and limited capacity to facilitate their colleagues' action ideas within the school and district. *Their challenge is to develop sufficient authority in their leadership relationships that their individual voices on behalf of learning are heard.*

TENDING TO THE STREAM OF ACTION-IN-COMMON

Principals and teacher leaders bring significant assets to the important leadership work of nurturing a belief in action-in-common. If their relationships with staff are sufficiently strong, their own belief in action-in-common can carry great influence with colleagues. Their shaping of group agendas, their respect for gathering and sharing feedback data, and their ability to facilitate meaningful learning and planning give both principal and teacher leaders key roles in the mobilization of staff to action. Busy schools tend to fragment efforts and isolate teachers from one another. Exhaustion and pragmatism can gradually grow into a culture of do-your-own-thing, paralyzing whole-school improvement. Leadership as I have defined it in this book cannot thrive in such a culture for it undercuts the very possibility of mobilization for institutional growth.

The litmus test for this third leadership stream is that adults are learning together from the major challenges in their work and actively improving their practices with students, parents, and each other. Principals, although saddled with administrative duties, profoundly affect this learning-to-action transfer in part through their convictions about the interdependence of staff work and in part through their insistence on whole-school reflective practice. If the principal accepts the planetary culture, she implicitly supports individualistic, disconnected, and even contradicting actions. If she offers feedback, facilitates group decisions, and actively supports inventiveness and collaborative work, she sends a very direct message that "we can do the best by every child but we need to work together to do it."

Teacher leaders are natural keepers of their colleagues' hopes, aspirations, and values. The egalitarian ethic of teaching and the natural opportunities teacher leaders have to build relationships give them ready access to acting-in-common with those colleagues. So too does their capacity to empathize, to "walk the walk" through the highs and lows of colleagues' experience. More than principals, teacher leaders can be in-action partners in generating practices that legitimately support a belief that "we are making a positive difference for these kids and this community."

This third leadership stream relies heavily on the first two for its strength. Without a solid working relationship and a mutual purpose to which staff are committed, leaders' abilities to coalesce their colleagues around the risky work of addressing adaptive challenges and fashioning new action are sorely handicapped. Reciprocally, with each new success at collaboration and action, staff come to feel more efficacious—a feeling that feeds their level of commitment to their purposes and strengthens the working relationships among them. In this manner, the leadership relationship integrates the interpersonal and the philosophical with the action of work. Personal and professional fulfillment can grow both from meaningful partnerships with colleagues and from clear evidence that those partnerships are helping each person fulfill the school's purposes in his or her daily work with children.

CHAPTER 8

Leaders Put Relationships
at the Center

Whether we will be able to move [ahead] . . . will depend on our collective ability to think in new ways about the meanings and the responsibilities of shared leadership . . . Teachers and principals can hold leadership roles and, working together, they can help the schools to build a professional culture.

—Lieberman (1988b), p. 653

The realities of our public schools dictate distinctive conditions for leadership. Being a leader there is quite unlike leading in many other contexts. Chapters 5 through 7 depict the special assets and liabilities that principals and teacher leaders bring to this important work. Administrators and teachers (among others) play vital complementary roles in each of the three streams that create a flow of leadership for the school. In the next three chapters, I look more directly at these leaders, their activities, and the skills and qualities that help to maximize their assets. Two central questions focus these chapters: "How can I cultivate leadership in our school?" and "How can I develop within myself the talents necessary to do this?"

I find that many principals and teacher leaders ponder these two questions over their entire careers. They can be heard at professional development conferences and in graduate courses, and I'm sure they swirl within the heads of many educators trying to make a difference in their schools every day. Within the framework of this book, however, these questions require immediate reformulation because "I"—the individual—do not, by myself, "make leadership happen." Leadership ebbs and flows as the relationships among faculty shift with changing people, their experiences with one another, and the intrusion of external factors such as state mandates, budgets, and community politics. Individuals who aspire to be leaders engage purposefully in the web of relationships in their building. But such work, as Margaret Wheatley (1999) describes it, is multifaceted, simultaneous, and impossible to reduce to a linear plan. Instead, leaders need to "tolerate unprecedented levels of 'messiness' at the edges" of the school's work while assuring "clarity of purpose" at the core (p. 157). Ultimately, what leaders do to mobilize others looks more, as Wheatley puts it, like "a dance, not a forced march" (p. 160). The talents they need, it follows, are those more befitting a choreographer than a general.

Leaders, then, participate as dancers in an ongoing dance of working relationships, purposes, and teaching and learning action. As they whirl around the floor, their goals are to build relationships, clarify purposes, and facilitate action-in-common so that all people train their energies and talents on learning. Leaders are moment-by-moment immersed in the work of balancing logic and artistry (Deal & Peterson, 1994). They thus enliven the three streams of leadership, energizing the dancers to step more energetically, more fluidly, and more in harmony with one another. In this chapter and the two that follow, I describe the activities, skills, and qualities that leaders engage in and use as they blend the three streams into one. Each chapter begins with a synopsis of activities that leaders undertake as they strive to cultivate leadership among those around them. Each synopsis highlights activities that cut across many roles, situations, and contexts. Each chapter concludes with observations about the skills and knowledge needed by school leaders and about the ways that they might be developed.

PUTTING WORKING RELATIONSHIPS AT THE CENTER

To do something new, people invariably experience periods of profound discomfort. Confronting the threat and uncertainty such change brings is best done together, not in isolation.
                                                                              —Vaill (1998), p. 67

Too many American public schools function as if the relationships among staff and between staff and parents are unimportant, unmanageable, or simply unmentionable. Schools are structured to maximize adult contact with students and to make interactions among adults as efficient as possible. This system appears to make sense, as "students are the client" and we do not want to "waste" public money by reducing the "time on task" of either students or adults—whose task is students. The result is an organization where the work is decentralized and its quality is left up almost totally to the individual competence of the teacher, counselor, aide, or coach. As we have seen, when the school confronts a major challenge to its success with children—that is, when leadership is needed—the relationships among educators and between educators, students, and parents are often too fragmented to permit effective improvement.

Leaders working in cultures so inhospitable to planful working relationships face a major challenge simply to make these relationships a priority. In the grand scheme, their work is to put relationships at the center of what they and others do, to value "how we work together" as much as "what work we do." *The litmus test for leadership in this stream is that the relationships among staff are trusting, open, and affirmative enough so that, when faculty and staff gather to address a challenge, their attention can dwell upon the important educational and moral questions at the heart of the challenge.* How is it, then, that leaders foster healthy relationships? This question clearly deserves more consideration than one chapter in this book (see for more extensive treatment Donaldson & Sanderson, 1996; Evans, 1996; Fullan & Hargreaves, 1994; Garmston & Wellman, 1999; Helgesen, 1995). I offer four relationship-building leader activities as an overview:

• Fostering ways to bring people together rather than to separate them.
• Acknowledging the importance of a working relationship by honoring how people feel in their work and about one another.
• Speaking explicitly about their working roles and relationships with others, clarifying and redefining these as necessary.
• Facilitating the group's capacity to work within its natural limits—preventing overextension.

Fostering Connections Among Staff

Relationships happen, whether leaders contribute to them knowingly or not. In many larger schools and in more heavily structured schools such as high schools, relationships are less fluid, more compartmentalized, and sometimes more oppositional than in smaller units where the entire adult staff can assemble more easily. The leader's challenge, at the simplest level, is to maximize opportunities for staff to come together for positive purposes—whether they be personal rejuvenation or professional problem-solving and growth. Although some administrators operate on the opposite principle—keeping staff separated makes them more compliant and less able to organize in opposition—such practices are ultimately destructive to true leadership. Knowing one another well enough to establish basic trust, openness, and affirmation is a precondition for forming the relationships that can mobilize people for professional improvement and personal support.

Principals and teacher leaders can do a myriad of structural things to encourage connections: assign rooms in configurations that spawn collaboration and teaming; make the schedule serve common planning needs that teachers have; cultivate mentor-pairs and colleague-critic circles where sharing problems and solutions can occur; conduct meetings through facilitated group dialogue instead of reports and lectures; hold dine-and-discuss conversations at breakfast or dinner around focused issues; set aside space and time for staff to gather for social as well as business purposes. Basic to all of these suggestions is a linking function. The leader's work is to listen to staff, parents, and students and to link them to others who have similar concerns, possible solutions, and the potential to assist.

This leadership work is encapsulated in numerous small phrases uttered directly to people whom active leaders interact with and seek out: "What if you stopped by Ms. McElmore's room this afternoon and shared this with her? I think she'd be interested." "That's a great idea you're trying. Christine is working on exactly the same thing in her literacy lessons—I'll set up a time when we can all get together over this." "I don't have an answer to that, but let's put out a memo to see who has some ideas and make it the topic of our next open-agenda coffee." At the heart of these utterances is a positive spirit and optimism—what some are now calling "appreciative leadership" (Srivastva & Cooperrider, 1990).

This leadership work calls upon principals and teacher leaders not only to encourage convening but to facilitate connections interpersonally. For principals, whose management responsibilities can overtake these more important relationship-building functions, the expected role is to structure agendas, be task-oriented, make decisions, and "see that things get done." Their greatest challenge is to fulfill these expectations in arenas where they are appropriate—such as the "business" portion of the faculty meeting—and to avoid the executive role in the many other arenas where other people have the wisdom, the responsibility, and the access to resolve problems and implement solutions. Rather than minimizing a teacher's feelings or avoiding the stresses among staff, principals honor them by listening, empathizing, and helping others manage relational issues.

Teacher leaders—particularly informal ones—come to this facilitator role more naturally, as they are not expected to be primarily managers and they are viewed as one-among-equals. They usually work in more intimate groups and teams that share a more coherent focus than the whole school. The growth of a leadership relationship among eight colleagues can occur more naturally through problem-solving and planning activities for their common students or curriculum. Teacher leaders can make meetings informal, can include personal time to "check in" with feelings about the day, and can devote attention to group ground rules that honor all voices and views.

In fostering connections among others, the leader's daily actions convey to others the belief that "we are in this together; your challenges and successes are ours and ours are yours." By visibly connecting with people and putting them in touch with others, the leader asserts an invitational, collaborative norm that says, "We depend on each other here."

Honoring Staff Feelings About Their Work and One Another

A second activity in the relationship-building of leaders is recognizing the emotional and personal realities of colleagues. Robert Evans (1996) emphasizes how essential "authenticity" is to healthy schools and healthy school leadership. He finds that denying members' feelings about issues that impinge on their work through avoidance, compromise, and outright dismissal undermines the individual's and the group's ability to take on the tough challenges they face as learners and innovators. When staff are upset about an interchange with a parent, elated by a successful teaching experience with a difficult class, or frustrated by the interminable debate of a faculty meeting, those feelings themselves come to dominate their participation in the school's activities. By honoring them, leaders serve notice that these feelings—and the people who have them—matter. The leader directly affirms and respects each individual and conveys the message that "we all count here."

How is this done? Teacher leaders and principals acknowledge feelings by inquiring about them and by stating them. In daily contacts, as Michael Fullan and Andy Hargreaves (1998) put it, they "manage emotionally as well as rationally"; they "ask people directly how they feel . . . ask for help not just when [they] are delegating busywork . . . but when [they] genuinely do not know what to do . . . [and] show empathy for other people's viewpoints and what gives rise to them, even though [they] may disagree" (p. 117). Mostly it means tuning into others' nonverbal cues—behaviors and expressions that indicate how they are feeling and, when appropriate, acknowledging their excitement, fatigue, elation, worry, or frustration. Sometimes it means inquiring directly: "I'm not sure how you're feeling about this decision. Can you share that with me?" Sometimes it means confirming what you are sensing: "You seem worried about the meeting with Matt's mother. Is that right?" or "You must be feeling that this is just one more duty on top of many others. Is there some way we can deal with that as a group?" Evans (1996) lists among the four "strategic biases" for school leadership "recognition" and "confrontation," two clusters of activities that engage leaders directly in acknowledging the emotional dimensions of working with people.

Leaders care not just about their mission but about their colleagues (Noddings, 1984; Sernak, 1998). Acknowledging the emotional realities of others' work naturally builds caring relationships and creates a level of authenticity that strengthens the group's capacity to respond to challenges. In this respect, leadership relationships emerge from individual efforts to honor the personal feelings intertwining the busy and very human work of teachers, principals, counselors, and other staff in schools.

Clarifying and Redefining Roles to Strengthen Relationships

As adaptive challenges confront the school, different expertise, talents, and energies are needed from the staff. An assault on eighth-grade test scores from disgruntled parents requires a different profile of responses and responders than does an internal challenge to develop personalized learning plans for all students. Leaders facilitate the group's allocation of its talents and energies to respond in the best way it can to these challenges. The relationships they foster help each person—including themselves—to know his or her own special talents and to be willing and able to contribute them to whole-school or team problems when the need arises.

Leaders do this by explicitly talking about roles and responsibilities. They can put frankly on the table the questions: "Can we do this?" and "What does this mean each one of us will do?" They can invite others to "get straight" how their time, energy, and talents can play into an emerging group plan. Leaders say, "If this is worth doing, how are we going to get it done?" "What parts of this can we do together? What can you do? I do?" They facilitate both an understanding of the plan and a clarity about each person's commitment to it; these are common under-standings and commitments that strengthen the working relationships among the members through clarifying expectations and making commitments a matter of choice.

Through individual conferences and group dialogue, leaders need constantly to reaffirm the voluntary nature of this relationship for it is essential to sustaining commitment. Here, the leader's attention to norms within the relationship that stress honesty and openness, that honor straight talk and problem identification, and that celebrate people and accomplishments plays a central role. These collaborative planning activities can be found in a number of resources (Donaldson & Sanderson, 1996; Garmston & Wellman, 1999; Schwarz, 1994).

This leader work is often trying. Staff in many schools are quite comfortable in their specialized roles; it is often easier to dismiss a problem as somebody else's than to accept responsibility for a piece of it oneself. So leaders often find themselves helping colleagues to accept what Peter Senge (1999) calls "the abandonment of what doesn't work" (p. 64) and, simultaneously, forming a commitment to in-venting something that works better. Some staff will prefer to leave school-wide issues in the lap of the principal and to others who are empowered and paid for those responsibilities. Still others will see the principal's or department head's invitation to collaborative leadership as a ploy to get them to work longer hours for the same pay. And some will—if the relationships and their own commitments to school improvement are strong enough—welcome the opportunity to invest themselves in activities that might enhance their success with students.

Changing roles and relationships is something that can only happen willingly. Leaders can articulate the need for it, can encourage colleagues to see how they can contribute, and can organize and manage the work. But assigning a teacher to a new group of students to teach them in a more effective manner will not succeed unless the teacher understands and supports the change. Robert Evans (1996) de-scribes the personal challenges inherent in this transformational process in *The Hu-man Side of School Change*. It is a process in which leaders help themselves and their colleagues "unfreeze . . . to face realities they have preferred to avoid," "commit ourselves to something new . . . to new competence," "become clear about the new structural alignment and its implications for responsibility, authority, and decision-making" (pp. 57–67). Leaders, by naming these realities of the process that the leadership relationship is likely to entail, prepare their partners for the journey and invite their participation in shaping it.

Principal and teacher leaders are apt to approach the "making public" of these issues quite differently. Teacher leaders often continue to think of themselves as teachers and adhere to the egalitarian norms of the teacherhood. For them, negoti-ating roles is likely to come quite naturally (and there is evidence in the work of Lynn Brown & Carol Gilligan (1992); Sally Helgesen (1995); and Constance Buchanan (1996) that women are more naturally inclined than men to give relationships and roles their due). The fact that they are authoring change and "staying on the front lines" to experience it give them instant credibility with colleagues, if not influence with them. With informal teacher leaders, particularly, colleagues feel little threat of manipulation or control.

Principals and some formally appointed teacher leaders, however, face quite a different challenge. Their roles give them legal and bureaucratic authority; many assume the legitimacy of principals' unilateral powers to assign staff, restructure, or dictate standards. Questions of authority, power, and control, however, inevitably enter into attempts to redefine working relationships (Fullan, 1998; Sarason, 1982). Because they can poison relationships instead of improving them, such questions must be put on the table. In the interests of clarity and honesty, principals in particular need to acknowlege how they intend to use—or not use—the authority of their position. They can facilitate discussions that clarify whether participation in an initiative is elective, how staff performance evaluations will be effected by participation, and how decision-making, action, and supervisory responsibilities will be shared. Principals or formally appointed teacher leaders bring different power, access, and information to the leadership relationship. Their responsibility to others centers on recognizing these differences and offering them as strengths that can be brought collaboratively to bear on the challenges facing the school.

Good working relationships require conscious care. Leaders make matters of role and responsibility part of their dialogues and meetings with colleagues as they form and nurture these working relationships. In the process, they grow within the group a level of authority that supersedes any individual's authority. Douglas Smith (1999), remarking on American organizational change in general, put it this way: "Only by practicing the team discipline . . . by living the change, are you going to ground yourself in a genuine authority that I, as a subordinate, am going to respect. And only then will both of us—you and I—have confidence in the advice you are giving" (p. 101).

Helping the Group to Work Within Its Natural Limits

Beyond the matter of each individual's place and participation in the leadership relationship lies a fourth arena of leader activity: monitoring the group's collective health and capacity to succeed at the challenges it takes on. Leaders keep an eye on the whole group, how its energy and morale are influencing its progress. They help the group to know whether the emerging work load promises to be manageable or overtaxing. If leaders cannot help their groups to monitor, they run the risk of losing participants and eroding commitment because the group has not realistically matched its capacities for work with the demands of that work. In schools where change and reform are a priority, these are two prime reasons that leadership fails to materialize—two reasons that efforts at improvement spawn exhaustion and defeat rather than energizing and mobilizing.

The challenge for leaders is to help staff to stretch without overreaching, to attain what Peter Vaill terms the "envelope of optimal realism" in the school's effort to transform its work with children (Evans, 1996, p. 293). Of immediate concern are the natural limits of the people who share in the leadership relationship. Typically in schools, nobody has time, regular access to others, or energy to commit to school change. Leaders must absolutely honor teachers' primary commitments to students, their learning, and their development. Where they do not, they often end up as the sole proponents of change, working among a minority of increasingly pessimistic advocates against a growing majority of "resisters" and "recalcitrants" (Muncey & McQuillan, 1996). The history of school reform is strewn with efforts that never substantially improved student learning because increasingly anxious administrators (and more recently, formal teacher leaders) kept pressing changes on staff despite abundant evidence that those staff could not—and increasingly would not—implement the spirit of those reforms (Elmore & McLaughlin, 1988; Tyack & Cuban, 1995). Indeed, inattention to relationships in such displays of "leadership" assured its very failure.

Leaders place value on the group's reading of its own capacity to sustain an effort to change. They help the group monitor its progress in two ways: toward its goals and in relation to the human and other resources it must draw upon to reach those goals. Leaders, in this way, care for the group; they help it stretch its performance, but not at the cost of overreaching. In addition to facilitating the "task" side of leadership—needs assessments, goal-setting, problem-solving, decisions, action-planning, and evaluation—leaders attend constantly to the "people" side. In team and faculty meetings as well as one-to-one, they foster honest dialogue within the group about its work—open sharing of what is frustrating and exhausting about the project and frank feedback about aspects of the work that are simply beyond their capacity to influence. Patricia Wasley (1995) describes how leaders encourage "straight shooting" and assessments of progress by establishing clear ground rules, focusing on students, and accepting staff feelings about how their work is "costing" them in time, energy, worry, and diverted attention from primary responsibilities. Addressing such questions with individuals who show signs of flagging energy or commitment both signals that the leader cares about each person and gives leaders vital information for gauging the capacity of the group to sustain its effort.

Teacher leaders, because they live the dual existence of classroom and leadership, are more apt to detect stresses in colleagues because they may be feeling them as well. They are also closer to the action than principals typically are. Their conversations and meetings can more naturally encompass this stock-taking function through both problem-solving and recognizing and celebrating successes among their team and department mates. Principals' daily routines permit them more opportunity to understand long-range and global aspects of the group's work. They can sometimes both anticipate and address obstacles "from the outside" before they become frustrating impediments to the group. On the other hand, principals can be blinded to the practical limits facing their teacher colleagues. Sometimes the pressures on them to solve a problem or implement a reform throw leadership-minded principals into "pushing the envelope" and challenging their staff to give more and do more just when teachers, mindful of their first commitment to their students, are feeling overwhelmed and contrary-minded.

As leaders engage in these four sets of activities—fostering connections, acknowledging feelings, clarifying roles, and facilitating the group's ability to work within its limits—they are subtly cultivating patterns of behavior, values, and relationships within the staff that enhance the health of the work environment. These are active, face-to-face patterns. Leaders who model them spread them through the life of the school, shaping how the teachers' room talk goes, who sits with whom at faculty meetings, whether memoranda from the principal are received with cynicism or eagerly read. They help to form the culture of the staff. Despite the fact that staff are often physically separated, very focused on students, tired, and developmentally and philosophically disparate, leaders' energetic and confident investment in these relational activities will grow environments that are healthier for them all. Ronald Heifetz (1994) calls these the "holding environments" for leadership, cultures where norms are personally supportive *and* professionally honest, where all members' freedom to speak and assuredness of being heard on matters of professional conscience are secured within a personally trusting and affirming relationship (pp.103–114).

THE STUFF OF LEADERS: THE CAPACITY TO GROW STRONG RELATIONSHIPS

What is it that enables a person to cultivate leadership through these four key relational activities? What are skills, talents, and qualities those leaders need in order to practice those activities well? These are perplexing and important questions that move the focus from "what leaders do" to "who they need to be." I devote the remainder of this chapter (and comparable sections in Chapters 9 and 10) to these questions. Four clusters of qualities and skills equip a person to contribute to the relational leadership stream.

A Predisposition to Trust and Respect

At the heart of leaders' capacity to foster strong relationships lies the capacity to trust in others. This capacity blends philosophical and psychological features. Leaders believe that all people are worthy and deserve respect. Carrying this into their interactions, they approach others with the assumption that their interaction will be reciprocal: It takes two or more to "make" a working relationship, and the trust and affirmation that cement the relationship emerge from each person's ability to trust and respect the other (Block, 1996; Lambert et al., 1995). Leaders approach people believing that they can make the relationship work.

Leaders initiate this reciprocal process by bringing to each individual and each group a predisposition to trust and respect. They enter into conversations, meetings, and conferences *believing that others will reciprocate if they are trusted and respected to begin with.* They demonstrate a faith that others' motives are to help the school do better and a respect for their ideas and values, however different they may appear to be. Lifelong experience and personality no doubt shape this disposition in us. So do our past relationships with teachers, administrators, and community members where we work. But philosophy shapes it as well: Leaders who believe in the importance of working interdependently can, through their conviction and persuasion, carry others toward a similar belief and to the relationship that lies at its core.

Interpersonal Awareness

The fostering of relationships stems far more from nonverbal, interpersonal qualities than it does from cognitive, verbal, or philosophical talents. In its simplest form, leaders are people who are attuned to relationships. They not only intellectually know the importance of relationships to the success of the school, but they emotionally understand the interpersonal dynamics that constitute those relationships. Books and articles abound describing the skills that influence strong working relationships: communication skills, conflict management and resolution skills, consultation skills, group process skills (see, e.g., Garmston & Wellman, 1999, Rees, 1991, and Schwarz, 1994). As these books often argue, these skills can be developed through coaching and practice. But, in a more fundamental sense, a person's ability to "tune into relationships" grows from aspects of personality and personal background. It is to a degree "hard-wired," a function of what Howard Gardner (1983) labels "interpersonal and intrapersonal intelligences" and what Daniel Goleman (1995) presents as "emotional intelligence." Both Gardner's and Goleman's research equates these intelligences, when well developed, with successful leadership.

How do these intelligences work to help create a capacity to be attuned to relationships? In my experience, they emerge in two demonstrable ways: first, to permit leaders to read the feelings of those around them; and second, to give them sensitivity as they generate interpersonal connections among staff and other. The first of these talents engages leaders in *understanding behavioral, verbal, and expressive cues and deducing from these the emotional states of those around them.* They are comfortable with the emotions that populate their busy workplaces—elation, frustration, resentment, happiness, sadness, anger, and more. For example, when a group is frustrated by its task or by criticism, leaders can detect these feelings before they boil over. They can say, "I sense that some of us are feeling frustrated with this. Can we talk about that for a few minutes?" This requires interpersonal sensitivity but takes a measure of courage, too. Most of us have grown up in organizational cultures that suppress the expression of feelings; men often have learned to subjugate their feelings to the goal of "getting the job done." Feelings and relationships are unruly, explosive, and literally unmanageable. Talking about feelings or about relationships that are not functioning well usually means that emotions will spill into conversations and meetings and this makes some people uncomfortable and even paralyzes others. The mere possibility of this leads many aspiring leaders and administrators to avoid acknowledging them and to deny their significance in the school's work (Evans, 1996; Fullan, 1997).

Yet these feelings determine how unified or how fragmented the staff's relationship will be. The leader's posture toward others needs to *invite and make safe the sharing of both opinion and feeling.* These are vital to a secure professional culture that can function as a holding environment for everyone's leadership. One way leaders do this is by consciously limiting their own talk and increasing their active listening, permitting them to detect strong feelings and opinions creeping into discussion. Their words and their body language can say, "I hear you," and, when the person or group is ready, can say, "Now how will we handle this and move on?"

Leaders will often need to *manage their own feelings* in this process. This is especially poignant for principals and formally appointed teacher leaders who feel obliged to run a smooth ship and to ensure that all problems are resolved "on my watch." For some leaders, the need to feel essential to others or the need to be in control makes listening and facilitating difficult; these needs overpower their interpersonal sensitivity and propel them toward unilateral action. Sally Helgesen (1995), who writes about women's ways of leading, suggests that this posture comes more naturally to women than to men because women tend to think of their work as forming "webs of inclusion" rather than primarily directing people toward tasks and goals.

Leaders, of course, need to help their schools move beyond feelings and connections to help mobilize action among staff and others. Here, *interpersonal and group facilitation skills* are core competencies. In the midst of an intense meeting or an exhausting dialogue, the principal or teacher leader needs skills for active listening, posing options, restating agreements, and checking for consensus (Goleman, 1998a; Rees, 1991; Schrage, 1989). When the leader senses a readiness to agree or to resolve, she articulates that: "Have we identified our options? Are we ready to make a decision?" If the others are not ready, the leader accommodates them (unless he or she is willing to risk losing commitment and participation by forcing premature resolution). Finally, leaders negotiate roles and tasks people will have in the follow-through to action. In these ways, leaders enable others both to voice their feelings and ideas and to honor each others' voices, strengthening rather than weakening relationships and commitment.

Just as leaders need to be interpersonally attuned so they can help clarify roles and responsibilities, their sensitivity allows them to monitor the group's success at working within its natural limits. Principally, this means having *a working knowledge of the staff and an understanding of the interplay between individual motivations and energy levels, on the one hand, and group productivity on the other.* Leaders listen to their groups and they are adept at "hearing" signs of successful group functioning or, on the contrary, of frustration and exhaustion. They can pose to the group questions that help it to evaluate how it is doing and to reassess personal commitments to its initiatives. They devote time in meetings and with individuals to reflecting on how each person "sees us progressing with this new unit." They can, as well, facilitate periodic stock-taking where staff examine data regarding student and school progress, identify factors that are enhancing or restraining their work, and plan forward.

Intrapersonal Awareness

Underlying our capacity to foster relationships are two other qualities: our success at forming authentic relationships ourselves and, in turn, our own intrapersonal self-awareness. We need to understand ourselves well enough to gauge accurately how our behaviors will be received by others and, then, be skilled at consultation with others to discuss and mediate feelings of fear, uncertainty, and even hostility that our behaviors might provoke. Robert Evans (1996) emphasizes the leader's ability to "acknowledge and affirm a truth about a person or situation" (p. 254), including oneself, as essential to the leader's "authenticity" in establishing a frank, aboveboard relationship. He notes that leaders use informal means of communication and consultation to face up to "the inevitable conflict that change creates" by surfacing concerns so they can be counted and so people's thoughts and feelings can be appreciated (p. 251). These require leaders with confidence in their own interpersonal skills, a confidence that is contingent on having sufficient intrapersonal awareness to trust their own intuition and feelings about people as well as their ideas and beliefs.

A principal's or teacher leader's self-awareness permits that person to see how behaviors, words, ideas, and feelings are entering into his *relationships with others.* He is attuned to emotional "nonverbals." Here is how Daniel Goleman (1995) puts it:

> When a person's words disagree with what is conveyed via his tone of voice, gestures, or other nonverbal channel, the emotional truth is in how he says something rather than in what he says. . . . Ninety percent or more of an emotional message is nonverbal. And such messages . . . are almost always taken in unconsciously, without paying specific attention to the nature of the message, but simply tacitly receiving it and responding. (pp. 97–98)

As school leaders, the skills and "intelligences" we draw on to cultivate relationship-building permit us to tune into these interpersonal and intrapersonal signals.

Goleman's (1995) five domains of emotional intelligence help to depict the skills central to this capacity. He argues that more emotionally mature leaders are more successful at giving honest and consistent feedback to others, fostering diversity and tolerance, nurturing teamwork and collaboration, and acknowledging and encouraging informal networks among others (see Chapter 10). Briefly, Goleman's research claims that leaders benefit from:

1. Knowing their own emotions as they come into play in their interactions at work (self-awareness).
2. Managing those emotions so they contribute to unified rather than fragmented relationships (appropriate expression).
3. Motivating themselves (marshaling emotions in the service of the goal).
4. Recognizing emotions in others (empathy).
5. Facilitating the expression of emotions so they contribute to strong working relationships (social competence; skill in managing emotions in others and with others). (p. 43)

Goleman's more recent work, *Working With Emotional Intelligence* (1998b), offers suggestions for developing sensitivities and skills in these domains. Other work by Barth (1990), Sergiovanni (1996), and Lambert et al. (1995) are helpful as well.

The Female Advantage

The small but growing literature on women's natural leadership styles suggests that gender can play a significant role in a leader's disposition toward relationships. Sally Helgesen (1995) found that women leaders she studied tended to be more concerned about relationships, to devote more time to building and maintaining connections to others, and to think of their leadership not so much in a hierarchical fashion as in a "web of inclusion" that relies "on the value of interconnectedness" (pp. 223–224). Others document an emphasis on caring over competition, on encouraging participation over compliance, and on learning over telling among women (Buchanan, 1996; Noddings, 1984; Regan & Brooks, 1995; Rosener, 1990; Sernak, 1998). Helgesen argues that women who lead are apt to see authority in the relational web, not in themselves or in their position; leading is "from the center" of the web, from "connections *to* the people around rather than distance *from* those below" (p. 55). In women's natural leadership, she wrote, "there is an aspect of teaching that accompanies authority as it flows from the center of the web. The process of gathering and routing information, of guiding relationships and coaxing forth connections, strikes an educational note" (p. 56).

Applied to public schools, where the majority of teachers and other staff are women and where leadership requires relationship-building, these qualities have clear relevance. Women may, more naturally and confidently than many men, engage their interpersonal sensitivities and trust their own emotions and intuition to address the quality of relationships around them. Although men can and do demonstrate these qualities and dispositions—and conversely, some women do not—the predominance of women on many school faculties suggests that, were we to recognize teacher leadership as it should be, schools could readily mobilize themselves to address instructional and organizational challenges. Given the poor success record of bureaucratic and executive leadership models designed and executed so predominantly by men, it is high time we looked not only elsewhere for a different model but also more often to women for leadership.

We should not pretend that raising the relational, emotional, and intrapersonal components into the light of leadership work will be easy. In too many school districts, the established norms keep people separated from one another, make them dependent upon administrative authority for resources and workplace rights, and disempower them even within their own classrooms, laboratories, and offices. Intractable school cultures, politics, and the occupational framework of teaching itself dampen hope and ambition, open-mindedness, and commitment to learning. I have noted many of these in preceding chapters: isolation; an embattled and subservient attitude; association-management rifts; persistent competition for inadequate resources; and the fragmentation caused by classical leadership models and bureaucratic press.

Our new generation of leaders must champion informal connections and authentic interaction among teachers and staff. As they trust others, draw out their talents, and connect them in pairs, small groups, and as a whole faculty, the entire professional community becomes more capable of meeting the school's challenges than each individual is alone. These connections enliven the webs of relationships among adults, bringing individual recognition and value to their work and to themselves. These connections cultivate recognition from colleagues whom they trust and value in return. When the school is pressed to change or to respond to a crisis, it is this web of relationships that determines how and how well the school's professionals will care for their students. Importantly, it is this web that permits each teacher, secretary, principal, counselor, and coach to care for one another and for themselves. In the webbing created by leaders who put relationships first lies the school's capacity to mobilize wisely for action to adapt and improve its service to children and community.

CHAPTER 9

Leaders Face Challenges
and Renew Commitment

[Schools face] conflict-filled situations that require choice because competing, highly-prized values cannot be fully satisfied. . . . They become predicaments when constraints and uncertainty make it impossible for any prized value to triumph.
                                                                                    —Cuban (1992), p. 6

Ronald Heifetz, in *Leadership Without Easy Answers* (1994), makes the case that a leader's true authority is "given and can be taken away" by those who deem him or her a leader (p. 57). It is earned from the group as part of a social contract that the group makes with the leader where the group sees in the leader someone who can help mobilize it for the good of its mission. This seems especially true in schools where professional standards, decentralized work, and loose coordination give staff and faculty little daily reason to need a Type A executive leader. Instead, they need a leader "when we need one." Usually that is in moments of emergency, when they see that their efforts are not succeeding, or when their programs and goals are under attack from without—or sometimes from within. The rest of the time, schools need managers, people who can keep the organization as a whole running smoothly, feeling safe, and supportive of each adult's and each child's work.

This conception of leadership reinforces Joseph Rost's (1993) contention that leadership is "episodic." Although a strong working relationship is always desirable, our public schools have experienced in their history periods of relative calm in which neither the public, the profession, nor the families sending their children to school found reason to question deeply the school's performance. Teachers are teaching and principals are attending to routine management tasks such as discipline, community and district relations, and supervision of the building and staff. We have, as well, experienced intense periods of distress when the school's current practices clearly and persistently failed in some respect and, as people recognized this predicament, they came into conflict with one another or with their own ideals and values. Tyack and Cuban (1995) have charted cycles of public and professional discontent followed by sustained reform at roughly 20 year intervals during the 20th century. Each cycle marked a time of adaptive change nationally when our public schools truly needed leadership.

This chapter examines how school leaders help their school communities respond constructively to such periods of adaptive challenge. Heifetz (1994) claims that "Every time we face a conflict among competing values, or encounter a gap between our shared values and the way we live [and work], we face the need to learn new ways" (p.275). Leaders emerge as they help the group understand the challenges facing it and engage staff and community in reexaminations of mission and purpose in light of evidence that the school is no longer adequately serving them. These activities are quintessential to the second or purposive stream of leadership. *The litmus test for leadership here is that when a school encounters fundamental challenges to its effectiveness, its members can reinvent their purposes and practices and renew commitment sufficiently to meet those challenges.*

PUTTING SELF-ASSESSMENT AND INQUIRY AT THE CENTER

What do leaders do to help their colleagues and constituents face essential challenges and renew commitments to a freshened mission? Leaders engage in three clusters of activity in this regard. One cluster revolves around facing questions of mission and moral purpose. A second cluster helps people openly identify the school's adaptive challenges by understanding discrepancies between what the school espouses and aspires to and what it actually accomplishes with children. This gives rise to a third cluster of activities: owning the challenge through understanding what part each person plays in its continuation and in its solution.

Facing Questions of Mission and Moral Purpose

In times when schools face adaptive challenges, their performance is brought into question. At the heart of this questioning lies doubt that the school is fulfilling its mission or, perhaps, satisfying its moral purpose in society. We have witnessed such challenges repeatedly in recent decades. For example, the civil rights movement confronted public school systems with the contradiction that they were obligated to serve all children well yet were doing so in segregated, tracked, and unequally funded schools. We faced similar questions regarding children with special needs and from poor families. More recently, public schools have been assaulted by politicians, business leaders, and parents for weakening America's competitive edge by failing to produce "world-class" results in every child. And within schools themselves, staffs have been divided over deep dilemmas regarding the purposes and methods of literacy instruction, whether there is a core curriculum and what values should be embedded in it, and how to respond to physically and psychologically unsafe intrusions. Each challenge to current practice is precipitated by people who feel deeply about the issues. They evoke emotion, distress, and often conflict. Each challenge persists and becomes, in Cuban's terms, a predicament. It is about fundamental purposes, values, and practices and cannot be met with Band-Aids or window dressing.

The leader's initial activity in this arena is to help others "approach the danger"—to recognize the emerging challenges to their work and the school. Public schools' stated missions encompass many purposes, from building intellectual skills and imparting factual knowledge to shaping social attitudes and eradicating asocial behaviors. Communities, parents, and students often expand the mission to include, for example, weekend recreation, the inculcation of traditional values, and vocational preparation. In the current accountability era, these diverse purposes have created a cross fire of demands, ranging from state "outcomes" tests to the record of the girls' softball team to community scuttlebutt about a particular teacher's handling of students. The public school leader's work, contrary to much common practice, is to help teachers, staff, parents, and school boards see that, because their school is public, it is morally committed to *considering seriously* each goal a member of the community brings to it. Leaders listen and empathize. They seek to understand what it is that parents, students, citizens, and educators value and believe the school is for. They honor the feelings and articulate the conflicts. And they restate these views and feelings for the school community to consider.

From this initial acknowledgment of the many goals in the public school mix, leaders ask those involved to revisit the core purposes of the school in an effort to ground deliberations in the school's past mission. They do this in two main ways: through facilitating discussion and debate about basic goals and values in groups; and by "walking the talk" in their interactions so that they and others can continually recenter on what they are there for and what their work is aiming to do for students. In the first of these, leaders conduct periodic visioning, mission-writing, and goal-setting meetings. They do so with diverse groups—staff, parents, administrative teams, teaching teams—and they do so *across* these groups, especially when differences between them threaten to split them apart. The products of these efforts are circulated widely, committed to poster board, made public—and always dated with the implication that they must be revisited. In a world where the broad moral purpose of preparing the next generation of Americans is indisputable, there will always be disagreements over the particulars and these will change with the times. But the fundamental mission of educating children intellectually and socially for productive futures remains at the core.

In routine group and faculty deliberations, they also raise the question, "Which of our central purposes does this issue address?" By raising this question, they provoke their colleagues and partners to anchor their thinking and their decisions in the core values of the school: "How will this alternative serve our goals? How will that alternative? Which one is more promising?" Further, leaders encourage others to clarify and articulate their own purposes by making their own values and core purposes apparent. Rather than simply spouting the doctrine of the school mission or vision, leaders "commit time, focus, and feelings to it, communicating the purposes by example, by attention, and by the moral passion [they] feel for it" (Vaill, 1998, p. 50). They embody in their public and private behaviors the student-centered and learning-focused values that justify the school's existence. As they do so, principals and teacher leaders establish as "the source of legitimate power in the organization its guiding ideas" and revalidate them as "lofty standards against which every person's behavior can be judged" (Senge, 1999, p. 60).

Principals, by virtue of their public exposure, find themselves regularly with the opportunity for this sort of articulation and revalidation. As I note in Chapter 6, their ability to represent the essential learning goals of the school in many different contexts, for many different audiences, and to do so with moral conviction often spells the difference between others' seeing them merely as managers or as leaders. People look to principals to enunciate the vision and to serve as keepers of the school-wide flame. Principals, then, can use their prominence not only to clarify existing purposes but, most importantly, to acknowledge the challenges to them brought forward by others. Staff, students, and public look to them for the moral direction of the whole organization. Their most fundamental obligation is to be open to all views and all people who offer their views as champions of student learning, of a just and healthy environment, and of democratic participation. The principal's response to adaptive challenges signals what moral keel and what end purposes are guiding the school.

Teacher leaders typically operate in more limited circles than principals and, within those circles, they can have immense influence over the extent to which their colleagues understand the broader challenges facing their work. Teacher leaders bring to the teachers' lounge, team meeting, or department a working knowledge of the "at-risk student issue," the growing community unrest over a curriculum, or the soon-to-be-implemented new assessment system. They can be mediators of these challenges where they most need to be: as teachers and staff mull them over, resist them, try them out, and ultimately decide how to respond to them in their own practice. Their abilities to help colleagues face-to-face reinvent purposes and practices and to renew their commitment to new work are essential to successful mobilization.

Inviting Evidence of Success and Failure

The second cluster of leader activities engages school leaders in specifying the challenges facing the school in practical terms. This work involves seeking assessments of the school's performance from the outside as well as listening to the evidence from inside. Leaders actively seek from community, parents, students, ex-students, and staff information that will help the school understand how it is succeeding at its purposes.

In its most structured form, this is evaluation work: They help to organize surveys, testing, follow-up interviews, focus groups, and other structured methods of determining how students are faring and tend to fare after they leave the school. More realistically and perhaps more productively, leaders in their daily routines keep an eye out for evidence of results: "How do we know that our science program is actually developing kids' problem-solving skills? Environmental awareness?" "What is it in this parent's complaint that tells us how we're not reaching her child?" They assemble individuals, teams, students, and parents to look more systematically at such evidence. Leaders focus these assessments to help the group conclude, first, what the nature of their challenge is and, second, what teaching and learning practices and school structures and norms appear most in need of adaptation. Their attitude and their skill at evaluating and planning help others to feel confident that seeking out the challenges—rather than avoiding them—can in fact bolster the school's success.

This search for evidence takes another form: inviting and honoring dissenting voices from within as well as from without. Adaptive challenges stem from evidence that the school's performance is falling short of its mission; but they also stem from deep differences of value and purpose within staff and community. By directly inviting "counterfluent" participation from individuals and groups who appear dissatisfied with current practices, the leader opens dialogue and spurs questions, criticisms, and even attack on the existing way. The leader's purposes are twofold: to value and respect the dissenting voices as legitimate; and to surface their values and perceptions of the school's performance so that they can become a part of the more general deliberation regarding change and improvement. This "ripening the issue" activity is not geared toward assuring that the school will respond to each person's desires; rather it is designed to communicate to all players a novel viewpoint or a silenced perspective so that it can be legitimately considered in the mix of purposes and practices. Inevitably, this helps to recenter and redirect efforts; often it challenges teachers, coaches, parents, administrators, school boards, and students to justify how their activities are contributing to the general good. This encourages others to seek out valid evidence and to share it.

The partnership of principals and teacher leaders in this endeavor is vital to the school's success. In many schools where the mandate to change is handed down by school board and administration, teachers have little choice but to resist, protect, and polarize their position from those taken by management. The result has too often been a standoff, and little progress occurs. If, however, a strong leadership relationship exists, the diverse perspectives and valuable information held by all participants can flow into the deliberations. Principals, with their access to the public, parents, and administration, are critical to the staff's current knowledge about external matters; they are as well key communicators to the outside about the staff's planning. Teacher leaders, plugged into the daily realities of students and teachers, can put faces, names, and classroom evidence on the school's challenges, anchoring them in ways that can assure that school-wide deliberations pay off in the classroom.

By inviting evidence of success and failure, leaders themselves demonstrate the courage and skill to ask tough questions of themselves and to meet conflict and difference face-to-face. Their efforts to involve all parties in open assessment of the school's work seek out the challenges. They thus draw attention to issues central to the school's improvement, bringing them to the center of the faculty's and community's working agendas.

Owning the Challenges

The final cluster of leader activities involves helping group members to acknowledge their own parts in the school's challenges. Understanding that the school needs to improve or that people differ over the core goals of the school is not the same as accepting responsibility for working on the challenge. Leaders, in this third arena of purposive activity, translate institutional challenges to the personal level and help colleagues to see how their work, attitudes, and behaviors are implicated in them.

They do this principally by taking public responsibility for _their own part_ in the predicament. With the challenge on the table and evidence of the school's need to improve plain, principals and teacher leaders demonstrate that they are willing to learn more deeply how their own habits of work and thought contribute to it. They openly inquire about their own practices with children. They are candid about what they do not know. They do not blame others or "parents these days" or "society" for the plight of the school. They demonstrate, in Joseph McDonald's (1996) terms, their willingness to "unlearn prevailing habits of practice and values" (p. 9). Leaders, in other words, publicly manifest to others how their methods of teaching, their attitudes toward certain students or parents, their knowledge base about certain ideas or practices might need to change. As they do so, they not only own responsibility for addressing the challenge, they send a powerful message to their colleagues and others that they can do likewise.

Leaders can, to a degree, help others to accept their responsibility by directly pointing it out. Teacher leaders working in close teams of colleagues are positioned well to model this form of ownership. Principals, however, are more often disadvantaged by their roles as staff evaluators. Their efforts to point out a challenge can easily be misunderstood as a declaration of staff deficiencies, perhaps motivated by a desire to "stick teachers" with the responsibility for it rather than by a desire to share ownership of the challenge. But where the working relationships are strong, colleagues, students, and parents will hear clearly the leader's depiction of the challenge and her or his opinion of what role they have in it. This is especially true where the leader is a skilled facilitator of self-assessment among group members and can cultivate clarity about the challenge and ownership for the solution among all. Through skilled leadership of consultation protocols, leaders can help individuals and groups to examine how their current practices are contributing to the general challenge facing the school. (See, e.g., Annenberg Institute for School Reform, 1998; Cooperrider, 1998; Garmston & Wellman, 1999). Action research, self-study procedures, and colleague-critic circles are all useful in this regard; they are particularly well adapted methods for teacher leaders to employ. (See Elliott, 1991; McDonald, 1996.)

In encouraging others to own the challenge, leaders convey an attitude about their work that embraces inquiry and improvement. At its root, this attitude rests in a belief system that holds that schooling is a complex and dynamic process, not reducible to formulas and "proven techniques." The individual's role in this process is not precise; it is truly professional, depending heavily on an inquiring mind, a creative and caring hand, and wise judgment. The leader's words and deeds say, "We all must constantly examine how well our methods are working and be ready to try new things, both individually and as a school." Integral to this is a view of change as incremental and experimental. As Fullan and Miles (1992) put it, "Change is a journey, not a blueprint. . . . There can be no blueprints for change, because rational planning models for complex social change (such as education reform) do not work. Rather, what is needed is a guided journey. . . . [where] 'do, then plan. . . . and do and plan some more' [is the means of progress]" (p. 749).

THE STUFF OF LEADERS: THE CAPACITY
TO FACE CHALLENGES

Leaders help bring focus to others' behaviors as well as their own. . . . They know which few things are important, and in their statements and actions they make these priorities known. . . . It is an ongoing process of choosing what to emphasize and what to leave alone.
—Vaill (1998), p. 53

What skills and qualities help leaders succeed at these purposive activities? At their heart, they call upon leaders to understand adaptive challenges and how they touch the daily work of staff and students. But beyond this are the skills and dispositions necessary to invite and address conflicting views and the frustration and distress they create in the system while preserving basic consensus about moral purpose. Finally, leaders need the self-confidence to be honest with themselves about their own contributions to the school's current condition and their own responsibility for moving it forward. These are critical to the leader's ability to assist others in owning their part, as well.

Understanding and Articulating the Challenge

What is it that helps us to understand adaptive challenges? How can leaders know when and how their schools are out of synch with their surroundings? *A wide-angle grasp of public schools' historic relationship with American society* is a good starting place. If we see how social, political, and cultural trends have brought to bear on schools fresh demands for learning, teaching, and school organization in the past, we can begin to see the source and the motive for presentday demands. Leaders' understanding of the press of "outside forces" on the "inside" of a school requires insight about the public school's roles in its community. This is a translating function for staff and people inside.

For example, when schools nationwide faced the challenge of integrating special-needs populations, they desperately needed help broadening their missions, assisting staff to reconceive their work to accommodate more varied learning styles, learning technologies and assessment, definitions of "equal" and of "free," and the redesign of teaching and of learning environments for new sorts of students. Or, when schools face parents, local businesses, and state leaders demanding evidence of "high achievement across the board," their own leaders need to be conversant philosophically with alternative conceptions of achievement and fluent in matters of assessment, learning and teaching styles, and the diagnosis and remediation of poorly performing students, classrooms, and teachers. Leaders can facilitate clarification of purpose in the midst of adaptive work only when their own *knowledge about societal trends and educational approaches* is sufficient to help others verbalize their differences and explore practical alternatives.

The breadth and depth of knowledge required here is indeed a tall order for any single person: philosophical underpinnings of public education; the school's role in American society and economy; understanding students' psychological and social development; cognitive, behavioral and social learning; teaching and curriculum; assessment; and the impacts of school and home environments. Any individual leader is unlikely to be proficient in all these arenas. Here again, the strength of the relational leadership model is that multiple leaders draw from one another; each leader need not be "expert" in everything. Ideally, leaders from the ranks of staff, teachers, parents, administration, and students can each bring vital perspective and knowledge to this mix.

Stepping back and summoning up a broader perspective is itself a leadership skill. Ronald Heifetz (1994) calls this "getting on the balcony"; he compares our leadership work to being one of many dancers on a ballroom floor who are

> engaged in the dance [where] it is nearly impossible to get a sense of the patterns made by everyone on the floor. Motion makes observation difficult. Indeed, we often get carried away by the dance. Our attention is captured by the music, our partner, and the need to sense the dancing space of others nearby to stay off their toes. To discern the larger patterns on the dance floor—to see who is dancing with whom, in what groups, in what location, and who is sitting out which kind of dance—we have to stop moving and get to the balcony. (p. 253)

With the perspective from the balcony, we can *detect sources of stress and the patterns of practice they press upon.* We can then present these to the group and together clarify the larger challenges that are impinging on our success and our feelings. Principals' and teacher leaders' powers of reflection and analysis come into play here. Cognitive strengths in sorting complex information and framing choices and decisions play into leader's success or failure (Hallinger, Leithwood, & Murphy, 1993). Increasingly, leaders are finding that collegial circles, reading and journal writing, regular professional development, and diversions such as exercising and recreation help them gain the temporary distance needed to see more accurately the whole school picture. (See, for detail, Barth, 1997; Covey, 1991; Louis & Kruse, 1995; Schön, 1983).

Another cluster of skills revolves around the leader's ability to *focus staff attention and skills on diagnosis and problem-solving.* In schools, this means examining evidence that the school's performance is in jeopardy; to lead such self-examination, we need to be knowledgeable and skilled in assessment and evaluation. Our colleagues will look to people who can guide the gathering of evidence, its examination, and the drawing of lessons and strategies for improvement from it. In the past decade, the importance of this type of literacy has risen dramatically as first noneducators and then educators have called for schools to demonstrate their effectiveness and to use "hard data" to drive school improvement. Leaders who can bring their own knowledge of children, learning, behavior, curriculum, and assessment to bear in problem-centered conversations are invaluable resources. (See, for detail, Darling-Hammond, 1997; Garmston & Wellman, 1999; Schlecty, 1991; Wiggins, 1998.)

Principals and teacher leaders can, for example, take student and parental worries about rising violence and incivility and convene groups to specify what they see as evidence and causes of the situation. They can then engage staff, parents, and students in a more systematic examination of incidents and the climate at school. Reconvening people, they all can use such data to judge whether new action—beyond the school's existing practices—needs to be invented. Whatever the outcomes, most participants in this sequences of vital activities should emerge with a clarified sense of purpose and renewed commitments to take responsibility for student safety.

Fostering Interpersonal Safety and Authenticity

This work is delicate work. It demands considerable interpersonal skill. As we "ripen the issues" by helping the group explore evidence of their successes and their failures, we invite discomfort, resistance, and even outright denial. These are natural responses from hard-working and perhaps wary teachers, staff, and parents. In drawing attention to problems, we invite dissent, division, and feelings of incompetence and loss. To succeed, leaders themselves need to *feel comfortable facilitating the expression of conflicting opinions and face-to-face confrontation.* They need to reassure colleagues and other participants that differences of opinion do not mean personal antagonism. They must help the group moderate the stress they are feeling and move from there to problem-finding discussions so that issues, options, and implications become more concrete and manageable. Binney and Williams (1995) describe this leader work as follows:

> What is needed is to hear the discontent, not to judge it or deny it, but accept that it is what others perceive. This simple act of listening, of seeking to understand the nature of the discontent, is enough to begin to shift staff's perception. [While] many managers refuse to listen because they fear the dissatisfaction . . . or do not see it as balanced by positive views, once they take the risk of listening they are often surprised by the good news which arrives along with the bad. (p. 104)

The activities and leader qualities explored in Chapter 8 that contribute to a mature, open relationship among the adults of the school community are essential building blocks for the interpersonal dimension of this "ripening" process. Our ability to *foster an environment with strong norms of interpersonal safety and professional honesty* makes it possible for staffs to withstand the stress and buffeting that come when people are discontented with how the school is spending its public money to educate their most treasured possessions. Roland Barth (1990), Linda Darling-Hammond (1997), Karen Seashore Louis, Sharon Kruse, and Anthony Bryk (1995), and Ann Lieberman (1988b) offer helpful descriptions of such norms and the processes for creating them.

Robert Evans (1996) describes the tasks that a school staff addresses as it meets a major challenge, adapts its beliefs and practices, and renews its commitment. Figure 9.1 summarizes these five tasks, starting with "unfreezing old practices and beliefs" and ending with "moving from conflict to consensus." I have adapted Evans' summary by adding skills that leaders need as they help colleagues through the renewal process.

Many of these leader skills are *interpersonal:* fostering straight talk, honest feelings, and interpersonal safety as colleagues let go of old beliefs and practices and accept their loss; facilitating issues that arise among staff as their working relationships change; openly renegotiating roles and responsibilities as the group rearranges schedules, teaching assignments, and partnerships in moving from "confusion to coherence." Some call on leaders' *cognitive* knowledge: focusing others on relevant diagnostic data to highlight the need to change; sponsoring widespread dialog about new practices and goals; coaching colleagues in new practices as they work to create "new competence" from old. Finally, leaders call upon a set of *intrapersonal* skills that help them to monitor their own feelings and behaviors as they interact with others and participate in renewal themselves: acknowledging their own needs to "unfreeze;" changing their own behaviors and beliefs, particularly as they apply to their leadership relationships with others; "getting on the balcony;" and maintaining their own personal optimism and faith in the action-in-common emerging from the group's work.

FIGURE 9.1   Skills for the Leadership of Renewal

Tasks Facing Staff	*Leader Skill Clusters*
Unfreezing old practices and beliefs Goals: Motivate need to change; reduce fear of failing	Acknowledge own need to unfreeze Focus others on diagnostic data: Is there a need to change? Celebrate old practices and beliefs for their past usefulness
Moving from loss to commitment Goals: Accept the loss of old practices, beliefs, and routines; embrace the learning of new practices, beliefs, and routines	Foster straight talk, honest feelings, and interpersonal safety Engage in public learning; encourage others to do likewise; facilitate collaborative exploration of the new Listen and provide opportunities to gather
Moving from old competence to new competence Goals: Develop new behaviors (skills), beliefs, and ways of thinking	Facilitate skill development and application, integrating it with daily practice; participate in this yourself Develop norms of reflective practice and learning; support colleague-critic teams and experimentation
Moving from confusion to coherence in staff relationships and roles Goals: Realign school structures and individual functions and roles to support new behaviors and beliefs	Regularly "get on the balcony" and facilitate such perspective-taking among others Face issues of role and responsibility; clarify new arrangements as people develop them Advocate for new structures, schedules, and resources with powers outside the school
Moving from conflict to consensus Goals: Generate broad support for change	Articulate the conflicts and mediate the search for mutually agreeable and beneficial paths or compromises Share personal optimism; persevere in the emerging mission

Accepting Responsibility and Expecting Success

Leaders engaged in the vital work of helping their schools to define their adaptive work often encounter resistance. Our own optimistic resolve, our own clarity about why it is essential that the school confront the task of changing, sustains us in school environments that seem intractable and stuck in routine. Evans (1996) sees in many schools a "tradition of avoidance" that permits faculties to deny that their performance has fallen out of step with school purposes; they sometimes explain deep challenges away, retreat into classrooms, and blame the school's inability to adapt on administration, school board, community, and state (pp. 274–276).

So leaders' approach to their work must have a hopeful and steadfast quality. In approaching colleagues and communities, leaders need both to celebrate and to problem-solve, to see the best in others and to hold our collective feet to the fire. Here, we return to the importance of relationship among adults that constitutes our leadership: Without building trust, openness, and affirmation and faithfully promoting the high purposes of the school, leaders will find that their words and actions will not ring with credibility when the chips are down.

A leader's credibility with others, that is, starts with him or her. If we acknowledge that our own attitudes, knowledge, and behaviors have contributed to the current condition of the school, we signal to others that we have the courage and the commitment to begin work on our part of the problem and to generate our part of the solution. This *acknowledgment that "change begins with me"* carries extraordinary weight among colleagues. It says to others, "I am ready to look hard at what I do and to entertain changing my own behaviors and beliefs." It expresses the leader's personal and professional self-confidence and her or his belief that the school can be a place for improvement. It is also, then, an invitation to others to join in learning and in the "move from confusion to coherence" (Evans, (1996), p. 56). At the root of this confidence is a belief in our own efficacy and in the collective efficacy of our fellow staff members.

Michael Fullan's (1997) exploration of "hope and emotion" in school change and the growing literature on professional efficacy (Bandura, 1997) suggest that leaders come with *a disposition toward hopefulness, a philosophical and psychological leaning toward optimism.* They expect success. A key aspect of this disposition is faith in others and in the power of collaborative relationships. It is this faith that distinguishes relational leaders from the "heroic" leader (Murphy, 1988). Thus leaders do not see their work as "manipulating" others or "managing" relationships to ensure that staff fulfill the leader's purposes for them. Leaders who believe that all staff, parents, and students share responsibility for the school's successes and failures do not need to coerce or trick others into action they do not endorse or understand. Rather, they "work with students, parents, and other educators, even when it seems like a lost cause . . . and participate in the politics of altering the structural conditions of schools so that reform and quality have a greater chance of being built into the daily experiences of the majority of educators and students" (Fullan, 1997, p. 19). In short, our capacity to lead hinges on our capacity to trust and to foster strong working relationships that help us as well as others remain committed.

In my own work as a principal and as a facilitator of leadership development, I encounter many leaders who feel caught between the expectation that "I should handle this myself" and their own belief that "in the end, it's not me, it's us" who will make the difference. The line between executive action and collaborative deliberation is often indistinct. We will always be pestered by doubts about our own place in the leadership mix: Is it my place to demand that staff recognize where we are failing students? If the community seems satisfied with the school on the whole, who am I to upset the apple cart by pointing out where we are neglecting some students? Deprived of resources as we are, is it fair to step up the demands on everybody? At what point will I push people past their tolerance level and lose them and perhaps my job?

These *are* the questions that leaders must ask. They have an "on the balcony" quality that marks them as leadership domain. And that places them in everybody's domain. Leaders invite colleagues and parents to find essential questions like these to ask about their individual and collective performance. They encourage them to join in the reinvention of purposes and practices. The deep renewal of public school purposes and of staff and community commitment to them can occur in no other way. By helping those around them to face persisting adaptive challenges, leaders thus feed the second stream of leadership in the school and community. The array of interpersonal and intellectual skills and the breadth of knowledge about public schools that this requires is dizzying. That is why, once again, leadership must come from a number of people, not from one. That is why, too, the working relationship among this multitalented, hopeful, and committed group of leaders is so important to the school's success at mobilizing for growth.

CHAPTER 10

Leaders Blend Learning and Action

We must have an approach to reform that acknowledges that we don't necessarily know all the answers, that is conducive to developing solutions as we go along, and that sustains our commitment and persistence to stay with the problem until we get somewhere.
—Fullan & Miles (1992), p. 746

Leadership mobilizes people. It generates new action, above and beyond—or replacing—"old" action. The relationships formed in leadership are breeding grounds for ideas and energies that, together, spin individuals and groups into new practices with children that meet challenges pressing on the school. A junior high school faculty, after long discussions about the disengagement of students, reconstitutes itself in teams to design project-centered learning. A high school staff adopts advisory groups and student-led conferences as a way to generate greater student responsibility for learning. A grade-level team, in concert with parents, replaces unit tests and the grading system with continuous assessment and monthly parent-teacher-student conferences.

We often mistakenly assume that the new actions that result from leadership will appear as a coherent, carefully choreographed package or must result from a "policy initiative" or "reform program." Nothing could be further from the truth in the planetary cultures of our public schools. Actions newly created to serve children are crafted largely on observations and intuitions from yesterday's—if not last hour's—experiences with those children. Improving learning for children grows from adults' "incremental" and "situational" shifts in knowledge, beliefs, and behavior, classroom by classroom and day by day, more than it does from wholesale changes in the materials, curriculum, or structures of schooling (Jennings, 1996; McDonald, 1996; Tyack & Cuban, 1995).

A staff's capacity to change is directly contingent upon their own opportunities to reflect on their work with children. New practice, as Chris Argyris (1991) puts it, stems from teachers, principals, parents, and students "connecting learning to real . . . problems, . . . learning by examining their own ineffective behavior . . . [having] plenty of opportunity to practice new skills . . . [and by] legitimizing talking about issues they have never been able to address before . . . so they can act more effectively in the future" (pp. 106–107). *The litmus test for leadership in the mobi-*

lization stream is that adults in school are adapting their own practices and attitudes with children and with one another to be more effective. Learning, that is, is what leads to new action.

PUTTING ADULTS' LEARNING AT THE CENTER

Leaders, then, foster learning as a core activity. Their activities encourage active questioning and open dialogue. Supported by strong, affirming relationships and commitment to purpose, leaders draw their colleagues into thinking outside the box and, most vitally, into acting outside the box. This is the essence of what makes them leaders; it is what helps them mobilize those around them to action in the effort to succeed more fully in the future. Leaders thus build the group's belief in its action-in-common, reaching individual members by fostering collective learning-to-practice activities. Their activities cluster around four themes:

- Modeling an attitude and practice of inquiry.
- Gathering people together to learn and to consider alternatives.
- Demonstrating a bias for action and the confidence to try.
- Seeking evidence of results.

Modeling Inquiry in Attitude and Practice

Leaders show others by their example that they are learners. They operate from a disposition of inquiry, not a disposition of control. They, as Peter Senge (1999) puts it, "genuinely ask questions to which they do not have an answer" (p. 66). Roland Barth (1997) frames the leader's inquiring disposition this way:

> Would I describe my school or classroom culture as one supporting "inventive irreverence," a "sense of wonder"? Do I have high expectations that all student and all teachers and all parents—and I, myself—can be profound learners, or do I think of some as learners and others as bottom ability group, voc ed, "brain dead," "burned-out," "lemons" or "learn-ed?" Is the nature of the relationships among the students in classrooms and adults in the faculty room in my school collegial? Or is it isolated, competitive, adversarial? (pp. 27–28)

This by no means indicates that all decisions and routines are uncertain or up for grabs. Indeed, busy educators *are* knowledgable; they make hundreds of decisions, invent routines, structure policies, and devise teaching and curricular systems to make the learning process dependable. The same is true at the school level: Systems for moving students, for controlling their behavior, and for making interactions and relationships predictable push principals, teachers, and other staff to respond to a cascade of requests and problems every day. Leaders, however, engage in these stabilizing activities with the understanding that no solution, plan, or policy is ever safe from the question, "Is this helping our students learn?"

In their daily activities, leaders are magnets for problems, issues, and new ideas because they offer others ways to work on those problems. Although it is often easy to fall into the trap of providing solutions, directing responses, and serving as "answer men," leaders operate more as consultants to others. A teacher leader responds to a teacher's puzzlement about students by asking questions that clarify the teacher's understanding, focus the challenge, and explore available alternatives: "What have you tried? What happened? How did you follow up? What could you do differently? How can we help?" Leaders give time in team meetings, faculty workshops, and parent-teacher sessions to focused examination of issues vital to participants.

Because they are so engaged with those around them, leaders become nodes in a web that carries information about students' experiences, teachers' efforts, and their learning to many others. Teacher leaders are particularly well positioned to feed this running inquiry about what students are learning, who is struggling, and what is working that others can use. Principals often have greater opportunities to facilitate learning around student behavior, cocurricular experiences, and linking to the home.

In facilitating inquiry, leaders are unabashed learners themselves. Principals and teacher leaders publicly share questions and evidence about their own performance, seeking feedback and help from others. A principal asks a teacher for suggestions on handling of an irate parent. A teacher leader takes time in a team meeting to present a recent teaching activity he or she used and to seek suggestions and reactions. As they read about useful ideas, talk to others about their work with students, and attend professional development events, the questions and ideas that pique their interest become part of their ongoing conversations with colleagues or more structured discussions in team or faculty meetings. In this very personal way, principal and teacher leaders say, "I am not the 'answer man' for every question; I need your help with people and tasks that are frustrating me, too." They model for everyone an openness about tough problems and even about mistakes. Their deeds say to all that interdependence among us is critical to the success of each one of us, that learning, not knowing, as the norm among adults in the school.

Gathering People Together to Learn

Advocating and facilitating learning among adults is problematic in many schools, and it can be particularly troublesome for principals. At the heart of learning-from-practice is a vulnerability, a willingness to admit that one's practice is flawed. To acknowledge publicly that "our school is not giving 75% of our students sufficient basic tools in math by grade 6" or that "we let our most able students die on the vine" requires the confidence to "unfreeze" old beliefs and practices and to believe that "we can do something about this." Leaders help their schools do this delicate work by convening those who are invested in or responsible for the challenge and facilitating their learning. Michael Fullan and Andy Hargreaves (1991; 1994; 1998), in their *What's Worth Fighting For* trilogy, offer superb advice about this process of building security to support risk, moving "towards the danger" instead of avoiding it, "steer[ing] clear of false certainties," and "respect[ing] those you want to silence" (1998, p. 105).

In schools, leaders can gather people in small groups more easily than in large. Many schools are moving toward permanent staff teams who work with a given set of students. These manageable, student-focused teams are proving the richest ground for the cultivation of teacher leadership around the model advanced in this book (Darling-Hammond, 1997; McDonald, 1996; Meier, 1995). Here, leaders routinely devote time to professional dialogue about issues group members face. Instead of administrative or leader-initiated agendas, teacher, counselor, and parent agendas about their students are the reason staff and parents are asked to convene. Turn-around time between a problem's surfacing and the invention of new alternatives is minimized.

Patricia Wasley (1995) recommends developing norms in these circles that encourage "straight-shooting within and between these groups":

- The point of the group is not evaluation, but learning from one another.
- Diversity of membership (e.g., many disciplines) and perspectives enriches suggestions and alternate possibilities.
- Administrators, too, have a place here; they need help with their issues and their perspectives need to be in the mix at the ground level.
- We talk about our work with children here, our actual work in progress—not "best lessons" or "war stories"—so that the feedback can be put to use immediately.
- We all need to set the goal and process for each session to meet our needs; and we all need to evaluate how well each session works. (Adapted from Wasley, 1995, pp. 58–59.)

As groups of teachers circle around their own problems of practice, they multiply their meager resources to meet one another's most pressing challenges. Teacher leaders seem quite naturally to do this in the course of their conversations over coffee or the copier. Principals, however, are often hampered by administrative roles and duties. The challenges for them in gathering staff are extensive: Faculty and staff are very busy; they often need to refuel when they are not teaching; faculty meetings and public meetings are often difficult places to establish norms such as those listed above. Principals, nevertheless, are uniquely positioned to advocate with central office and others for a schedule and structure built around the principle that educators do their best work in teams. When they loudly and clearly argue that adults, too, need time to learn together, they say to all that children's learning cannot improve unless staff work in conditions that promote their own learning, planning, and new classroom practices. Few acts can contribute more mightily in both symbolic and instrumental ways to a group's belief in its own action-in-common.

Try It Out: Demonstrating a Bias for Action

The first two leader activities have emphasized learning as a central adult responsibility in schools. But this learning must generate action in the form of new practices and behaviors if it is to meet the litmus test for leadership. Historically, we have been taught that new institutional action results from "strategic planning" and "curriculum development." We have been taught to begin with a needs assessment and proceed through goal-setting, examination (and perhaps pilot-testing) of alternative new procedures, and on to full-scale implementation. (See, e.g., Lipham, Rankin, & Hoeh, 1985, chap. 6.) This process has proven useful in long-range planning for program and policy adoption, but it has not served schools well as a method of improving teaching and learning activities in the classroom (Lieberman, 1995; Oakes, Quartz, Ryan, & Lipton, 2000).

New practices follow from practitioners' thoughtful decisions to try something new. Those decisions grow from dissatisfaction with current practice and a belief that something different holds promise. "Trying it out and seeing what happens" is the predominant means for changing educational practice (Darling-Hammond, 1997; McDonald, 1996; Tyack & Cuban, 1995). Karl Weick (1985) puts it this way: "Be willing to leap before you look. If you look before you leap, you may not see [ready opportunities to succeed]. Action generates outcomes that ultimately provide the raw material for seeing [what can work]" (p. 133). The leader's contribution is to inject a bias for action into thinking and planning. Leaders encourage colleagues to experiment and tinker. Critically, they constantly query, "What are we learning from this and what does that tell us we should do next?"

Leaders exude a courageous empiricism. Instead of carefully planning every step and preparing for every eventuality, they pull heads together to assess the situation, check their moral compass, and, partially on the basis of intuition, plunge ahead (Sergiovanni, 1992; Sernak, 1998). Sensing adequate information after a 5-minute diagnostic consultation, for example, a grade-level leader pushes the agenda to "What are two or three things we could do tomorrow to begin to address this problem?" The next afternoon, he or she seeks out two team members to "see how it went," what worked and what did not. After 3 weeks of discussion, a school's leadership team recruits a few teachers to try the new writing-skills rubric. At the next faculty meeting, a half hour is devoted to debriefing the learning of these pioneers for the benefit of all. This thoughtful on-the-fly adjusting of practices often fits the realities better than a highly refined plan. Teacher leaders and principals encourage and legitimize such tinkering. For staff who hesitate to change or who will change only with a master plan in place, they may need to push and cajole. The principle is: We do not have to be right with every move; rather, we need to be able to learn from what occurs and to adjust our next steps.

Leaders can encourage and model this learning-into-action by being public risk-takers themselves. Their own bias for action communicates to others that continuing routines that they know have not succeeded in the past is a greater price to pay than falling on their faces trying something new. In their own work as principals and teachers, they freely share their experiences with a new method of organizing their workday or dealing with a difficult parent or motivating a sullen student. In group settings, they invite opinions about the new schedule they advocated, the three programs staff visited on the last inservice day, or their own pet project.

But they also have an ear for consensus and know when to say, "Is there a way we can try this for a week and see how it works?" They hold such draft plans in the group's mind and gather resources to support ad hoc efforts to "work the plan." They thus organize the faculty, committee, or team to work in tandem on a new schedule, a new approach to a difficult child, or a new assessment technique or learning resource. And then they reconvene them to see how it went.

How Did It Go? Seeking Evidence of Results

Nothing mobilizes people better than seeing how their new actions are influencing the quality of students' experience. In the thick of daily school work, staff often cannot know how well their efforts are leading to student learning: Effects are hidden or overcast by the newness of the activity; or "results" don't surface until well down the road. Leaders help the school community to gather evidence on how it is doing and thus to carry its impact on students "beyond talk."

In contrast to the more systematic methods of assessing and evaluating practices described in Chapter 9, leaders here participate in more frequent and less formal "checking in" activities. Their efforts are formative: "How did the kids react to the new checklist today?" "What did Fred do when you asked him to show his work to the class?" "Did splitting the class into groups do what you'd hoped today? How did they handle the freedom?" Key to these informal follow-through conversations is the leader's emphasis on evidence. Leaders chat with a colleague or assemble a team for brief, informal assessments before a new practice has been in trial very long.

Their inquiries, however, are not limited to "How'd it go?" They probe beyond colleagues' descriptions of *what they did or felt to how students' responses indicated whether learning was occurring.* Their interactions with faculty, staff, coaches, and parents generate talk about what students appear to be gaining—or losing—from the activities adults are structuring for them. They all identify valid evidence of their effects: daily observation, work samples, attendance records, test results, parental reports, performance data from the years after students leave the school. This attention to results is critical to anchoring planning and action in well-focused goals and objectives. It is the most essential way that leaders help colleagues' actions remain purposeful.

Leaders' attention to results is as important as is the information the group gleans from these running reflections or from more formal feedback such as testing or surveys. The message is: We have leaders who care about this attempt to improve; they are willing to follow through and to ask the tough question, "Is it working?" They are not simply bringing staff to the brink of implementation and sending them off alone to carry it out. Implementation is for leaders, too! In fact, it plays an extremely important role in creating a leadership relationship. Principals put the wieght of their office behind risk-taking and experimentation for better student learning. They unapologetically encourage staff who fail. They find resources to support ad hoc innovation and participate in gathering evidcence and learning from it. Teacher leaders, perhaps more naturally than principals, can work side-by-side with colleagues, sharing the trial of new teaching practices. They can more easily follow through with team members and share how a new twist might work better the next day or in the coming instructional unit.

Leaders' emphasis on looking at results, although it can sometimes be uncomfortable and even demoralizing, is the cornerstone of staff confidence. They not only help colleagues face rather than avoid evidence of results but also constantly run interference in the busyness of school for these critical assessment activities. They protect time and bring in special expertise if necessary so that teachers, teams, and the whole faculty can "pause the action" long enough to learn how well that action is paying off. In the process, they are attuned to staff morale and energy levels so they can shepherd the group to new action on its own schedule and without overextending its members. Success then generates stronger belief in the group's future capacity to act. As one small school faculty described it, the process works this way: "We began by sharing ideas and convictions, which brought us closer together and spurred us to try some things [in our classrooms] which, in turn, led us to try still others things" (Goldsberry, Holt, Johnson, MacDonald, Poliquin, & Potter, 1995, p. 155).

THE STUFF OF LEADERS: THE COURAGE TO ACT AND TO LEARN

"Leader as teacher" is not about "teaching" people how to achieve their vision. It is about fostering learning for everyone.

—Senge (1990), p. 356

Schools are places of constant and unruly action. Despite our long-standing attempts to improve learning through controlled, centralized and uniform procedures, the planetary and tribal cultures of adults and students alike have fragmented and undercut those efforts. We have found instead that leaders who mobilize others do so through daily personal contact, a reverence for learning, and a dauntless commitment to action. They cultivate learning among everyone—teachers, counselors, principals, parents, coaches, aids, secretaries. They do it more through modeling, convening, coaching, and incremental trials of new practices than they do by directing overnight makeovers (Darling-Hammond, 1997; Oakes et al., 2000; Tyack & Cuban, 1995). At the core of this leadership activity *is not simply learning but learning to do better what they do with children.*

What helps us as leaders to accomplish this integration of learning and action? The leader attributes in Chapters 8 and 9 are a foundation: fostering relationships that will permit honest attention to performance and improvement; grasping the philosophical principles of effective schooling; and knowing how children learn and grow and what adults can do to foster their development. The blending of learning and action, however, further calls upon leaders to possess these qualities:

- The ambition to find a better way
- Trust in experiential knowledge
- Active caring

These three qualities and their attendant skills largely engage leaders' intrapersonal understandings—their capacity to monitor and shape their thoughts, feelings, and interactions—as they go about "shaping and being shaped" by colleagues.

The Inspiration to Find a Better Way

Fostering learning and action calls on leaders who themselves are inspired by the pursuit of a better way. Their own ambition sustains them and it fans the hopes of others. It originates partly in their deep convictions about their work and partly in the intellectual and intrapersonal rewards they feel when the school makes strides. Leaders' inspiration (some would call it passion) has an uplifting and a sustaining quality to them and it spreads to others a hopeful vitality that does not fade over time. They are optimistic people; their optimism flows from *a disposition that welcomes and enjoys tough challenges.* Some might identify this as confidence; some might also see it as the courage to ask tough questions, to listen attentively to others and to news that is not necessarily welcome, and to jointly—and even joyfully—press on to hypothesizing solutions and taking action in uncertain circumstances.

Leaders *bring their own hopefulness to their circles of colleagues.* Their belief that "we can make something of this" contributes energy and hope to the relationship that is difficult to measure yet, in the minds of those in the group, is undeniably present. In doing so, leaders draw from their own moral and philosophical convictions as well as from practical and hard-nosed assessments of obstacles and opportunities.

They are not blind idealists or ideologues; rather, they anchor their optimism in experience and in faith in the group. These qualities blend into the leader's conviction that, in Michael Fullan's (1997) words, "persistent negative emotions lead to ever greater individual and organizational illness and diminution of capacity and, on the other hand, that being hopeful is a critical resource, especially in the face of seeming lost causes" (p. 18).

Peter Vaill (1998) captures an element of this quality in his term "pushy collegiality," a style of approaching colleagues that blends a deep respect for others with a transparent desire to "get on with it," that combines the pragmatic with the idealistic, action with thought (p. 242). This hopeful pushiness is not unfamiliar to teachers. It is often what makes them successful in bringing children through the challenges of new skills, new material, new frameworks for understanding. It is captured in protypical teacher language: "I know you can do it"; "It may not feel like it, but we're making progress"; "Let's just try this"; and "Let me know how this works." Many skills and qualities that work for teachers transfer to this aspect of leadership: approaching a problem or challenge with conviction and, perhaps, the "thrill of the hunt"; developing jointly an understanding of it; carving out manageable aspects of it to learn about; seeking new knowledge about these aspects; and examining how that new knowledge "works" to respond to the initial problem or need.

This inspired search for a better way should not be misunderstood as a hell-bent-for-election effort to push colleagues where they do not see a reason to go. The leader's inspiration sparks confidence and action among others but does not overflow the bounds of *a respectfulness for others that remains the heart of the leadership relationship.* Ronald Heifetz (1994) puts it this way:

> Listening and intervening go hand in hand. Each action [is] viewed as an experiment. Improvisation demands ongoing assessment. . . . A person who leads must intervene and then hold steady, listening for the effects of the intervention. She moves from balcony to dance floor, back and forth. She has to allow for silence. Holding steady gives the system time to react to her intervention. It also gives her time to listen. By listening, she refines her interpretation of events and takes corrective action. Based on what she hears, she intervenes again. By this approach, interventions are not simply proposed solutions; interventions are ways to test the waters and gather information to refine the strategy. (p. 272)

Trust in Experiential Knowledge

Leaders also bring to the blending of learning and action *a sophisticated and pragmatic understanding of learning-in-action.* Although leaders do not devalue formal or "book" learning, they have a special appreciation for "craft knowledge" or "tacit knowledge" and know how to feed its development (Sternberg & Horvath, 1999). Since the onset of the professions, we have been pestered by the disjunctions between formal knowledge of the work (the "science" we are taught in university and inservice courses) and the "on-the-ground" knowledge that we discover works in practice (the "art" of practice). In recent years, we have come to understand the importance of this latter kind of knowledge for it is what most powerfully shapes what educators do minute-by-minute and thus what shapes students' learning (Darling-Hammond, 1997; Lave & Wenger, 1991; Schön, 1983).

Joseph Horvath, who together with Robert Sternberg has led recent research into professional tacit knowledge, finds that three elements mark craft knowledge. First, it derives "intimately from action" and, in turn, shapes a person's or group's future action. Second, we tend to favor it because we have learned firsthand that it works—that it leads to the attainment of valued goals. And third, it is usually acquired with little help or external validation by others (Horvath, et al., 1999, p. 44). Often, what we have learned from experience is so obvious to us and so much a part of our everyday practice that we have never articulated it or thought consciously about it. Much of what we do in the busyness of schools, that is, derives from knowledge and beliefs that we might not even be aware of.

As leaders seeking to help colleagues learn and to turn that learning into new action, we are helping each other literally to make sense of our own tacit knowledge. Leaders, then, are *skilled mentors who help others to see how their current knowledge does and does not work* in different situations and with different students and *to reformulate this craft knowledge* in a more widely applicable and successful form. A principal, after observing a teacher's lesson, begins by asking the teacher to talk about how the lesson went. Rather than impose the district's checklist or her or his own professional values on the teacher, the principal asks questions designed to help the teacher see how his or her actions and attitudes affected students' experience. Similarly, a team leader uses questioning, reflecting, and summarizing skills as he or she leads a debriefing of this week's team unit. The leader's ability to help the group articulate what worked and why and then to focus on "what next" propels their learning from action.

Leaders' success at facilitating such learning stems from their beliefs about their own knowledge and the role it plays in their leadership relationships. They do not value their own knowledge (or an expert's knowledge) above a colleague's or the group's. Learning with others is a reciprocal process. They enter into it *believing that they will both contribute to the learning of others and learn from others—that together they will construct knowledge* that is informed by immediate practicalities and by relevant literatures and other "stored" knowledge (Barth, 1990; Heifetz, 1994; Lambert et al., 1995; Senge, 1990). The principal's skill at listening to others, showing that she or he has heard by reflecting back, and exhibiting authentic interest in others' ideas and beliefs is basic to establishing others' responsibility for learning and action. Because school cultures can value knowing answers and dictating solutions over active inquiry (Rait, 1995), formal leaders must be sensitive to the way they are heard. This can be challenging work, particularly for principals (who often feel a need to have answers and to be in control).

As leaders push to establish such collegial learning as the core culture for school change, their own willingness to learn from their experience in this more public way will have the most telling impact on others. Our reciprocal relationship with our colleagues as we learn our way forward means that *leaders too need the courage to raise the learning bar for themselves.* Given expectations on leaders, this will require the resolve and personal confidence necessary to, as one principal friend of mine put it, "put myself out there, warts and all." Few actions, however, could do more to convince others of the importance of "unfreezing," acknowledging the "loss" of old ways and beliefs, and opening up to learning new competencies and new relationships (Evans, 1996). Our capacity to enter into this authentic reciprocity, where we are truly interdependent with our colearners, permits us not only to share in learning but also to share in the action that results from it.

Active Caring

Individuals who aspire to lead in the three-stream model assume less sole responsibility and power than do old-style leaders. They work at relationship-building and at holding firm to moral purposes and challenges, not at knowing solutions and compelling or persuading others to carry them out. They approach their daily work and the school's challenges as learning opportunities; their actions are guided by what the group learns, not just from what they learn. They believe and ultimately trust in action-in-common over fragmentary action. These are fundamentally caring activities. They derive not only from leaders' commitment to the quality of student learning and staff performance but also from caring about students and staff as people.

I call this third cluster of leader qualities "active caring." They address our willingness to accept our school's challenges and our current working conditions and relationships and, despite the odds, to act on them. The leader who actively cares sees the need to change and is moved to action. In contrast, the person who is paralyzed by fear, hopelessness, power, or "the odds" contributes little to leadership (Noddings, 1984; Sernak, 1998). Jentz and Wofford (1979), from their case studies of school leaders, observe that "the opposite of caring is indifference." Leaders help to mobilize those around them by not being indifferent in their words, their attitudes, or their actions. They do not settle for "good enough." They literally care enough to take action despite objections and discomfort.

What are the qualities that contribute to active caring? One is *deep conviction about the goodness of our work.* School leaders understand their career choice as a philosophical and moral one. Typically, they believe that their work contributes to the betterment of American society and humankind through service to children. So when their team, their department, their school, their community, or their profession is faced with deep challenges, their motivation to grapple with these challenges is strong. The roots of their commitment to public education nourish a form of courage (Palmer, 1997; Sergiovanni, 1992). It is this courage that helps leaders face attacks on their schools or teams. It helps leaders "face the dangers," remain open to opposing, counterfluent voices, and able to learn from them.

Active caring stems as well from the ability to *communicate authentic respect and personal affirmation to all others*. Others need to believe that you care not only about children and the school's mission but about them. Robert Evans (1996) describes this as "authenticity." Bennis and Nanus (1985) found that leaders' interpersonal values and motives were public and consistent, allowing others to trust them on personal and professional levels. I understand it as comfort with oneself, a quality that some might equate with self-confidence and maturity. In the thick of a contentious faculty meeting or during a staff picnic, a teacher leader's personal style and expressed values remain constant even while his or her words and behaviors vary. In stressful situations, these leaders can separate their own egos from the points and words of others. Team members, staff, or parents leave the meeting confident that the leader is above personal retribution or political manipulation to "get his way." They can rest assured that this person they view as a leader is one who trusts that the facts will come to light and one who will abide by a fair and open process of coming to agreements and to action.

Active caring, too, means that the leader *honors others as people, not only as coworkers or neighbors*. The principal, despite her or his long-standing disagreement with the social studies department over their inquiry approach to history, respectfully acknowledges the different philosophies and logics of department members. Moreover, the principal recognizes their feelings while repeatedly proposing an evaluation of the merits of their program, articulating their frustration and expressing her or his own. In honoring coworkers, the principal projects an on-the-balcony skill that permits her or him to separate the professional disagreements from an abiding personal respect. Others come to see her or him as dependable in this steady affirmation of others, even in the heat of battle or the depths of a crisis. This capacity to separate the professional from the personal builds confidence in others that the leader's focus on action-in-common is motivated by professional goals, not personal idiosyncracy or interpersonal grudges or affiliations.

Active caring, finally, is rooted in *leaders' caring for themselves*. Their own optimism, their belief in the school and the faculty, and their personal confidence and satisfaction as leaders will be tested in their attempts to lead in this more unruly, learning-centered fashion. Especially in times of adaptive challenge when conflicts, raw emotions, and open questioning about purposes and practices are the talk of teachers' rooms, coffee klatches, and board meetings, school leaders are exposed and vulnerable. Others look to them to settle things down or to come up with solutions that work for everyone. In the intense work of learning what needs to change and whether alternatives are successful, leaders themselves feel interpersonal stresses and personal exhaustion. Their own ability to care for themselves can have profound effects on others' ability to care for themselves and for students, school, and community (Ackerman, Donaldson & van der Bogert, 1996).

How do leaders care for themselves? They stay in touch with themselves, with how they are feeling and with the emotional effects of other people and events that naturally and spontaneously shape their thinking and actions. Goleman (1998b), among others, claims that our ability to monitor our emotions is by far the most significant factor shaping our actions. As leaders participate in the busyness of their schools, their intrapersonal antennae help regulate the wash of people, feelings, and events. In particular, they need constantly to judge what they can control and what they cannot, what they personally can be responsible for and what others must be responsible for.

We gain this perspective in part by "getting on the balcony" and watching ourselves in relationship with others. In routinely reflecting on how we typically behave in leadership situations, leaders quite literally learn about their part in the complex of interactions that constitute leadership relationships: How does our personality type, for example, kick off reactions in other people? How does our age, gender, and personal background constrain and enable our relationships with others? Which of our skills work particularly well with what sorts of people, in what sorts of situations? The more deeply and more accurately leaders understand themselves in these regards, the more possible it is for them to grasp the particular ways they can contribute—and, more important in our culture of superhero leaders— the particular ways they cannot. Heifetz (1994) describes this as "listening to yourself, using yourself as data" (p. 271). Caring for yourself, in this sense, means not shouldering responsibility solely for the entire school's or team's challenges or for aspects of the school's shared responsibilities over which you have little control and about which you, personally, have little expertise.

Leaders care for themselves, as well, by clinging doggedly to the conviction that they are only a part of the leadership necessary for a school to grow. Leaders, in this sense, "find partners," confidantes to share in their personal and professional reflections and colleagues who, as fellow leaders, can together cultivate enough "leadership density" in the school to mobilize many others. As perhaps the most fundamental act in the leadership process, finding partners is about growing relationships one-by-one with others that will permit the group, team, or whole school to function better. Heifetz (1994) sees it as follows,

> Even if the weight of carrying people's hopes and pains may fall mainly, for a time, on one person's shoulders, leadership cannot be exercised alone. The lone-warrior model of leadership is heroic suicide. Each of us has blind spots that require the vision of others. Each of us has passions that need to be contained by others. Anyone can lose the capacity to get on the balcony, particularly when the pressures mount. Every person who leads needs help in distinguishing self from role and identifying the underlying issues that generate attack. (p. 268)

CHAPTER 11

Choosing to Lead

It is impossible to reduce natural leadership to a set of skills or competencies. Ultimately, people follw people who believe in something and have the abilities to achieve results in the service of those beliefs. . . . Who are the natural leaders of learning organizations? They are the learners.

—Senge (1990), p. 360

The afternoon sun is low on the horizon, infusing the west wing of Acadia High with orange warmth. Twelve people sit in a circle amid a jumble of student desks, papers, soft drinks, and pretzels. They bend earnestly toward each speaker as she or he picks up on the preceding person's idea or comment. Though they show the ragged edges of the day's work, every member of the group is intent on the dialogue. They are the members of Acadia's Leadership Team: six teachers, one counselor, a district curriculum coordinator, two principals, a parent, and a school board member.

The team has been meeting for 16 months. They convened in the aftermath of a long and bitter faculty debate over an administrative initiative to change teaching periods from 43 minutes to 85 minutes and press teachers into more student-centered teaching. The proposal's defeat had left staff divided; many, including the principal, wondered whether leading Acadia toward more learner-centered practices would ever be possible. But it had also left many staff and some parents even more committed to meeting head-on the long-standing criticism that Acadia was "only good for doctors' and lawyers' kids." And it had convinced a critical mass of Acadia High members that a different and more broad-based form of leadership needed to emerge if the school was to improve its practices with students.

So the Leadership Team had formed at the invitation of the principal and three core teachers. From the outset, its members were determined to "go slow to go fast." Their first goal was to create open and honest communication within the team, to build themselves into a working group that could express ideas and feelings without fear of rejection, reprisal, or subversion. That work took the bulk of a year and is ongoing. After 4 months of developing their own working relationship, the team was ready to begin a series of individual and small-group discussions with all faculty and staff, representative parents, and the school board. They focused on two questions: "What do you see as the greatest obstacles to our success with all students?" and "What are our strongest assets as a school and community?" This initial "audit" generated a rich assortment of purposes, assessments of current practice, and inquiries about "Where is this going?"

The Leadership Team spent long hours examining themes from their conversations with their school community and blending these with a growing pool of "harder" data: the results of the accreditation team visit; annual state-wide achievement test scores; trends in SAT's, attendance, disciplinary referrals, transfers in and out of Acadia High, and the like. In the ensuing months, the team shared these themes and data widely with staff, students, parents, and the board, always with the caveat that "this is what we're seeing and hearing about Acadia." During this period, they also invented three new practices at Acadia: a format for faculty meetings that turned them into highly participative, data-based explorations of issues rather than principal-led information-giving; opportunities for teachers in pairs and trios to visit other schools where detracking and integrated teams were successful; and replanning staff development activities to dovetail with the Leadership Team's work.

And now the team is wrestling with two issues: "How will they facilitate ways for staff, parents, and students to explore personalizing learning through regular teacher-student-parent goal-setting and assessment conferences?" and "How will the team itself find the time, skills, and resources necessary to continue their leadership of the process?" Although some members of the group remain discouraged by the faculty naysayers, most are frankly surprised at how widespread acceptance of the team itself has become. Each member of the team can count six to eight non-team members with whom they converse regularly about their budding focus around personalizing learning. The principal and her assistant principal have managed to extract substitute-teacher funds from the central office for visitations and now for members of the Leadership Team who will work with willing colleagues around new classroom practices. Although they are far away from new teaching and assessment practices and a schedule that permits collaborative planning time, they are feeling optimistic that the school board, administration, and leaders in the community are understanding better the need for these changes.

Acadia High School is not just exploring a new path toward improved learning and teaching, it is charting new leadership waters for itself. From the failure of an administratively initiated reform emerged an informal consensus that the school does not meet the needs of all students equally well. Turning to widely respected teachers who shared in this consensus, the principal courageously acknowledged the impossibility of, as she put it, "imposing on 20-year teaching veterans my formula for better teaching." The result was the Leadership Team, a group of staff and citizens who shared a sense of urgency about the adaptive challenge facing the school. The team's path was not clear nor did its members have a mandate from anybody to change the school. Quite to the contrary, they set out to grow within themselves a strong enough working relationship to sustain their leadership of the school.

Over the first 2 years of their existence, they not only created among themselves a more robust confidence that they could make a difference, but they also extended through a variety of relationship-building strategies this growing belief in action-in-common to many others. Out of dialogues, workshops, new issue-centered faculty meetings, and visitations to other schools came a new way to think about the purpose of Acadia High as a place where students need to develop more responsibility and more personal control over their own learning goals and activities. Central to the process of rethinking and replanning has been widespread learning among staff, parents, and even the school board. From this somewhat chaotic and diffuse activity, Leadership Team members and a number of other teachers feel a strengthened commitment to changing how they work with students in their classrooms and how they must grow to include parents more openly in their work.

Acadia's experience hitching itself along toward a new form of leadership is being repeated in other schools across the nation. Their stories are documented in the work of Debbie Meier (1995), Linda Darling-Hammond (1997), Joe McDonald (1996), Roland Barth (1990), Carl Glickman (1993), Robert Evans (1996), and Jeanne Oakes et. al. (2000). What is common to them is that schools that are improving are meeting the leadership litmus tests put forth in this book. They are growing strong enough relationships among adults, robust enough purpose and commitment, and faith enough in common action to generate self-reinforcing patterns of productive work.

Relationships within the school community are valued and cared for. Respected and trusted teachers, principals, staff members, and citizens place importance on the interpersonal connections and practices of the school—starting with their own. They do so in formal ways through ground rules, compacts, and explicit meeting and decision-making procedures; but they also do it informally by acknowledging feelings, conflicts, and each person's integrity.

What is also common to these schools is a purposefulness among many staff that grows up around this relationship. Questions of purpose are commonplace: How does this current practice serve—or not serve—our goals for children? How might this alternative better serve them? From the examination of practices in this way, purposes are clarified and, importantly, commitments to fulfilling them are renewed.

Common to many of these schools, finally, is a healthy confidence that "we can together make a difference." This belief in action-in-common is not based on dreamy idealism alone; it is the product of direct experience among staff working together to improve the way they work with students in practical ways. The result is not identical work from teacher to teacher; rather it is a collaboration that assures that most adults are working for the same ends and that ensures the sharing of resources, techniques, and partnership along the way. Leadership merges the streams of relationships, purposes, and action, and in that merging are born new knowledge and beliefs, new attitudes, and new practices to support student learning.

What is most noteworthy about these schools is that their leadership is not readily apparent. We cannot see a strong working relationship in one visit to a school. We do not sense a robust sense of purpose and deep commitment without listening intently to conversation and experiencing it in classrooms, corridors, offices, and playgrounds. We cannot know whether collaborative self-assessment leads to action-in-common without observing how staff deal with students and with each other over time. Certainly, if we look only to those who hold a leadership title, we can be misled. Principals, assistant principals, team leaders, and department chairs must continue to manage the affairs of the school. If they are leaders as well, however, we will clearly see that they put relationships ahead of rules, face challenges instead of avoiding them, and nurture learning and experimentation among their colleagues.

A more accurate reading of the litmus tests of leadership can be found among the teachers themselves. Do *they* feel that their working relationships are strong enough and their purposes and commitments to children robust enough to nourish a confidence in their school's chances of succeeding with all children? We cannot identify school leadership by asking teachers to name from among them their leaders; the culture of the teacherhood and the continuing prevalence of classical leadership models make us hesitate to say, "She's the one" or "He's it." We can tell, however, by listening to teachers and other staff talk about who fosters connections among them, who honors their feelings and their perspectives, who "always has the best interests of children at heart," who will speak up about significant issues even in hostile company, and who is ready to act either by tinkering with practice or by reinventing whole structures that stand in the way of student learning. What we are apt to learn from school staff is that leadership is everywhere in a school where they believe that together they can improve.

LEADING IS A CHOICE FOR EVERYONE

I began this book with a query: Do schools need leadership? Clearly, they do. But the leadership they need is this more diffuse, relational type of leadership, a type that is more apparent in the action and spirit of a school than in its structures and entitled leaders. Most schools do not need leadership simply to run from day to day. But all schools need it when existing ways and values are deeply and persistently challenged. When voices in the community or from within the staff or student body question the usefulness or wisdom of current practices or when they actively proclaim their failure, can the adults of the school respond? Can they openly and carefully consider these counterfluent voices, "unfreeze" old beliefs and behaviors, and learn new competencies and practices that adapt the school to the challenges it faces? Or does the staff fragment and turn in on itself? Or circle their wagons around past practices and purposes and fight? Or close their classroom doors, turning passive and expecting only their appointed leaders to "deal with it"?

Such adaptive challenges pose the question: "Are you willing and able to join with others to address this challenge?" This question does not fall on one person's shoulders more than on another's. Because every employee and every parent hold so much responsibility and capacity to make learning succeed for their children, the challenge touches them all. Leading, for each one of us, is a choice. Facing that choice, educators and parents typically have two concerns:

1. *Will it be productive?* If I join in, I want there to be a good chance that by doing so we will mobilize ourselves to improve the learning of our students.
2. *Is it sustainable for me personally?* If I join in, I need to feel reasonably confident that the personal demands on me will not, when added to my "regular work" as teacher, parent, spouse, be unmanageable or unhealthy for me.

Ultimately, as we work on growing leadership in our schools, we need to return to these two concerns. Any form of leadership that does not address them is doomed to fail. Such forms, that is, are not forms of leadership at all.

This book has amply documented how public school realities give many educators reason to wonder about investing themselves in leadership. The conspiracy of busyness, the planetary culture, and the interpersonal strains of meeting difficult challenges head-on will not magically disappear. In fact, as we think about investing in leadership it is vital that we recognize these and the specific challenges they pose to principals and teacher leaders. I have devoted little attention to the roles of school districts, communities, and states in influencing these realities on behalf of leadership. Plainly, school boards and central offices carry enormou responsibility for the conditions that make school leadership both productive for the school and personally sustainable for those who undertake it.

They too must choose to lead. Their attitudes and administrative practices, the working conditions and negotiated contracts they agree to, and the availability of resources signal to staff in very concrete ways whether "being a part of the solution" is feasible and wise (Johnson, 1996). Other factors such as the sheer size and bureaucratic nature of a school or the legacies of past attempts to mobilize staff will leave some teachers and administrators more hesitant than others to join in the leadership stream.

Superintendents, school board members, state education commissioners, and other policy members are unlikely to change their assumptions about who leaders are and how leadership functions without evidence that the old way does not work. Thankfully, the past 20 years of reform debate and school improvement experience constitute a rich pool of such evidence. Much of the literature I have drawn from in writing this book can bolster local leadership teams as they advocate to their central office administrators, school boards, and communities this more potent means of improving their service to children. For leadership teams like Acadia High's, convincing decision-makers to support their leadership activities with resources and commitment is a major investment—one that extracts precious time, energy, and optimism from the team's members.

Imagine how much closer to their goal they would be if the central office stood behind their teamwork, underwriting it and even joining in it. Imagine, too, how Acadia's team would feel supported if grants and policies gave resources and authority to school-based teams where true leadership could thrive. And imagine how all schools would benefit if university graduate programs, professional associations, and policymakers promoted relational leadership and a model where successful leadership meant better learning for children. Finally, imagine how vibrant the leadership of schools would be if we all held to the conviction that women, teachers, parents, support staff, and even students are essential to it.

MAKING THE CHOICE

The choice to lead begins with the resolve that taking on challenges is best done with others, not alone. For busy educators and parents, *the first step in leading is toward a colleague or friend*, into the stream of relationships that runs deepest in the leadership river. Find partners and consciously attend to one another's affirmation, trust, and respect. Actively care for the members of the group as well as for its mission. In our resolve to act, both our productivity and our capacity to invest in this wider work will hinge on the replenishing qualities of group membership for each of us.

The choice to lead means resolving to infuse within these working relationships healthy dialogue about purposes and performance. Strong *relationships tilt toward leadership when they feed professional commitment to better educational performance.* Their value to leadership is as a working relationship. They nourish the purposive stream of the school's life, pulling adults and children alike along in a steady current with clear direction. Teachers, principals, and parents question goals and investigate evidence of performance. They actively wonder how both might be reinvented so that children benefit more from their time at school. They remind one another of their commitment to kids and rejuvenate those commitments when they flag.

And those who choose to lead resolve to act. They do so within the compact they have formed with others. The energies and commitments flowing from colleagues *foster their faith that they can act to improve student learning.* They talk. They pose questions from their work with children. They listen. And they test out new strategies, feeding their bias for action with a steady diet of new possibilities. What they find that works, they share and refine. What they find that doesn't work does not cripple them. Their incremental experimentalism nourishes a stream of belief in their vital influence over the quality of their students' learning and development. And their action-in-common continues.

The great potential of this three-stream model of leadership lies in its open invitation to everyone who cares about his or her school. We can each help to propel our schools forward if we choose honest relationships, child-centered purposes, and a commitment to act in concert. We can all be leaders if we choose, even if *our* contribution to the relationship looks quite different from somebody else's. This inclusive and ultimately democratic quality of the three-stream model is what makes it most appropriate for American public schools. How well our schools adapt to the deep challenges they face has in the past hinged upon how well those who care have mobilized themselves to change. As long into the future as we have public schools, their capacity to adapt to the evolving needs of children, communities, and American society will likewise hinge on such leadership.

References

Ackerman, R., Donaldson, G., & van der Bogert, R. (1996). *Making sense as a school leader: Persisting questions, creative opportunities.* San Francisco: Jossey-Bass.

Annenberg Institute for School Reform. (1998). *National school reform faculty training materials.* Providence, RI: Author.

Argyris, C. (1991, April). Teaching smart people to learn. *Harvard Business Review,* 69(3), 99–109.

Argyris, C. (1993). *Knowledge for action.* San Francisco: Jossey-Bass.

Argyris, C., & Schön, D. A. (1974). *Theory in practice: Increasing professional effectiveness.* San Francisco: Jossey-Bass.

Bacharach, S., & Mundell, B. (Eds.). (1995). *Images of schools: Structures and roles in organizational behavior.* Thousand Oaks, CA: Corwin.

Bandura, A. (1997). *Self-efficacy and the exercise of control.* New York: W.H. Freeman.

Barth, R. (1988). School: A community of leaders. In A. Lieberman (Ed.), *Building a professional culture in schools* (pp. 129–147). New York: Teachers College Press.

Barth, R. (1990). *Improving schools from within.* San Francisco: Jossey-Bass.

Barth, R. (1997). *The principal learner: A work in progress.* Cambridge, MA: International Network of Principals' Centers, Harvard University.

Bascia, N. (1994). *Unions in teachers' professional lives.* New York: Teachers College Press.

Bennis, W., & Nanus, B. (1985). *Leaders: The strategies for taking charge.* New York: Harper and Row.

Berry, B. (1995). School restructuring and teacher power: The case of Keels Elementary. In A. Lieberman (Ed.), *The work of restructuring schools* (pp. 111–135). New York: Teachers College Press.

Berry, B., & Ginsburg, R. (1990). Effective schools, teachers and principals: Today's evidence, tomorrow's prospects. In L. Cunningham (Ed.), *Educational leadership and changing contexts: 96th Yearbook of the NSSE* (pp. 155–183). Chicago: University of Chicago Press.

Biklen, S. K. (1995). *School work: Gender and the cultural construction of teaching.* New York: Teachers College Press.

Binney, G., & Williams, C. (1995). *Learning into the future.* London: Nicholas Brealey.

Blase, J., & Anderson, G. (1995). *The micropolitics of educational leadership: From control to empowerment.* New York: Teachers College Press.

Blase, J., & Blase, J. (1994). *Empowering teachers: What successful principals do.* Thousand Oaks, CA: Corwin.

Blase, J., & Kirby, P. (1992). *Bringing out the best in teachers: What effective principals do.* Thousand Oaks, CA: Corwin.

Block, P. (1996). *Stewardship: Choosing service over self-interest.* San Francisco: Berrett-Koehler.

Bolman, L., & Deal, T. (1991). *Reframing organizations: Artistry, choice, and leadership.* San Francisco: Jossey-Bass.

Bolman, L., & Heller, R. (1995). School administrators as leaders. In S. Bacharach and B. Mundell (Eds.), *Images of schools: Structures and roles in organizational behavior* (pp. 115–138). Thousand Oaks, CA: Corwin.

Brown, L.M., & Gilligan, C. (1992). *Meeting at the crossroads: Women's psychology and girls' development.* Cambridge, MA: Harvard University Press.

Buchanan, C. (1996). *Choosing to lead: Women and the crisis of American values.* Boston: Beacon Press.

Burns, J. M. (1978). *Leadership.* New York: Harper and Row.

Callahan, R. (1962). *Education and the cult of efficiency.* Chicago: University of Chicago Press.

Carnegie Foundation for the Advancement of Teaching. (1990). *The condition of teaching: A technical report.* Princeton, NJ: Author.

Carter, S. B. (1989). Incentives and rewards to teaching. In D. Warren (Ed.), *American teachers: Histories of a profession at work* (pp. 49–65). New York: Macmillan.

Clifford, G. J. (1989). Man/Woman/Teacher: Gender, family and career in American educational history. In D. Warren (Ed.), *American teachers: Histories of a profession at work* (pp. 293–332). New York: Macmillan.

Coalition of Essential Schools. (1997, January). Why small schools are essential. *Horace, 13*(3) 1–12.

Cooperrider, D. L. (Ed.). (1998). *Organizational wisdom and executive courage.* San Francisco: New Lexington Press.

Covey, S. (1991). *Principle-centered leadership.* New York: Summit Books.

Crosby, B. (1988, Fall). Women: New images of leadership. *Social Policy, 18*(2), 40–44.

Cuban, L. (1984). *How teachers taught: Constancy and change in American classrooms 1890–1980.* New York: Longman.

Cuban, L. (1988). *The managerial imperative and the practice of leadership in schools.* Albany: State University of New York Press.

Cubberly, E. P. (1916). *Public school administration: A statement of the fundamental principles underlying the organization and administration of public education.* Boston: Houghton Mifflin.

Cunningham, L. (1990). Educational leadership and administration: Retrospective and prospective views. In L. Cunningham (Ed.), *Educational leadership and changing contexts: 96th yearbook of the NSSE* (pp. 1–32). Chicago: University of Chicago Press.

Darling-Hammond, L. (1997). *The right to learn: A blueprint for creating schools that work.* San Francisco: Jossey-Bass.

Deal, T., & Peterson, K. (1994). *The leadership paradox: Balancing logic and artistry in schools.* San Francisco: Jossey-Bass.

Devaney, K., & Sykes, G. (1988). Making the case for professionalism. In A. Lieberman (Ed.), *Building a professional culture in schools* (pp. 3–22). New York: Teachers College Press.

Donaldson, G. (1991). *Learning to lead: The dynamics of the high school principalship.* Westport, CT: Greenwood Press.

Donaldson, G. (Ed.). (1997). On being a principal: The rewards and challenges of school leadership. In *New directions in school leadership* (Vol. 5). San Francisco: Jossey-Bass.

Donaldson, G., & Marnik, G. (1995). *Becoming better leaders.* Thousand Oaks, CA: Corwin.

Donaldson, G., & Sanderson, D. (1996). *Working together in schools: A guide for educators.* Thousand Oaks, CA: Corwin.

Donaldson, M., & Poon, B. (Eds.). (1999). Reflections of first year teachers on school culture: Questions, hopes and challenges. *New directions in school leadership* (Vol. 11). San Francisco: Jossey-Bass.

Education Digest. (1996). Ann Arbor, MI: Prakken Publishers, *61*(7).

Elliott, J. (1991). *Action research for educational change.* London: Open University Press.

Elmore, R., & McLaughlin, M. (1988). *Steady work: Policy, practice and reform of American education.* Santa Monica, CA: RAND Corp.

Evans, R. (1995). Getting real about leadership. *Education Week, 14*(29), 36.

Evans, R. (1996). *The human side of school change: Reform, resistance and the real-life problems of innovation.* San Francisco: Jossey-Bass.

Fellers, G. (1992). *The Deming vision: SPC/TQM for administrators.* Milwaukee, WI: ASQC Quality Press.

Foster, W. (1989). Toward a critical practice of leadership. In J. Smyth (Ed.), *Critical perspectives on educational leadership* (pp. 39–62). New York: Falmer Press.

Fraser, J. W. (1989). Agents of democracy: Urban elementary teachers and the conditions of teaching. In D. Warren (Ed.), *American teachers: Histories of a profession at work* (pp. 118–156). New York: Macmillan.

Frech, P. (1997). *The nature and perceived value of informal teacher talk.* Unpublished doctoral dissertatiion, University of Maine, Orono.

Fuhrman, S. (1993). *Designing coherent education policy: Improving the system.* San Francisco: Jossey-Bass.

Fullan, M. (1997). Emotion and hope: Constructive concepts for complex times. In A. Hargreaves (Ed.), *Rethinking educational change with heart and mind* (pp. 14–33). Alexandria, VA: Association for Supervision and Curriculum Development.

Fullan, M. (1998, April). Breaking the bonds of dependency. *Educational leadership, 55*(7), 6–10.

Fullan, M., & Hargreaves, A. (1991). *What's worth fighting for? Working together for your school.* Toronto: Toronto Public School Teachers' Federation.

Fullan, M., & Hargreaves, A. (1994). *What's worth fighting for in the principalship.* New York: Teachers College Press.

Fullan, M., & Hargreaves, A. (1998). *What's worth fighting for out there.* New York: Teachers College Press.

Fullan, M., & Miles, M. (1992, June). Getting reform right: What works and what doesn't. *Phi Delta Kappan, 73*(10), 745–752.

Gardner, H. (1983). *Frames of mind: The theory of multiple intelligences.* New York.: Basic Books.

Gardner, J. W. (1990). *On leadership.* New York: Free Press.

Garmston, R., & Wellman, B. (1999). *The adaptive school: A sourcebook for developing collaborative groups.* Norwood, MA: Christopher-Gordon Publishers.

Geisert, G. (1988). Participatory management: Panacea or hoax? *Educational Leadership, 84*(3), 56–59.

Glickman, C. (1993). *Renewing America's schools: A guide for school-based action.* San Francisco: Jossey-Bass.

Goldsberry, L., Holt, A., Johnson, K., MacDonald, G., Poliquin, K., & Potter, L. (1995). The evolution of a restructuring school: The New Suncook case. In A. Lieberman (Ed.), *The work of restructuring schools* (pp. 136–156). New York: Teachers College Press.

Goleman, D. (1995). *Emotional intelligence.* New York: Bantam Books.

Goleman, D. (1998a, November/December). What makes a leader? *Harvard Business Review,* *76*(2), 93–102.

Goleman, D. (1998b). *Working with emotional intelligence.* New York: Bantam Books.

Goodlad, J. (1984). *A place called school.* New York: McGraw-Hill.

Gutmann, A. (1987). *Democratic education.* Princeton, NJ: Princeton University Press.

Hallinger, P., Leithwood, K., & Murphy, J. (Eds.). (1993). *Cognitive perspectives on educational leadership.* New York: Teachers College Press.

Hallinger, P., & Murphy, J., (1991). Developing leaders for tomorrow's schools. *Phi Delta Kappan, 72*(7), 514–520.

Heifetz, R. (1994). *Leadership without easy answers.* Cambridge, MA: Belknap Press/Harvard University Press.

Helgesen, S. (1995). *The female advantage: Women's ways of leading.* New York: Currency-Doubleday.

Herbst, J. (1989). Teacher preparation in the nineteenth century: Institutions and purposes. In D. Warren (Ed.) *American teachers: Histories of a profession at work* (pp. 213–236). New York: Macmillan.

Hesselbein, F., & Cohen, P., (Eds.). (1999). *Leader to leader: Enduring insights on leadership from the Drucker Foundation's award-winning journal.* San Francisco: Jossey-Bass.

Hoffman, N. (1981). Woman's "true" profession: Voices from the history of teaching. New York: The Feminist Press at City University of New York.

Horvath, J., Forsythe, G., Bullis, R., Sweeney, P., Williams, W., McNally, J., Wattendorf, J., & Sternberg, R. (1999). Experience, knowledge, and military leadership. In R. Sternberg and J. A. Horvath (Eds.), *Tacit knowledge in professional practice: Researcher and practitioner perspectives* (pp. 39–57). Mahwah, NJ: Lawrence Erlbaum Associates.

Jackson, P. (1968). *Life in classrooms.* New York: Holt, Rinehart, and Winston.

Jackson, P., Boostrom, R., & Hansen, D. (1993). *The moral life of schools.* San Francisco: Jossey-Bass.

Jennings, N. (1996). Interpreting policy in real classrooms: Case studies of state reform and teacher practice. New York: Teachers College Press.

Jentz, B., & Wofford, J. (1979). *Leadership and learning.* New York: McGraw-Hill.

Johnson, D., & Johnson, F. (1995). *Joining together: Group theory and group skills.* (5th ed.). Boston: Allyn and Bacon.

Johnson, S. M. (1990). *Teachers at work: Achieving success in our schools.* New York: Basic Books.

Johnson, S. M. (1996). *Leading to change: The challenge of the new superintendency.* San Francisco: Jossey-Bass.

Johnson, W. (1989). Teachers and teacher training in the twentieth century. In D. Warren (Ed.), *American teachers: Histories of a profession at work* (pp. 237–256). New York: Macmillan.

Labaree, D. (1989). Career ladders and early public high school teachers. In D. Warren (Ed.), *American teachers: Histories of a profession at work* (pp. 157–189). New York: Macmillan.

Lambert, K., Walker, D., Zimmerman, D., Cooper, J., Lambert, M. D., Gardner, M., & Slack, P. J. (1995). *The constructivist leader.* New York: Teachers College Press.

Lave, J., & Wenger, E. (1991). *Situated learning: Legitimate peripheral participation.* Cambridge: Cambridge University Press.

Lieberman, A. (Ed.). (1988a). *Building and professional culture in schools.* New York: Teachers College Press.

Lieberman, A. (1988b, May). Teachers and principals: Turf, tension, and new tasks. *Phi Delta Kappan, 69*(9), 648–653.

Lieberman, A. (Ed.). (1995). *The work of restructuring schools: Building from the ground up.* New York: Teachers College Press.

Lieberman, A., & Miller, L. (1992). *Teachers: Their world and their work: Implications for school improvement.* New York: Teachers College Press.

Lipham, J., Rankin, R., & Hoeh, J. (1985). *The principalship.* New York: Longman.

Little, J. W. (1982). Norms of collegiality and experimentation: Workplace conditions of school success. *American Educational Research Journal, 19*, 325–340.

Little, J.W. (1988). Assessing the prospects of teacher leadership. In A. Lieberman (Ed.), *Building and professional culture in schools* (pp. 78–108). New York: Teachers College Press.

Lortie, D. (1975). *School teacher: A social study.* Chicago: University of Chicago Press.

Louis, K. S., & Kruse, S. (Eds.). (1995). *Professionalism and community: Perspectives on reforming urban schools.* Thousand Oaks, CA: Corwin.

Louis, K. S., Kruse, S., & Bryk, A. (1995). Professionalism and community: What is it and why is it important in urban schools? In K. S. Louis and S. Kruse (Eds.), *Professionalism and community.* Thousand Oaks, CA: Corwin.

McDonald, J. (1996). *Redesigning school: Lessons for the 21st century.* San Francisco: Jossey-Bass.

McLaughlin, M., Talbert, M. J., & Bascia, N. (Eds.). (1990). *The contexts of teaching in secondary schools: Teachers' realities.* New York: Teachers College Press.

McLaughlin, M., & Yee, S. (1988). School as a place to have a career. In A. Lieberman (Ed.), *Building a professional culture in schools* (pp. 23–44). New York: Teachers College Press.

Meier, D. (1995). *The power of their ideas: Lessons for America from a small school in Harlem.* Boston: Beacon Press.

Meyer, J., & Rowan, B. (1978). The structure of educational organizations. In M. Meyer (Eds.), *Environments and organizations* (pp. 78–109). San Francisco: Jossey-Bass.

Milstein, M., Gresso, D., Cordeiro, P., & Wilson, P. (1993). *Changing the way we prepare educational leaders: The Danforth experience.* Thousand Oaks, CA: Corwin.

Moller, G., & Katzenmeyer, D. (Eds.). (1996). Every teacher a leader: Realizing the potential of teacher leadership. *New Directions in School Leadership.* San Francisco: Jossey-Bass.

Muncey, D., & McQuillan, P. (1996). *Reform and resistance in schools and classrooms.* New Haven, CT: Yale University Press.

Murphy, G. (1988). The unheroic side of leadership: Notes from the swamp. *Phi Delta Kappan, 69*(9), 654–659.

Murphy, J. (1992). *The landscape of leadership preparation: Reframing the education of school administrators.* Thousand Oaks, CA: Corwin.

Murphy, J. (Ed.). (1993). *Preparing tomorrow's school leaders: Alternative designs.* University Park, PA: UCEA.

Nanus, B. (1992). *Visionary leadership: Creating a compelling sense of direction for your organization.* San Francisco: Jossey-Bass.

National Center for Education Statistics. (1994). *America's teachers ten years after "A Nation at Risk."* Washington, D.C.: Office of Educational Research and Improvement, U.S. Department of Education.

A Nation at risk: The full account. (1983). The National Commission on Excellence in Education. Cambridge, MA: USA Research.

Newmann, F., & Wehlage, G. (1995). *Successful school instruction*. Madison, WI: Center on the Organization and Restructuring of Schools.

Noddings, N. (1984). *Caring: A feminine approach to ethics and moral education*. Berkeley: University of California Press.

Oakes, J., Quartz, K. H., Ryan, S., & Lipton, M. (2000). *Becoming good American schools*. San Francisco: Jossey-Bass.

Palmer, P. (1997). *The courage to teach*. San Francisco: Jossey-Bass.

Persell, C., & Cookson, P. (1982). *The effective principal in action*. Reston, VA: National Association of Secondary School Principals.

Peters, T., & Waterman, R. (1982). *In search of excellence: Lessons from America's best-run companies*. New York: Harper and Row.

Public Agenda. (1996). *Given the circumstances: Teachers talk about public education today*. New York: Author.

Rait, E. (1995). Against the current: Organizational learning in schools. In S. Bacharach & B. Mundell (Eds.), *Images of schools: Structures and roles in organizational behavior* (pp. 71–107). Thousand Oaks, CA: Corwin.

Rallis, S. (1994). Professional teachers and restructured schools: Leadership challenges. In L. Cunningham (Ed.), *Educational leadership and changing contexts: 96th Yearbook of the NSSE* (pp. 184–209). Chicago: University of Chicago Press.

Rees, F. (1991). *How to lead work teams: Facilitation skills*. San Francisco: Jossey-Bass/Pfeifer.

Regan, H., & Brooks, G. (1995). *Out of women's experience: Creating relational leadership*. Thousand Oaks, CA: Corwin.

Reyes, P. (Ed.). (1990). *Teachers and their workplace*. Thousand Oaks, CA: Sage.

Rosener, J. (1990, November/December). Ways women lead. *Harvard Business Review, 68*(10), 119–126.

Rosenholtz, S. (1986). *Teachers' workplace: The social organization of schools*. New York: Longman.

Rost, J. (1993). *Leadership for the twenty-first century*. New York: Praeger.

Rury, J. L. (1989). Who became teachers? The social characteristics of teachers in American history. In D. Warren (Ed.) *American teachers: Histories of a profession at work* (pp. 9–48). New York: Macmillan.

Rusch, E., & Marshall, C. (1995, April 18–22). Gender filters at work in administrative culture. Paper presented at the Annual Meeting of the American Educational Research Association, San Francisco, CA.

Sarason, S. (1982). *The culture of school and the problem of change*. Boston: Allyn and Bacon.

Schein, E. (1985). *Organizational culture and leadership*. San Francisco: Jossey-Bass.

Schlecty, P. (1991). *Schools for the 21st century: Leadership imperatives for educational reform*. San Francisco: Jossey-Bass.

Schön, D. (1983). *The reflective practitioner*. New York: Basic Books.

Schrage, M. (1989). *No more teams! Mastering the dynamic of creative collaboration*. New York: Currency-Doubleday.

Schwarz, R. M. (1994). *The skilled facilitator: Practical wisdom for developing effective groups*. San Francisco: Jossey-Bass.

Senge, P. (1990). *The fifth discipline: The art and practice of the learning organization*. New York: Doubleday.

Senge, P. (1999). The practice of innovation. In F. Hesselbein and P. Cohen (Eds.), *Leader to leader* (pp. 57–68). San Francisco: Jossey-Bass.

Senge, P., Kleiner, A., Roberts, C., Ross, R, & Smith B. J. (1994). *The fifth discipline fieldbook: Strategies and tools for building a learning organization.* New York: Doubleday.

Sergiovanni, T. (1992). *Moral leadership: Getting to the heart of school improvement.* San Francisco: Jossey-Bass.

Sergiovanni, T. (1996). *Leadership for the schoolhouse.* San Francisco: Jossey-Bass.

Sernak, K. (1998). *School leadership: Balancing power with caring.* New York: Teachers College Press.

Shakeshaft, C. (1989). *Women in educational administration.* Newbury Park, CA: Sage.

Shedd, J., & Bacharach, S. (1991). *Tangled hierarchies: Teachers as professionals and the management of schools.* San Francisco: Jossey-Bass.

Sizer, T. (1986). *Horace's compromise: The dilemma of the American high school.* Boston: Houghton Mifflin.

Sizer, T. (1992). *Horace's school: Redesigning the American high school.* Boston: Houghton Mifflin.

Sizer, T. (1996). *Horace's hope: What works for the American high school.* Boston: Houghton Mifflin.

Smith, D. (1999). Making change stick. In F. Hesselbein & P. Cohen (Eds.), *Leader to leader* (pp. 95–108). San Francisco: Jossey-Bass.

Spring, J. (1997). *The American school: 1642–1996.* (4th ed.). New York: McGraw-Hill.

Srivastva, S., & Cooperrider, D. (Eds.) . (1990). *Appreciative management and leadership: The power of positive thought and action in organizations.* San Francisco: Jossey-Bass.

Sternberg, R. J., & Horvath, J. A. (Eds.). (1999). *Tacit knowledge in professional practice: Researcher and practitioner perspectives.* Mahwah, NJ: Lawrence Erlbaum Associates.

Titone, C., & Maloney, K. (1999). *Women's philosophies of education.* Upper Saddle River, NJ: Merrill.

Tyack, D. (1974). *The one best system: A history of American urban education.* Cambridge, MA: Harvard University Press.

Tyack, D. (1989). The future of the past: What do we need to know about the history of teaching? In D. Warren (Ed.), *American teachers: Histories of a profession at work* (pp. 408–422). New York: Macmillan.

Tyack, D., & Cuban, L. (1995). *Tinkering toward utopia: A century of public school reform.* Cambridge, MA: Harvard University Press.

Tyack, D., & Hansot, E. (1982). *Managers of virtue: Public school leadership in America, 1820–1980.* New York: Basic Books.

Urban, W. J. (1989). Teacher activism. In D. Warren (Ed.), *American teachers: Histories of a profession at work* (pp. 190–212). New York: Macmillan.

Vaill, P. (1989). *Managing as a performing art: New ideas for a world of chaotic change.* San Francisco: Jossey-Bass.

Vaill, P. (1998). *Spirited leading and learning: Process wisdom for a new age.* San Francisco: Jossey-Bass.

Wasley, P. (1991). *Teachers who lead: The rhetoric of reform and the realities of practice.* New York: Teachers College Press.

Wasley, P. (1995, April). Straight shooting. *Educational Leadership, 52*(7), 56–59.

Weick, K (1985) Sources of order in underorganized systems: Themes in recent organizational theory. In Y. Lincoln (Ed.), *Organizational theory and inquiry: The paradigm revolution* (pp.106–136). Beverly Hills: Sage.

Weick, K. (1976). Educational organizations as loosely coupled systems. *Administrative Science Quarterly, 21,* 1–19.

Weick, K., & McDaniel, R. (1989). How professional organizations work: Implications for school organization and management. In T. Sergiovanni & J. Moore (Eds.), *Schooling for tomorrow: Directing reforms to issues that count* (pp. 330–355). Needham Heights, MA: Allyn and Bacon.

Wheatley, M. (1992). *Leadership and the new science: Learning about organization from an orderly universe.* San Francisco: Berrett-Koehler.

Wheatley, M. (1999). Good-bye, command and control. In F. Hesselbein and P. Cohen (Eds.), *Leader to leader* (pp. 151–168). San Francisco: Jossey-Bass.

Wiggins, G. (1998). *Educative assessments to inform and improve student performance.* San Francisco: Jossey-Bass.

Wimpelberg, R. (1990). The inservice development of principals: A new movement, its characteristics, and future. In P. Thurston & L. Lotto (Eds.), *Advances in educational administration: Vol. 1, Part B. Changing perspectives on the school* (pp. 73–119). Greenwich, CT: JAI Press.

Index